WAVEFORM

TWENTY-FIRST-CENTURY
ESSAYS BY WOMEN

THE UNIVERSITY OF GEORGIA PRESS   ATHENS

WAVEFORM

EDITED BY MARCIA ALDRICH

© 2016 by the University of Georgia Press
Athens, Georgia 30602
www.ugapress.org
All rights reserved
Designed by Erin Kirk New
Set in 10.5/13 Minion
Printed and bound by Thomson-Shore, Inc.
The paper in this book meets the guidelines for
permanence and durability of the Committee on
Production Guidelines for Book Longevity of the
Council on Library Resources.

Most University of Georgia Press titles are
available from popular e-book vendors.

Printed in the United States of America

20   19   18   17   16   P   5   4   3   2   1

Library of Congress Cataloging-in-Publication Data

Names: Aldrich, Marcia, editor.
Title: Waveform : twenty-first-century essays by women /
    edited by Marcia Aldrich.
Description: Athens : The University of Georgia Press, 2016. |
    Includes bibliographical references.
Identifiers: LCCN 2016014714 | ISBN 9780820350219
    (pbk. : alk. paper)
Subjects: LCSH: American essays—Women authors. |
    American essays—21st century.
Classification: LCC PS683.W65 W38 2016 |
    DDC 814/.60809287—dc23 LC record available at
    https://lccn.loc.gov/2016014714

CONTENTS

ACKNOWLEDGMENTS

I feel a great swelling of gratitude and hope as *Waveform* sails out into the world. It is a book I have wanted to exist ever since I became aware of the bounty of essays being written by women. My first thanks therefore go to the writers who brought into being the impulse for this book.

Jill Talbot, friend and unacknowledged legislator, coplanned the contents and helped select contributors. I am grateful to Michele Morano and Barrie Jean Borich, who provided specific help at crucial spots along the way. Thanks to Patrick Madden, who shared his experiences in editing a collection of essays and offered practical tips. I owe a long debt of gratitude to Ned Stuckey-French, with whom I have conversed for years about the essay and who has been a champion of this volume.

Anonymous readers for the University of Georgia Press offered detailed, intelligent, and knowledgeable responses. I couldn't wish for a better guide through publication than the director of the University of Georgia Press, Lisa Bayer. She has been at my side from the beginning, when we drank some very bad coffee at the AWP Conference in Minneapolis, and has consistently brought to bear her promptitude and vision.

The longest debt of gratitude is held by Richard Isomaki, who has strengthened me over the years.

This book celebrates an exuberant field of contemporary literature, the literary essay as written by women. Women's essays today are exuberant in all the senses of the word—plentiful, energetic, lively, and unrestrained. The essay, along with other forms of nonfiction, has moved out of the shadows cast by the long-renowned genres of poetry and fiction. It is no longer a quaint and distant also-ran, conceived as an exercise in rhetoric with modest aims or a neutral narrative of fact. Innumerable types of essays are being written, and written in greater numbers than ever before, if we judge by the rising count authors send to journals and magazines and websites in hopes of seeing their work in a public forum. Many more essays are being published, and more are being recognized with accolades and prizes. The essays are coming in waves.

Essays abound today for many reasons. Social media have made everyone a potential author—all it takes is a few keystrokes and a post. Online publication has vastly increased the number of venues where essays are published. Nonfiction in general has gained respect as a coequal class of literature, and creative writing programs that teach it have multiplied. Boundaries between fiction and nonfiction, and poetry and nonfiction, have melted, and literary techniques now flood and enrich the essay, like the banks of the Nile. Reality television makes the claim that anyone's life is worth documentation. And so on.

Women have been instrumental in moving the essay to the center of the literary stage. They have been writing in the form brilliantly for decades and centuries, a lineage that runs back through Jamaica Kincaid and Joan Didion to Virginia Woolf, Harriet Martineau, and further still. Yet the current flourishing of the form is unprecedented in both variety and volume. The new hallmark of the essay is its versatility and range. It is large, expansive in definition, long in history. It contains multitudes. It encourages exploration regardless of the subject. It is expressed in a singular voice and makes use of (but is not complacent about) personal experience. It asks us to question assumptions and does so in ways made visible to the reader, who is encouraged to join in the process of thinking that the essay threads.

Contemporary women writers are exploring and pushing the formal possibilities of the essay, which assumes myriad forms in their nimble hands. Current examples take every configuration that writers can imagine and find a purpose for. The essay is now a shape-shifting thing. It can do many turns, take on any subject, and assume any structure demanded by the writer's aims and the requirements of the materials she wields. In sum, we are experiencing a wave of women's essays, and within it flow multiplicities of form. Thus the title of this book, *Waveform*.

This anthology presents some of the women shaping the essay today, mapping an ever-changing landscape. It represents the scope and flexibility of contemporary essays by women, capturing the sweep and achievement of our moment and representing recent trends and developments. There is no one-size-fits-all essay today, just as there is no one-size-fits-all woman. Individual women explore the form in their own way, and neither the writer nor her work can be pigeonholed. The contemporary essay is alive and breathing, and it changes, reshaping itself in every moment. This book samples the essay's contemporary development by putting one example next to another, displaying the idiosyncrasies of lived experiences and styles that the genre holds.

About half of the works included here have been written specifically for this anthology. The other contributions have previously been published. Some of these essays may be familiar to readers; all of them deserve a wide readership.

This collection champions the diversity of women's approaches to the structure of the essay. The essay is today a site of invention and innovation, with experiments in collage, fragments, segmentation, braids, triptychs, and diptychs. There are found essays, collaborative essays, list essays, not to forget the potent rise of the flash nonfiction essay. The contemporary model explores modes beyond the layout of words, in diagrams, video essays, graphic essays, and photographic essays. The selection here emphasizes the formal accomplishments of the authors.

Focused on explorations of form, this book is not wed to a fixed theme, or even women's experience per se. It is not driven by subject matter but highlights the writers' interaction with all manner of subject and circumstance, through the elements of style, voice, tone, and structure—all the fun literary stuff. The subjects fall where they may. Of course, in well-wrought essays, shapes are taken for the sake of themes. The essays included in this volume necessarily portray the stuff of women's experience. How could it be otherwise? Women do not check their lives at the door when they write. Some of the writers openly address issues of being a woman, but some do not. The authors aren't obligated to write about women's lives. If they do, it is because that is where their interests lie. There is in this collection the appeal of the miscellany, that is, the pleasure of unpredictable subject matter. The pleasures of surprise come to the fore in encountering what the writers have chosen to write about. Just as you settle into one woman's fascination with the puddling behavior of butterflies, you turn the page and are plunged into a daughter's fascination with her father's gun.

Let me briefly introduce a sample of the works that follow.

Questioning your place in the world is one kind of inquiry that motivates essaying. In the hands of one of the practitioners herein, Roxane Gay, the essay lets individuals reveal themselves, but it connects them to something larger than themselves. In such essays we read to see in what direction the writer will take her experience or vulnerability or revelation. Rooted in personal experience, the essay resonates beyond itself.

Herein are two startlingly different essays on the writer's discovery that her mother is a lesbian. Michele Morano offers a narrative-driven memoir on the time when her mother left Morano's father to form a new relationship. All the characters are upended by her mother's new choices, which they can't comprehend. Morano creates that moment in all its complexity and never lets us forget that it is she who remembers and reconstructs the scene. Wendy Rawlings's entry in this pair, a segmented essay about the demise of her parents' marriage after thirty years, is moody and meditative, reflecting on photographs and images culled from her family's history—an early portrait of her parents in love and, later, no longer in love. Rawlings asks how her mother could have been considered "successfully heterosexual" for so many years and then declare herself "crooked." Addressing a similar subject, these two essays could not be more different stylistically and temperamentally. One returns to a particular moment to look at the casualties that ensue from a personal choice, attesting to the moment's persistence in the author's own life as a writer, shaping her, while the other essay is deeply inquisitive and restless, troubling the waters of certainty.

Many of the essays here are memoir-like, personal, including those by Jocelyn Bartkevicius, Laurie Lynn Drummond, and Margo Jefferson. The writers revisit unfinished experiences, transporting us to past situations they didn't comprehend in their earlier life. Kyoko Mori reckons with her parents' unhappy marriage and her mother's suicide. She begins, in memoir fashion, with her mother's cat, who slept with Mori when she was a baby in her crib. Almost imperceptibly the essay moves forward through crucial relationships in which cats had their role. The narrative ends as the writer discovers her final preference for solitude.

Readers will discover here brief lyric essays, such as Dana Tommasino's cri de coeur, Sonja Livingston's almost unclassifiable entry, and Kristen Radtke's graphic flash. Flash nonfiction demonstrates how much can be said by saying very little ("Write an epic on the inside of a matchbook," recommended Charles Simic). These writers practice arts of omission and guided association, the mind leaping from one idea to the next, crossing a river on exposed stones. The space between words and sentences is offered for the meditative reader to fill. These works are not easily imitated, as each form evolves according to the specific occasion and need, a polished improvisation. To appreciate them, readers must learn how they operate.

Joy Castro's entry is a 365-word lyric built on the remembered image of a torn paper target she used in gun practice and then hung over her baby's crib. Her essay is both triggered by that image and responds to it. It relies on fragmentation and juxtaposition; linear time is disrupted or nonexistent. No narrative or backstory frames the ominous details. Allusive, the essay offers us small but telling fragments of a larger account. Most important, the essay is about things that can't be said directly but must be intuited.

Herein are diverse innovative forms. Brenda Miller's contribution takes the shape of what she has dubbed the "hermit crab essay," which lives in the shell of another type of writing, in this case, the letter of rejection, with its predictable phrases of unhelpful consolation. Miller composes a series of rejections to herself that grow more painful as the losses accumulate. Here the adopted shell gives the writer a covering in which she, with all her vulnerability, can endure despite the pelting.

Adriana Paramo's essay is abecedarian, written in sections arranged alphabetically. The form was used in ancient cultures for sacred composition of prayers, hymns, and psalms, and Paramo turns that tradition to a new subject and purpose, spelling her own body and making it holy through incantation.

Nicole Walker's contribution is a fact-filled, research-based, yet personal and idiosyncratic catalog. The "I" of the essayist brings herself forward, barreling along, dispensing witty asides, all the while marshaling facts about wolves and life in Flagstaff, Arizona. Torrey Peters's essay is also shaped as a litany of facts, the names and details of the trans people, mostly women, many women of color, who have been killed. Peters does not intervene in this roster, does not weave her own story through those of others who have come to a brutal end. She shapes what she finds, arranging it on the page, putting one name next to another, but ultimately this naming does not transfigure the violence. Peters finds, remembers, bears witness, and gives testimony, as the makers of obituaries and engravers and elegists have done for millennia in attempts to forge a history that will not disappear.

Some of the essays in *Waveform* are already justly lauded. We open with a piece from Cheryl Strayed's "Dear Sugar" advice column. Strayed has pumped new life into a familiar format by using requests for advice to launch personal essays in the form of an epistle. In response to a correspondent asking for help, Strayed tells a story about herself to illuminate a larger truth for the readers of her column. She has thereby created a collaborative personal medium from the ashes of the syndicated advice column.

The collection is bookended by two epistolary essays. It ends with my own entry, a letter written to my daughter, telling her the story of her birth, a story that rewrites the silence of the author's own unnarrated entry to the world.

The respective essays by Meghan Daum and Leslie Jamison are widely admired. They are drawn to uncomfortable subjects, unflattering revelations. Gimlet-eyed, Daum assesses her volunteer work with children, first as a Big Sister and then as a court-appointed advocate in the foster care system, while musing on her reluctance to bear children and its effects on her marriage. Neither objective reporting nor academic treatise, Jamison's essay tours the history of female suffering in art and literature while reflecting on her own past as a "wound dweller." Rigorously self-reflective, her essay keeps probing until you think it can go no further, and then it goes further.

This book is not a memorial. Although we need to remember the women writers who have come before, this book is about women writing essays now. The wave is an image that catches the sense and motion that define the current movement, its fluidity and momentum. I see a long body of water curling into an arched form that breaks on the shore. Waves are continuous, one coming after another, but a single wave shows the water's shape at a given time. This book is part of the larger motion of many women bringing essays into being, building on the energy and daring of other writers, essayists adding their work to what is bigger than any one writer, to any one manifestation of the essay, to the history of the essay. By necessity only a finite number of contributors could be included in these pages, but beside each writer included are many more deserving essayists, writing now and coming into being, who deserve an audience. The sea of contemporary women essayists is rich and deep.

This is a collection of contemporary voices that work on our imagination and may become necessary for generations to come. Women writers should be brought to the fore, so readers will know that they exist and discover what they have been missing. Many of us in the past have waited hungrily for the cadences, the rhythms of Jamaica Kincaid, the meandering line as Virginia

Woolf wanders through the streets of London looking for a pencil—even if we did not know what we were waiting for. This book is designed to get essays recently written by women into the hands of those who have been waiting patiently for something they could equally claim as their own.

As Ariel Levy says, "Writing an essay is like catching a wave."[1] And you have to read a wave to catch it.

NOTE

1. Ariel Levy, ed., introduction to *The Best American Essays of 2015* (Boston: Houghton Mifflin Harcourt, 2015), xvi.

WAVEFORM

Tiny Beautiful Things

Dear Sugar,
I read your column religiously. I'm twenty-two. From what I can tell by your
writing, you're in your early forties. My question is short and sweet: what would
you tell your twenty-something self if you could talk to her now?
Love,
Seeking Wisdom

Dear Seeking Wisdom,
Stop worrying about whether you're fat. You're not fat. Or rather, you're some-times a little bit fat, but who gives a shit? There is nothing more boring and fruitless than a woman lamenting the fact that her stomach is round. Feed yourself. Literally. The sort of people worthy of your love will love you more for this, sweet pea.

In the middle of the night in the middle of your twenties when your best woman friend crawls naked into your bed, straddles you, and says, *You should run away from me before I devour you*, believe her.

You are not a terrible person for wanting to break up with someone you love. You don't need a reason to leave. Wanting to leave is enough. Leaving doesn't mean you're incapable of real love or that you'll never love anyone else again. It doesn't mean you're morally bankrupt or psychologically demented or a nymphomaniac. It means you wish to change the terms of one particular relationship. That's all. Be brave enough to break your own heart.

When that really sweet but fucked-up gay couple invites you over to their cool apartment to do ecstasy with them, say no.

There are some things you can't understand yet. Your life will be a great and continuous unfolding. It's good you've worked hard to resolve childhood issues while in your twenties, but understand that what you resolve will need to be resolved again. And again. You will come to know things that can be known only with the wisdom of age and the grace of years. Most of those things will have to do with forgiveness.

One evening you will be rolling around on the wooden floor of your apartment with a man who will tell you he doesn't have a condom. You will smile in this spunky way that you think is hot and tell him to fuck you anyway. This will be a mistake for which you alone will pay.

Don't lament so much about how your career is going to turn out. You don't have a career. You have a life. Do the work. Keep the faith. Be true blue. You are a writer because you write. Keep writing and quit your bitching. Your book has a birthday. You don't know what it is yet.

You cannot convince people to love you. This is an absolute rule. No one will ever give you love because you want him or her to give it. Real love moves freely in both directions. Don't waste your time on anything else.

Most things will be okay eventually, but not everything will be. Sometimes you'll put up a good fight and lose. Sometimes you'll hold on really hard and realize there is no choice but to let go. Acceptance is a small, quiet room.

One hot afternoon during the era in which you've gotten yourself ridiculously tangled up with heroin you will be riding the bus and thinking what a worthless piece of crap you are when a little girl will get on the bus holding the strings of two purple balloons. She'll offer you one of the balloons, but you won't take it because you believe you no longer have a right to such tiny beautiful things. You're wrong. You do.

Your assumptions about the lives of others are in direct relation to your naive pomposity.

Many people you believe to be rich are not rich. Many people you think have it easy worked hard for what they got. Many people who seem to be gliding right along have suffered and are suffering. Many people who appear to you to be old and stupidly saddled down with kids and cars and houses were once every bit as hip and pompous as you.

When you meet a man in the doorway of a Mexican restaurant who later kisses you while explaining that this kiss doesn't "mean anything" because, much as he likes you, he is not interested in having a relationship with you or anyone right now, just laugh and kiss him back. Your daughter will have his sense of humor. Your son will have his eyes.

The useless days will add up to something. The shitty waitressing jobs. The hours writing in your journal. The long meandering walks. The hours reading poetry and story collections and novels and dead people's diaries and wondering about sex and God and whether you should shave under your arms or not. These things are your becoming.

One Christmas at the very beginning of your twenties when your mother gives you a warm coat that she saved for months to buy, don't look at her skeptically after she tells you she thought the coat was perfect for you. Don't hold it up and say it's longer than you like your coats to be and too puffy and possibly even too warm. Your mother will be dead by spring. That coat will be the last gift she gave you. You will regret the small thing you didn't say for the rest of your life.

Say thank you.

Yours,

Sugar

Girl Hood   *On (Not) Finding Yourself in Books*

Growing up, I was always the black sheep of my family—the loudmouth, the troublemaker, the practical joker. I was a juvenile delinquent who spent most of her time on the streets, a habitual runaway, a high school dropout. By the time I was seventeen, I'd attempted suicide and been arrested at least eight times. I was mostly home when it was legally required by house arrest. My family didn't know what to do with me, and I didn't care. I was the lost kid of an absentee father and an addict mother, being raised by an elderly grandmother who had no clue how to deal with my explosive anger or my recklessness or my drug use or my drinking. I lost count of how many teachers, court-appointed shrinks, juvenile probation officers, police officers, friends' parents, and drug counselors tried to save me. There was no saving me—I was on a path of self-destruction.

As an adult, I would come to understand that I was angry at my parents— at my father for not being around, at my mother for being abusive, at both of them because they didn't know me, or even *see* me. I needed to know that I mattered to someone, that I wasn't invisible. So I turned to my homegirls, who were escaping their own lives, trading the chaos of home for the chaos on the streets. One of them had left home after being sexually abused by an uncle and lived with her brother most of the time. Another had two babies before she was a junior in high school and decided they were better off with the father, a man in his thirties. And another had five siblings and what I thought was a perfectly good set of parents at home—a dad who owned a restaurant and paid for summer vacations in Spain and a mom who planned birthday parties and cooked dinner. Yet she preferred the madness of the streets. Maybe, like me, she was tired of not being seen.

But I'd be lying if I said that it was all about my parents. It was also about me. I was in the middle of a sexual awakening, what my homegirls would call "catching feelings" for boys *and* girls. But I couldn't talk about that, not to anyone, not in the early nineties, and certainly not in my neighborhood.

It was a high school English teacher who gave me books to read, who sat me down and asked me to think about what I wanted out of life, who wouldn't accept my lies or my bullshit. It was she who suggested I write about who I was and who I expected to be.

Unfortunately, there was nothing I wanted. I couldn't imagine a life past my eighteenth birthday.

My recovery was not instantaneous. There was no one person or one moment or even one year that made the difference. It was a collective effort that took several years and quite a few people and countless failures, until one day it was clear: not just that I was going to live but that I actually wanted to.

And yet, even during all the turbulence of my adolescence, one thing remained constant: I was a kid who loved to read. As cynical and angry as I was, I still believed that books were important, believed in their magic and their power. Even before I was a writer, I was a reader. My favorite books got under my skin. I returned to them again and again, gave myself to them entirely, and they kept me up at night. They grabbed hold of me, shook me, and even after they let me go, it would be a long time before I could see clearly again. You could say it was books that saved me.

Growing up bilingual—speaking Spanish to my parents and grandparents, English at school, Spanglish with my friends and siblings—it was difficult to find books that I could relate to. I read whatever I could get my hands on: *Dracula, The Catcher in the Rye, Pride and Prejudice, To Kill a Mockingbird.* The books I read were full of characters that were nothing like me, who didn't share my experiences, or my background, or my language, or my *anything.* I didn't see myself in books, and it was clear that these writers weren't writing with me in mind. No one was writing for me.

When you grow up poor, sometimes books are the only connection you have to the world that exists outside your neighborhood. You begin to imagine that the people in those books matter. You imagine that they are important—maybe even immortal—because someone wrote about them. But you? When you fail to find yourself in books—or people like you, who live in neighborhoods like yours, who look like you and love like you—you begin to question your place in the world. You begin to question if those people who make up your neighborhood and your family are worth writing about, if you are worth writing about. Maybe no one thinks about them or you. Maybe no one sees you.

It wasn't until I was nineteen that I discovered Sandra Cisneros's *The House on Mango Street* and Esmeralda Santiago's *When I was Puerto Rican.* In their books at least some of the characters were bilingual, even Puerto Rican, and we shared similar experiences. But Cisneros and Santiago wrote about "good" girls—girls who (for the most part) did what they were told and who seemed much more innocent than me. Girls who didn't have my problems. Something—I didn't know what—was missing.

Then, when I was senior at the University of Central Florida, my professor, the poet and writer Cecilia Rodríguez Milanés, introduced me to Junot Díaz's *Drown*. I was smitten. I read it twice in two days. I'd finally found the book I'd been waiting my whole young adulthood for—a book with realistic accounts of poverty, addiction, longing, and difficult familial relationships. These stories were each a study of gender roles, sexuality, and the duality of the immigrant experience. It was the reality I knew, and here was someone who understood. *Drown* introduced me to characters who were flawed, selfish, troubled, mentally unstable, who found beauty in their world in spite of their dire circumstances, who loved one another despite all the ugliness and suffering. Finally, after all this time, I found a writer who'd written a book for me.

Years later I heard Junot Díaz speak at the AWP Conference in Washington, DC, where he described his own childhood reading experiences, how he lost himself in comic books and science fiction, how he was an avid reader, but still, he never, ever saw himself in the books he read. So he wrote for that kid he was, who was always searching books for characters like himself and the people he knew and the places he lived, maybe as some sort of validation that these were all worth reading and writing about.

Now, in the middle of several projects, I find myself revisiting my Girl Hood, revisiting the places where I lived as a kid—the public housing projects in Puerto Rico, a handful of neighborhoods in Miami—and I'm back where I started, hoping to find even a speck of myself in books. I've found my Girl Hood in bits and pieces: I fell in love with Patricia Engel's *Vida*, Jennine Capó Crucet's *How to Leave Hialeah*, Adriana Paramo's *My Mother's Funeral*, and Amina Gautier's *At-Risk*. And for the past few years, especially while reexamining my Girl Hood, I keep coming back to Michelle Tea's *The Chelsea Whistle*, a memoir about growing up in the rough neighborhood of Chelsea.

And yet it's not enough.

I'm a queer woman.

This is something I was never able to say as a teenager.

And if you think it's difficult for a poor high school dropout/juvenile delinquent Latina to find herself in books, try adding LGBTQ to that equation.

These days, as I revise the third draft of my novel, I think about myself as a young reader. My main character is a lot like I was, although she's not entirely me—she's more like a mosaic of a handful of the street girls I knew growing up. Half of them I was secretly in love with. Girls who fought with me, got arrested with me, smoked out with me. Girls who snuck into clubs with me, terrorized the neighborhood with me, got jailhouse tattoos with me. Girls who picked me up when I was stranded and brought me food when I was starving, who sat with me outside the ER after my boy was stabbed in a street fight, and who held me and cried with me at my grandmother's funeral. Girl Hoods, of course, who were both strong and vulnerable and, much like the characters in *Drown* and *The Chelsea Whistle*, still found love and beauty and hope in the miserable world in which they lived. They are women now—the ones who are alive, the ones who made it. For a while there, we didn't know if any of us would.

These are the people I write about. These are the people I write for. For the girls they were, for the girl I was. For girls everywhere who are like the girls we were, troubled and angry and lost, who turn to books for a little bit of salvation or redemption or reprieve, in hopes that the story will find them and that they will find themselves in the story and not feel so alone.

When I Was White

Rachel Dolezal's recent unmasking as a white woman living as black sparked a debate about the legitimacy of "transracial" experience. I cannot speak for Dolezal or anyone else, but I can state for a fact that racial transition is a valid experience, because I have gone through it.

I was raised in a white family from birth and taught to identify as white. For most of my life, I didn't know that my biological father was black. Whenever I asked, as a child, about my darker skin, my mother corrected me, saying it was not dark but "olive." When others asked if I was adopted, my mother ignored them. Eventually everyone, including me, stopped asking.

When, as an adult, I learned the truth of my paternity, I began the difficult process of changing my identity from white to black. The difficulty did not lie in an unwillingness to give up my whiteness. On the contrary, the revelation of my paternity was a relief: it confirmed that I was different from my parents and siblings, something I had felt deeply all my life.

The dilemma I faced was this: If I am mixed race and black, what do I do with the white sense of self I lived with for twenty-seven years, and how does one become black? Is that even possible? Now, you may say that the rest of the world already saw me as black and all I had to do was catch up. True. But "catching up" meant that I had to blow the lid off the Pandora's box of everything I thought I knew about myself and about race in America.

My first instinct, as an academic, was to approach the problem intellectually. I read everything I could get my hands on about the creation of black identity. But that was only a safe first step down a path that would tear me apart—physically, emotionally, intellectually, and psychologically.

"Coming out" as black cost me my relationship with my mother and some of my closest friends. It cleaved my sense of self in two. As I struggled to come to terms with what the revelation meant for my family (are they my real family?), my integrity (my whole life I had been passing without realizing it!), and my core identity (if I'm not the person I was made to believe I was for the past twenty-seven years, who am I?), I began to experience symptoms of trauma such as exhaustion, weight loss, and constant all-over physical pain. My hair fell out in clumps. I couldn't concentrate. I developed acid reflux and could not tolerate most foods.

"You're making a big deal out of nothing," my mother said when I tried to impress on her the seriousness of what I was going through. "It's only important if you choose to make it important." Needless to say, her dismissive attitude toward race and my existential struggle did not help. For her, I was and always would be the little "white" girl.

We all have a raced understanding of ourselves and the world, regardless of the racial group or groups with which we identify. The notion of people changing their racial categorization is conceivable only in societies where race is policed, where it determines your access to or denial of social and economic status. Otherwise, why would it matter?

This is not something I learned growing up. In my family, it was understood, even if it was never directly stated, that only people of color had race; whites were just people. Perceived racial neutrality is endemic to whiteness, and so, growing up, I understood race as something that applied exclusively to other people. In my white family and white community, race was a problem for other people, but not for us.

And despite discredited notions of biological essentialism, race was assumed to be an intrinsic quality. If you were born black, well, too bad for you—you had race, like it was an incurable disease, deep in the bones and blood.

I remember being at a friend's house in first grade with another girl, who happened to be the only (other) black girl in our class. She got a nosebleed and ran to the bathroom to grab a towel, and I stood outside the open bathroom door, out of sight except for part of my face peering around the corner, reflected in the bathroom mirror. I stood transfixed as I wondered what color her blood would be when it came pouring out of her nose. She's black, dark-skinned, different, not like the rest of us, I thought. Surely her blood would be a different color, too. Such an important difference has to be more than skin-deep. Of course, the moment her bright red blood stained the white towel, I lost interest.

That was my first real lesson about race: black people still seemed different; they were just not as exciting or exotic as I had hoped.

I leave you to judge for yourself the sad irony of this absurd racism coming from a girl who had been so indoctrinated in the delusional psychology of whiteness that she could not see her own dark-skinned face staring back at her from the mirror. It took that girl years of therapy for post-traumatic stress disorder and depression, medication, broken relationships, and painful reckoning to shed that psychology and create a new one that allowed her to see and love her own blackness and to forgive the little white girl who did not know any better.

Did I change my appearance? No. I look pretty much the way I've always looked, just older. But I did change my last name. I needed to make a definitive break with the person I had been, with the person my family had told me I was. I no longer wanted to be complicit in the lie of whiteness; I needed to define my identity on my own terms. That caused a rift between me and the father who raised me, whose last name I had carried since birth. Until then he had been extremely supportive and understanding. Though he hardly spoke of it, I could feel his hurt and disappointment, and it broke my heart. But what could I do? Sarah Valentine is a different person than Sarah D., who had explained her darker skin as owing to her mother's southern Italian and her father's "black Irish" heritage.

It was both exhilarating and panic-inducing to be publicly black for the first time, to be able to answer, when someone asked, "What are you?" (and they always asked), that I was a mixed-race African American. Never mind that I felt like an impostor, that I didn't feel as if I knew "how to be black." Eventually I became comfortable in my own skin.

Ten years later I can look back at that painful period of racial transition and say that I came out of it with a cohesive sense of self that embodies all its contradictions. But there is still much that I am struggling to articulate and understand.

I don't know how others with stories like mine have handled the revelation of their racial identity, nor do I know if Dolezal's is merely a case of "passing" or something more. But I believe it is time to probe deeper into the nature of racial experience to see if we can entertain the possibility of authentic transracial identity.

This Is How I Spell My Body

Ass—Apology

He is an ass man. And because of this, he wants to turn me over, to flip me 180 degrees, so he can see me from behind. I kiss him the way he likes it, with an intrusive tongue that sucks, and gets sucked, with tendrils of saliva stretching the expanse between his lips and mine. I talk dirty. I moan and wriggle under his weight. I'm coy and brazen. I play whore, then I play virgin. Anything but exposing my butt, please. But he is an ass man, he tells me again, as he puts his hand firmly on one of my shoulder blades and tries, once more, to put me face down on his bed. At this point I don't know what I'm more tormented by: the way he handles me, like I'm a rag doll, or the fact that no matter what I say or do, he will see what he wants to see. Forget lengthy discourses about the objectification of my body or scintillating lover-to-lover pillow talks. I want to play-pound his chest, kick my legs in the air, turn my face away from him with a pouty lip, and insist he respect my desire not to be flipped over. But I don't want to ruin the moment. I adopt a pleading voice. Please, you don't want to see my ass, I tell him. His voice is raspy and needy when he whispers breathlessly that, Oh, yes, he'll see it, he'll lick it; he'll do things to it that nobody has done before. I don't doubt a word he says. So I spill the beans about that part of my body. It's flaccid, really, like a little girl's. I have stretch marks all over it. I'm a zebra woman. Zebra. I.Am.A.Zebra I punctuate, looking him in the eye. I warn him. He will be disappointed. It will gross him out. My ass, its broken skin like stab marks shining in the dark, the freckle on my right cheek. I'm a mother, I try to tell him, but before I know it, I'm facedown. He deems the sight exceedingly sexy. I collapse under his scrutiny. I'm no longer a woman but a curious artifact, something to be examined, explored, conquered. A cute panda at the zoo, a relic behind a glass, a black orchid about to be plucked, an exotic Maori dancer, a raw emerald. I forget about the pleasure I felt earlier and focus on the ugliness of my backside and the stigma of being a single mother. When is it too late to say no? Before, during, or after foreplay? Before, during, or after intercourse? When is the ideal time to delineate one's boundaries in bed? My mind searches for the perfect opportunity to bolt out of his bed, to tell him that my behind is off-limits; that this is not a matter of modesty but a personal preference; that no means no. Really. By now my face is buried in his pillow, and I'm left with his imagined face, the imagined disgust, the imagined frown, the imagined WTF that I'm sure I just heard. I'm mortified and aroused and humiliated and embarrassed, all in the same proportions. So I apologize. For the pregnancy that left the stretch marks on my ass, for not being the regular twenty-one-year-old girl he thought I was, for being imperfect and insecure and flat-chested and tremendously uncomfortable in my skin and new to this doggie-style business. Please, don't look, I plead. Then I apologize again as, sure enough, he does things to my ass that nobody has done before.

Breasts—Betrayal

I met Esmeralda in college. We were studying to become petroleum engineers, and we were the only girls in a classroom of twenty-five students. One night we went out to celebrate the end of our freshman year. Esmeralda had a little too much to drink, and I took her home with me. We shared my bed. In the middle of the night, she woke me up. I felt her hot alcohol breath on my nape. I pushed her away with my back. A few seconds, minutes, later, she came back to me. This time she kissed my shoulder, my earlobe; she whispered things in my hair. It was okay, she said. No one will ever know. I stayed still, calculating my next move, trying to reconcile the two girls: my best friend taking a calculus test next to me in the classroom and this needy girl wriggling in bed behind me, encircling my body with her warm arm, like she was drowning. I visualized the knobs of my spine pushing into her chest, my heart quietly thudding against her hand like the final notes of an anthem, like her own heart, and I wondered if after a while she'd be able to tell the two apart. Her heart and mine. I turned over with the full intention of saying something along the lines of *what the hell is wrong with you?* But as soon as I faced her, she kissed my eyelids, my cheeks, so gently, so lovingly, that I stored my words in the back of my throat for later, for when the fleeting moment was over. In the dark, I couldn't see her eyes, only the contours of her face, her angular cheekbones, the outline of her ear tucked like a fetus in a halo of messy hair orbiting her head.

Before I uttered a word, she held my face in her hands, and what used to be my chin and my forehead just seconds before became weightless, like vapor, under her touch. I thought of things to say, words of protest and discomfort, hushed short phrases to establish the end of my preferences and the beginning of hers. And that was when she used her hungry tongue to part my lips; her tiny hands galloped around my hipbones, drawing me closer to her; and whatever language I spoke, whatever ability I had to string words together and make myself understood, faded inside the dark cave of her fiery mouth. I made one false attempt to push her away, more for my own peace of mind than because I wanted to take her away from my lips, as if saying *I did everything I could*. We were still in our teens, but right at that moment it felt as though we were two grown-up women: one giving, the other receiving, one harboring thoughts of a steady relationship, the other already scheming a way out.

She placed my hands on her breasts; they felt soft and hard at the same time, two masses of warm flesh that failed to capture my attention. Touching her breasts was like touching my own. The last traces of the excitement I had felt earlier dissipated before the realization that I was in bed with a mirror image of myself. Another girl, like me, every part of my body replicated on hers; every part of hers existed on mine. A surge of sobriety washed over me. Whatever I had been drunk on: the dark, her mouth, the alcohol in her breath, or the end of the freshman year, had ran its course. I turned around to get out of bed, but she pushed me back in. Gently, like a promise. I took this as an apology and a truce. Stone cold sober, I rested my head on the pillow, smiling at the near miss, how close I had been to the other side and how unscathed we both had emerged out of tonight's dangerous game. But just like that, her mouth found its way to my breasts, the moment of clarity was gone, the lights once and for all went off, and my head exploded in multicolor shards of pleasure.

The following day the sun shone brightly and the quotidian cacophony of life was inescapable. There was no darkness into which to get lost, no amorphous shadows, no wandering tongues like blind women in a new place looking for landmarks. Reality was palpable with sharp edges and angular confines. I woke up to a black-and-white life devoid of gray areas. I couldn't look at her in the eye, let alone myself in the mirror. I was ashamed. The night before felt like a blemish on my otherwise impeccable record. Like shoplifting, like cheating on a test, like flirting with Father Thomas, like mocking the librarian's stutter. Before noon it was clear to me that only the weight of her sacrifice could quash my guilt, only her blood would wash away my sin. So I saved myself by crucifying her. I told everyone about Esmeralda. Not about my tongue in her mouth exploring this uncharted jungle of desire, not about the incomprehensible lightness I felt in her arms or the softness of her expert lips. No. At eighteen I had already mastered the art of betraying and lying. A quick stab in Esmeralda's back seemed the only plausible way to exculpate myself.

I went to work quickly before one kind of guilt trumped the other, before the remedy became worse than the disease. He who hits first hits twice. I went around telling anyone who'd listen my story of her, my version of her: a confused girl I thought I knew, a friend who took advantage of my hospitality and tried to seduce me in *my own* house, a messed-up chick who, sadly, couldn't hold her liquor. Who would've thought, right?

Three weeks later she dropped out of college.

I never saw her again.

Clitoris—Confusion

Where exactly is it and what is it for? My girlfriend and I exchange notes. She tells me it is somewhere down there, that if I use my fingers to rub the general area vigorously, I'll be able to find it. And it is to make me die. A little. The French call it *la petite mort*. A surge of panic comes over me. I don't want to die looking for my clitoris, this much I know. I didn't even know I had one and I've been just fine, thank you very much, but I don't want to disappoint Maribel, who allegedly has already died a few times. I act casual, like we are just shooting the shit, rather than trying to find an answer to the gnawing question: where the hell is my clitoris? She tells me it is the little hood we pee through, and the thought of every tinkle being a close encounter with death tones my curiosity down.

On the day I turn thirteen, I sit on the bathroom floor—mirror in hand, legs wide apart—and look for it. I pee a little to locate the hood and rub it and its vicinity like my life depends on it. But I don't die, not even a little. When the rubbing begins to hurt, I pull my panties back on and dismiss my girlfriend's guidelines. She is so full of shit.

Deltoid, Derriere, Duodenum, Diaphragm—Defiance

This is my body in the abecedarian form. Ass, breasts, clitoris. These first three letters were easy, but I'm struggling with the letter D. I have no emotion attached to my duodenum, no experience with my diaphragm worth writing about, nothing interesting to say about my deltoids. The experiences of my body parts are not tidy and sequential like an alphabet is. The journeys on which my body has embarked over the years are messy, incongruent at times, and in many occasions unwanted and unexpected. I'm using the alphabet as a guiding tool, but I will not strap my body to its rigidity. My body is too old, its stories choppy, its scars too stubborn to abide by sequential rules.

Ears—Emotion

"Do you want to see God?" my thirteen-year-old sister asks me.

"Yes, yes, with all my heart," I tell her.

She's been teasing me about my ears. She tells me I look like a Volkswagen Beetle with the doors wide open. At six, I'm already aware of my skinny legs, my frizzy hair, my big ears, and, to make matters worse, I'm about to lose my two front teeth. She catches me looking at myself in the mirror, moving my teeth with my tongue. I tell her that my face is too thin and that the Pocahontas-style braids make me look stupid.

"Nothing to do with the face," she says. "It's the ears, Dumbo. Trust me."

My sister stands in front of me and grabs me by my ears. "Are you sure you want to see God?" I nod, eager to look into his blue eyes. She gives my ears a good squeeze and lifts me off the ground. It hurts like crazy. I'm sure that by the time I see God, my sister would have ripped my ears off my head, but I suppose the reward is worth the pain. She puts me down and asks if I saw him.

"No, I didn't."

"Do you want me to try again?"

I say yes, and I don't know why she smiles. She grabs my ears; squeezes them flush against my skull, like she is closing the doors of the Volkswagen; and lifts me off the ground again.

"Can you see him? Can you see him? Can you see him?"

"No, no, no," and I start to cry.

She pats my head and tells me we'll try again tomorrow. If I want.

"Just don't get too emotional, Dumbo."

G-Spot—Guerrilla

If I need a quick job done, Fingers is my man. When Hubby fails *again* to deliver the goods, I send Fingers to town. Do not come back empty-handed, I warn him. He knows I mean business. So, I ask Fingers to pay the old hood a visit and find my man Gräfenberg. I've heard wonders about this guy, a little elusive fellow who goes by "G" and who, rumor has it, is like the Fountain of Youth and El Dorado combined. I want that combo. That little nugget of fun has to be mine. And so I show Fingers the way into that sticky part of the hood where G hides. The instructions are straightforward: Take no prisoners. Shoot first, ask questions later, guerrilla-style. If he can't find G nobody can. I leave Fingers at the gates of the hood and send him off. Dry-mouthed and breathless, I wait for what seems an eternity. I imagine the goods; I dream about G over and over, all the unleashed pleasure, the earth-shattering little moments, the rough texture of that sneaky bean. Go, Fingers, go. Find the bastard.

But Fingers comes back weary and sweaty. He reeks of hood and salt. No, he didn't find G. I can't be mad at him. The thing is, Fingers is my man. I rely heavily on him for the dirty jobs. He's been there for me when nobody has. He knows stuff about me that I wouldn't whisper to my best friend. I give him a good bath and try to forget about the little bean, although I know I'll send him looking for G again and again.

Iris—Infidelity

Ever since you read that pupil dilation occurs during moments of sexual arousal, you've been checking the size of your iris before and after having sex with your husband. You are not surprised to find that your irises barely change. With your husband, your iris is not just a flat ringlike membrane behind the cornea of the eye, controlling the pupil; with him, your iris is also a secret keeper, the irrefutable proof that your marriage is over. If your husband were to look into your eyes when he is inside you, it'd take him a second to know. But you close your eyes shut, depriving him of his right to know, and fantasize about your lover. With him, your iris is a gooey slinky.

You meet this other man in deserted beaches and vacant lots. You breathe out of each other's mouths like moribund fish. You unbutton his shirt; he undoes your skirt; you traverse each other's bodies, getting zapped in the process, the circuits in your bodies going awry, the four irises nearly evaporating.

But you are afraid of revealing too much too soon and you run home to certainty. There, you do it all over again. You unbutton your husband's shirt, and he undoes your skirt and you wait for the sparks. They never come. You don't want to compare, but you do. You don't want to cry, but you do. So you lie in bed thinking of your secret, of these two men's eyes, visualizing the electric war being waged in your heart. The married man's protons, your husband's nucleus, the secret locked away in your eyes, all crazy hungry for love.

Knees—Kinetics

The dance studio is empty when I arrive. I connect my iPod, put my hair up in a ponytail, and cha-cha-cha alone, relishing the reflection of my body in every single mirror. I'm lean and fit. I sashay right to left and left to right. I stop, make a 180-degree turn, gyrate my hips in a big slow circle, and yield to the temptation to whip my hair a little. I swear the mirrors curtsy to me. I look good. This is my domain. This spa where I teach Latin dances, this studio where I am followed, imitated, this wooden palace where I'm queen, makes me a salsa goddess. One-two-three, kick, turn. One-two-three, kick, turn. When I dance, I'm young. Through kinetics, I'm alive.

The young students never walk in the studio alone. They bring along their perky breasts, their perfectly shaped behinds, their torsos that cave at the waist. "If this is your first time," I tell them, "you might run out of steam quickly. Don't sit down (you don't want your heart rate to drop dramatically); keep hydrated; don't get discouraged if you can't follow the steps. It takes a few goes, don't worry."

I start the music. I'm a graceful bobcat when I play *bachata*, a waltzing kite to the beats of salsa, a merengue-possessed beast. I am high on music. So I go for a killer *quebradita*, and my line-dance kicks are higher and more vigorous than anybody's in many miles around. *Oh, the young girls want water? Puhlease! Oh, honey, you're gasping for air. Are you ok? Ha!* I'm the coolest grandmother you'll ever meet. *Push it, girls! Go, Go.* I lunge into twenty deep squats, but by the third one a loud creak stops me in my tracks. My left knee cap twitches, and the right one feels at the point of breakage. If I do one more squat, the patella, the meniscus, the bits of squishy cartilage, and the base of my femur will all go to shit. The pain is excruciating and familiar and old. Old. Like me. The young students could do squats all day, but not me. I stand up and walk around the gym *checking* on their form. I can hardly walk. Now the mirrors seem to recoil when I walk by them. The girls are panting. Eighteen, nineteen, twenty squats. I make them hold the last one. "Hold it," I say. "Hold it. No pain no gain." I'm leaning on the mirror, smoking an imaginary cigarette, a little charade that's supposed to make them feel worked hard on. "Work it, ladies," I shout while I puff away and sip my tea. But the truth is, I'm holding onto this mirror for dear life. The pain radiates from my kneecap; it shoots invisible rays of pain down my shin, my toes, all the way to the sole of my feet, tenderizing the flesh as it moves along. The next song is an energetic hip-hop tune. I drag my feet to the sound console and press skip. My knees. Oh, my knees.

Tonight I lie on the couch with bags of frozen peas over my knees. Tonight I don't rehearse a new routine; I memorize it from YouTube. Tonight I keep kinetics to a minimum. Tonight I think of the young girls in my classes and envy the quiet beauty of their knees.

Mouth versus Mind

1. To my mother who asks me for the fifth time why it doesn't get dark in Alaska in the summer:
   MOUTH: Because we are very close to the North Pole, love. Too far away from the equator [*sigh*].
   MIND: You ask me the same damn question again, and I swear I'm gonna pull my hair out.

2. To my husband who slaps my ass every time he passes me by:

   MOUTH: I appreciate that after all these years you still find my ass attractive, but it's not a toy, you know.

   MIND: Sonofabitch. Keep your bloody hands to yourself. I'm not a toy.

3. To my writer friend who sends me essays about how much she hates her body.

   MOUTH: I suggest you temper the self-loathing narrative with a combination of self-deprecating humor and praiseworthiness.

   MIND: What the hell is wrong with you? Grow up, Barbie. Can't you see you look like a fucking model?

4. To my daughter on the day she gets accepted into the U.S. Navy.

   MOUTH: You are going to do great. So happy you found your path.

   MIND: Don't screw up again. Please don't fuck it up.

5. To the editor who says that although he found lots of lovely moments in my essay, he regrets to inform me he won't publish it.

   MOUTH: Thank you for your feedback. I look forward to the opportunity to submit to your magazine again.

   MIND: Lots of lovely moments? That's my life in eight thousand words, jackass.

6. To my born-again Christian neighbor who is visibly appalled upon discovering that I'm Buddhist (for the most part).

   MOUTH: I'm not lost, really, but thank you for praying for me.

   MIND: You don't let your kids play with the black kids across the street. Why don't you pray for yourself?

Ovaries—Oncologist

During a regular pap smear, the nurse tells me I have an elongated uterus, and for reasons I can't explain, this makes me smile. I think bananas, boomerangs, crescent moons, sickles. I'm healthy, fit as a fiddle; an elongated uterus is the least of my worries. The nurse refers me to a gynecologist for further examination of my banana float. Big Deal.

The doctor is a handsome young man with spectacular blue eyes. I smile again, this time at the prospect of having this handsome devil exploring my elongated cave with his gloved fingers. There is a hmm, followed by a twitch of the mouth, followed by a squint of his eyes. Whatever he's found down there is making him think hard. He orders a battery of tests, and when the results come in, I pay the doctor a visit. I go with my husband.

One mass is the size of a tennis ball, the other of a Ping-Pong. The gravity in his voice doesn't keep me from chuckling at the thought of my uterus being turned into a sports facility. I've had those masses before. Birth control pills make them go away. Not this time, the doctor tells us. The masses are dark—the wrong color, and, as an oncologist, he recommends surgery ASAP. Wait, what? Did he say oncologist? My husband's voice trembles when he asks the doctor if it could be cancer. Yes, he says, there is a strong possibility.

I write my will; buy a life insurance policy; think about cancer, chemotherapy, hysterectomy; and go into surgery. An hour later, after removing one ovary, the appendix, and a cumulus of endometriosis, the doctor talks to my husband. No, of course, I didn't have cancer. What a silly question. Where did he get that idea from? My husband is grateful and confused, but mostly confused. Two weeks later I go in for a self-scheduled follow-up appointment (nobody ever called from the hospital to check on me).

It's January and the handsome oncologist seems particularly happy. We shake hands and exchange pleasantries. The weather is marvelous. I-75 is finally open. It's hockey season and our teams are doing fine this year. There are rumors of an impending recession. The handsome devil is not worried about the economy, though. He rubs his hands together and tells me that if this year is anything like the previous, he'd be able to schedule the same amount of surgeries before Christmas, maybe more, you never know, which means he could easily retire in two years. I lay flat on the stretcher, put my feet on the stirrups, and let his fingers and his words sink in. "Do you have any questions?" he asks as he presses down on the side of the surgery. *Yes, doctor, can I have my ovary back?*

Quadriceps—Quarrels

The truth is, I didn't need the operation. The orthopedist told me that my knee pain could be treated with physiotherapy. But I had this other hurt to deal with, the pain of constantly wriggling my way out of a toxic relationship only to be sucked into it again. He was a coworker, and I needed to distance myself from his savvy fingers, his expert tongue, the precision of his dirty talk, the calculated gifts of his young body, this flesh-centered patois we spoke to each other. I also needed to distance myself from the epic quarrels, his fiery insults, his public put-downs, and the back of his hand so quick to fly across my face at the slightest provocation. I needed time off from work and him.

He didn't visit me at the hospital. After the surgery I went home and drank a bottle of wine. The following day I went on a hunger strike—a subversive act of rebellion against myself. On my way to the first post-op physiotherapy session, I stopped by the wine shop, turned around, got drunk. On my way to the second session, I got distracted by a happy hour neon sign flashing two blocks away from the pain management center. On my way to the third session, I called some friends, made a U-turn, met them at a bar.

"Your right quadriceps is shrinking," the orthopedist told me during the follow-up appointment. "You need your physio." He sent me home with bands, and rings, and rubber weights. Later I stood naked in front of the mirror and confirmed, to my horror, that my right thigh was considerably smaller than the left. I opened a bottle of wine and drank it all. When I woke up, I was collapsed in front of the mirror. Still naked. Still alone. Through the blur of my drunkenness I found the telephone, placed it on my shrinking quadriceps, dialed his number, heard his voice, and hung up.

Skin—Sadness

I'm not supposed to call it a wrinkle. My friend Connie, a Botox/dermal-fillers/fat-transfer/implant veteran, tells me it's called the nasolabial fold.

"You have a fold, not a wrinkle," she says, as she stretches the right side of my face. When she does, the wrinkle disappears and I'm young again.

"See? Folds are reversible. Two shots of Juvederm and you'll be like new."

We're afflicted by a sort of middle-age melancholy, the realization that no matter how many hours we spend at the gym or what antiaging treatment we follow, we will never look or feel the way we did when we met twenty years ago: two women crossing the street in miniskirts and stilettos, drivers and passersby turning heads; two young executives walking into a bar after a hard day in the office, free drinks from the guys in the corner; two taut bodies coming out of the cinema, tight jeans, fashionable boots, both giddy with life, exuding sex-appeal, youth, health, confidence. *Do you remember when . . . ?*

We decide to dress up and hit a salsa club in Miami, but I have second thoughts as soon as we stand together in front of her mirror. The skin in my face wasn't sagging yesterday when I drove to South Beach to see Connie; it started sagging five minutes ago as I watched her struggle to tuck her brand new breasts into a tiny bustier. Her skin is flawless and the Botox has paralyzed some muscles just enough to keep her face looking natural. Her body is taut from cosmetic surgery and long hours in the gym. She's older than I'm and wrinkle-free.

"Repeat after me," she says. "I don't have a wrinkle. I have a fold."

That night all the beautiful Latinas in South Florida show up at the club, a dizzying parade of rock-solid bodies, cheeks bursting with collagen, curves, and luscious hair. No nasolabial folds in sight. I realize that we might be the oldest women at the club, that someone might be looking in our direction and thinking, "what a sad pair of cougars." I tap on my newly found wrinkle after the first *mojito*, follow its crease all the way from the curve of my nostril to the corner of my mouth. It feels deeper now than it did two hours ago in Connie's bathroom.

She looks around, scanning the club for a pair of eyes, any man with a pulse will do. Mind you, she is not looking for a husband, or a one-night stand, or a companion. She is way past that. Tonight, she just wants to lose herself to Latin beats in a man's arms, to remember what it was like to feel the heat of someone's hand firmly planted on her back, giving her silent cues to kick, connect, clap, turn, and sway in sync with him. I order another *mojito*. A heavy awkwardness envelopes me. I think of a hundred things I'd rather be doing: writing, reading, playing with my dogs, painting my toenails, walking down the beach, researching how safe Juvederm actually is. Connie disappears into the crowd, and a few minutes later I spot her dancing with an old man. He is bald and a terrible dancer. Halfway through the song her eyes meet mine. She looks desperate, like the song couldn't be over soon enough. I mouth, *what the fuck are you doing?* And just like that she is next to me at the bar laughing at the poor bastard, at herself for going hunting, at me for not having the balls to go hunting with her.

We had another *do you remember when . . . ?* Then I order another *mojito*.

Uterus—Unknown

I want to tell you a story: It's after seven and it's dark. There have been roadworks, and the lampposts flicker with weak rays of dim light. I'm walking from the convenience store to our apartment, and it's beginning to rain. In one hand I have a bag of groceries, in the other a teddy bear for you, and now an umbrella. I realize a second too late that, during the day, a little hill has been transformed into a set of steps. I lose my footing and fall hard on the concrete, the groceries spill out of the bag, and the umbrella is broken. I'm still holding your teddy bear. In the dark I can't see the next step and fall again, this time harder than before. The blunt of the fall makes the pain travel quickly from my hips all the way to my head. When I get up, I realize that I have a broken shoe heel. I wobble to you. By the time I make it home and hand you your teddy bear, my underwear is soaked in blood.

Blunt trauma, the doctor tells me the following day. Pelvic blood vessels must have been torn during the fall. Nothing major. Or, or, he says, it could have been a miscarriage. Would I like to take a pregnancy test? Of course not. I *know* I'm not pregnant. I'm positive. I'm 99 percent sure. I can't be. I'm just out of college. I have a real job at a big company. I'm on the pill. I'm a single mother.

Yet, twenty-four years after the fall, it is on dates like today that I think about my uterus, where you lived. And I wonder if maybe this other hypothetical child, unlike you, would have remembered my birthday; if maybe this younger sibling of yours would have called me first thing in the morning to wish me a happy birthday and tell me, "I love you, mom." If he or she would have called you to remind you to call me. Would a sibling have brought us closer? Would a triangle have been stronger than these two dots on a blank paper that you and I are? It is on dates like today that I wonder if you were the only inhabitant of my uterus; if this other improbable baby would have made us a real family, rather than planets that orbit one another by the sheer force of gravity but never collude. Were you my only child? I'll never know.

Y chromosome—Yes

My father wanted boys, lots of them. With boys he could play soccer, explore under the hood of a car, eat oysters, make up swear words, visit whorehouses, and get drunk.

He had one boy.

My father never wanted girls. He called us "hinges," because in his book that's what women's legs were good for: open, close, open, open.

He had five girls.

He was an absent father. A parent who traveled for business and pleasure, one who remembered he had a home only when he was out of clean underwear, or hungry, or sick, or bored, or heartbroken after a failed romantic conquest.

He left for one of his business adventures a few hours before I was born, just as mom had gone into labor. Six months later he called home.

"Is it a boy?" he asked my mother over the phone.

"Yes," she said, hoping that maybe he'd come back to us. That the promise of a little boy would finally make him want to stay.

My father abandoned us soon after he came to see his "boy." And, I wonder, if things would have been different had he passed his Y chromosome on to me; maybe had I been a boy this single piece of coiled DNA would have glued the seams of our lives.

Zygomatic bone—Zen

The first time he slapped me across the face, my cheekbone hurt for days. The second time I saw it coming, clenched my jaws tight, and tried to dodge the slap. I nearly missed it. From then on I turned every blow into a challenge: mind over matter, soul over body. *This zygomatic bone he is hitting is not mine. This smooth open hand crashing into my face is a misguided caress. This cigarette he is extinguishing into the palm of my hand is a fire burning in someone else's forest.*

The last time he slapped me, I felt nothing. Nothing. I looked him in the eye, and a wave of clarity came over me. I knew our six-month-long marriage was over. After he left for work, I packed my belongings methodically and unsentimentally. I made coffee, drank it slowly in a Zen-like trance, stared hard at a breadcrumb on the dining table until the breadcrumb, the table, the room, and everything around me disappeared into a fluid continuum of silence. I called a taxi. Left the water running in the kitchen sink. Left the garbage disposal on. Left the stereo blaring Gregorian chants—which he hated. Left the house door open. I walked across the garden. I trampled on his flowers.

"Where to?" the taxi driver asked.

I caught my reflection in the back passenger window. The image looking straight back at me was of a woman still in her twenties, still beautiful, still intact. To make sure that the image was not a fantastic optical illusion, I ran my fingers across my right cheekbone. There was no pain, no discomfort, no traces of his violence. It was just me inside a bubble of silence, crystal inside crystal. Unscratched, surprisingly unscathed, stubbornly whole.

"Just drive," I said.

On Puddling

1. I keep thinking about this girl I once knew who died from a fall and the construction paper we folded and cut in the shape of wings on the evening of her memorial service. We fashioned pipe cleaners into antennae. We glued on glitter and sequins like iridescent powder on the wings of butterflies. We pinned them to a clothesline and raised the thin rope high into the rafters of the college chapel.

2. I am driving on an unpaved road toward the house I rent in the woods, home from errands and a stop at the bar. In the rutted lane ahead, a small cluster of wings appears, milk-white, black, and orange against the pale mud. I slow just before a handful of them flutter from the ground and scatter like rice tossed in the air. I swerve, cursing at the brambles scratching my passenger door, then stop, engine idling, to watch them.

3. In a 1967 interview with the *Paris Review*, Vladimir Nabokov claimed, "It is not improbable that had there been no revolution in Russia, I would have devoted myself entirely to lepidopterology and never written any novels at all." His family's exile led to hunting trips in the Pyrenees, Berlin, Paris, and then on to North America, where his wife, Vera, drove on their epic journeys throughout the continent. Eventually, Nabokov landed in the east, where his butterfly collections remain on view at Harvard's Museum of Comparative Zoology—their wings pinned open in crucifixion, their names cataloged by species, by sex.

4. In town I meet a friend for drinks and listen to her inventory of woes, how she misses her college days, and I tell her that I've had it with the butterflies and country roads. But what I really mean is that I am terrified of running them over, terrified of adding to the losses I've collected between then and now. She laughs and orders another round and tells me about puddling—a phenomenon of lepidopteran species in which they collect

on the ground, regurgitate into the dirt, and extract liquid nutrients, salts, and amino acids from the soil. Puddling is a supplement to flower nectar, she tells me, which lacks nutrients the butterflies need to reproduce. In most species, puddling is restricted to males and increases reproductive success.

5. I don't remember the first time I made a list as a girl, but the obsessive tendency has been present ever since, which must have something to do with my fondness for classification. In the same way the card catalog is a way to navigate the vastness of libraries or as accession numbers give order to encyclopedic museum collections, we list things to honor them or because noting things somehow makes them exist.

6. When I say, "a girl I once knew," maybe I never really knew her at all. Maybe I've just filed away certain details, *things I remember*: her acute laugh, the dark waves of her hair, that she smoked Camel Lights and always left the filters wet, kept journals in high school, loved a good dirty joke and insects. And maybe I never really knew myself then either. Sometimes I can't recall my own name, don't recognize my handwriting when I find a scrap of paper, a sentence written on a bar coaster or a Post-it note tucked in a book somewhere. *Things I want to do before I die*: Travel to Africa, Alaska, and Berlin. Spend a year in Kyoto. Fold a thousand paper cranes. Learn French. Bear children. Pilot a plane, and parachute out of it.

7. Nabokov caught his first butterfly as a boy, age seven, in the woods of his family's country home, Vyra. Russia was at war with Japan. In *Speak, Memory*, he describes how he captured a swallowtail in his cap and stored it in a wardrobe only to watch it escape the next morning, dodging through the air with an intensity he dramatically revealed he would find again only years later in Colorado. When he found a set of dusty atlases and scientific periodicals, I imagine he might have looked up the creature's name and written it down somewhere—that this was the start of his life list.

8. What I remember most are the petri dishes she stole from the biology lab and kept in her dorm room. Like a curator, she filled them with insects: cicada wings, beetle backs, and fly legs—dried appendages like cellophane or tissue paper jewels. She had worked out a system, her own web of wisdom. Sealing our hand-rolled cigarettes with our tongues and pinching the tail end, we laughed when she told us about Nabokov's cabinet of insect genitalia. We studied the specimens scattered around her dorm room as we experimented with a selection of pills and powders, which

we wiped from our fingertips along our gums, hypothesizing the various effects: which would keep us from drying out, which would keep us up the longest with the gentle buzzing in our chests, which might let us fly.

9. Nabokov developed a particular passion for the *Polyommatus* blues, found largely in South America. By sampling the male reproductive organs, he theorized that the *Polyommatus icarus* originated from ancestors in Southeast Asia, crossed the Bering Strait, and moved down to South America in a series of waves millions of years ago.

10. I don't know when she caught her first butterfly, but at age twenty-two her last might have been in the Colorado mesa during an expedition for the field class she was taking on Nabokov's butterflies. She must have read about the *Polyommatus* blues, cracked jokes about courtship and mating behavior, while admiring their majesty—that blue a shade she might brush over her eyelids or paint on her toes. At the memorial a boy in her class with a soft crush in his voice described the sight of her: the windsweep of her hair, her laughter adding whimsy to the field as she hunted, bounding through the tall grass with her net.

11. Puddling is commonly observed post–monsoon season in India. During mud season in New England too. So I keep my eyes open as I walk along the wooded roads when the light is high and the ruts in the ground swell erect and eager to dry. When I see the clustered wings in the open road, I stop. Some days up to twenty-something butterflies gather at once. When one sees another they must be reassured that the puddle is rich and that beneath all the sludge there lies nourishment. In the same way, each time I know someone who has died, not fearing death gets a little bit easier. The list has grown and I am less afraid of the outcome than I am of the act of dying—the pain, the landing, the waiting.

12. On the night of her death, perched on her windowsill overlooking the athletic fields, she peered out too far. I imagine her there, craning her neck to see if the Frisbee that might have flown through the air below was a rare blessed blue. And when she fell four stories to the ground, having landed in the dirt and grass, she lay there as internal injuries began to kill her while the bells of Shove Chapel chimed.

13. Certain moth varieties found in Madagascar are known to puddle in tears. They hover over and probe the closed eyelids of roosting birds. I try to imagine that. Are we so different from the order of lepidoptera? We classify them with their segmented bodies and jointed limbs, but what about this

ability to drink away tears? Can such strange ritual soothe the heart? Can the single breath of a wing lull our obscure faith in chaos and disaster?

14. Nabokov died in 1977, surrounded by his family. Although fever and congestion were likely the cause, I have read that his health was further threatened after he experienced a fall during his last hunting trip to the Pyrenees. In *Speak, Memory* he wrote, "If my first glance of the morning was for the sun, my first thought was for the butterflies it would engender." I imagine his boyhood room filled with specimen boxes, and the way he might have placed his pins artfully through the thorax of his captures and into the cork board, dabbing them with cotton, spreading open their wings. Or, as an old hatless man in shorts, swinging his net, slipping and landing, taking a last sip from the ground before he went.

15. The morning after the fall, I cried into the armpit of a lover who let me grapple and pull at his skin, held me while I fought, flailing toward the stagnant and familiar pool of grief. Outside, the campus paths were tagged with graffiti—a colorful trail of stenciled wings stained the concrete. I was careful not to step on them, like cracks in a sidewalk I might have fallen through or puddles I dared not disturb.

16. If life were to consist of classified things—real or imagined, actualities or dreams—we might know ourselves by an index of correlatives, *things I will try to learn and likely never get right*: How to balance my checkbook. Hand-beaten egg whites. Punctuation. The difference between *rhythm* and *rhyme*, between *lay* and *lie*. The correct way to spell *guarantee*. Faith in a god. Faith in prayer. Patience. Stillness. Grace.

17. I think often about Nabokov's search for butterflies and the joy they held, how difficult they are to catch, how quickly they fly before you can ever really see them—that is the shame of the living. After the freak falls and car crashes, gunshots and overdoses, it is the *things themselves I've grown to hate*: the car, the road, the windowsill, bullets and needles and pills, the trees, the ocean, the air.

18. In 2011, after years of doubt, genetic-sequencing trials conducted by the Royal Society of London confirmed that Nabokov's hypothesis concerning butterfly evolution was correct, restoring his scientific reputation. I wish it were that simple. I have no proof to validate the details of her fall or to vindicate the butterflies that never flew that night. I can't help but wonder how if one of them had flapped its wings somewhere across the world at that very moment, perhaps she wouldn't have fallen, the breeze

instead rustling the wings on her desk to bring her attention back inside. I've been trying not to blame them. I've been trying not to add them to a list of regrets: our carelessness, our bad behavior, how fast the world rotated in our inebriated spiral.

19. In the chapel we raised the butterflies high into the rafters. For a long time I would fear ledges and then I would tempt them wherever I could, shuffling my feet to the cliff sides on the summit of Pikes Peak, standing on bridges and rooftops and peering below, trying not to believe that everything that had happened would happen all over again.

20. Soon after her death, I started seeing a new therapist. Through trial and error, a series of treatments, and a strange ritual of tapping lightly on my knees, she talked me through the raw tantrums and quiet moments of my childhood: the journals I kept in kindergarten when our class raised butterflies from larva, tracking their pupal stages like the stages of grief, which may well be the stages of living—so much shedding of our past selves necessary to grow, so much morphing and eclosion necessary to live. This is not to say that it's so immeasurably difficult being young, but it feels no less insurmountable than any other age. Again, my theory lacks proof. Perhaps this is no more probable than my notion of the culpable butterflies.

21. Now my lists, scrawled on lined pages, record mundane practicalities, *things I don't fear crossing out*: Pick up groceries. Fold laundry. Pay bills. Catch up on correspondence. Research odd butterfly behavior. Wash windows. Call home. I strip the lists down to squares, tonguing the edge of a crease for an easy tear, and then fold them up again into origami birds, fortune tellers, boats. Exacting each fold with my fingernail, I practice their Japanese names: *tsuru* for crane, *sakana* for fish, *chocho* for butterfly. I find them lying around my apartment, stuck between books on the shelves, thrown in the kitchen drawer, some pinned above my desk.

22. Here, again, I am pulled over, standing in the dry, caked road, watching the butterflies puddle in the dirt. Again, I am kneeling down with them. When we are young and too busy getting high, we don't recognize we are falling. But it is also true that when we are too busy falling, it is hard to recognize anything—the world too cruel and too exquisite to know that we have flown. If only I had a straw I might probe into the ground that somewhere on earth holds the bodies of my friends. If only I might extract from the muck some leftover salt or tear and add it to my list of home remedies, so I can keep on living, keep writing down words and crossing them out.

birdbreath, twin, synonym

I'm sucking soft figs at my mother's sink, and there he is, my brother, just out of prison. In, a year, for *all the crime*. The judge finally said, it's just too much. When first together we twinned iridescently. We've been unwound so long I don't recognize this scene: Shay and me in a room together.

There used to be random messages from phone booths outside the rehab buildings (where no outside contact was allowed)—"stronger," "different," "God" would float up from my message machine, brotherwords I could not place in him.

———

Recently, I've been in the loop of smashing small bits of others' tweets together into one tweet, my own words worked in, too. It's a sideways approach. A kind of multi, floating erasure poem with no obvious mother.

scuppernongs, exactitudes, swim-kissing, low tree testimonies

The fodder is good and infinite. It's some kind of oblique saying, divination. It calls, sometimes clears me.

———

When did it start?

Our father picked us up once a month as part of a divorce agreement and would take us to his mother's place, which reeked thirty years of Coors and cigarettes and, in some rough magic trick, had up-close views of the same LA freeway from both front and back door. She was sometimes hazy by eleven o'clock. She adored us. We'd sit, hands under thighs, on a sinking couch across from her.

perfumed pies, dis/solving elegance, your prayer skirt constellation

Or this: Shay, twelve, produced a bud-ee quarter bag from a friend one spring night, our parents out. We took long pulls through his new bong in the bathroom, my first time, one of his. Higher than Jesus. We could barely speak. I was up all night defuming with rose air spray so my parents wouldn't guess and freak; up all night in the dark staring myself down in a wide bedroom mirror. We took it from there.

Or this: my mother, broken in the bathroom, asks me which she should choose: my brother or my stepfather.

———

It's not like we didn't have smiling moments under trees. Or sun didn't pour through every back window of our house. Or we weren't cute as bull bits in adolescence. All of it true. And him kicked out at fifteen, on the streets at sixteen, his best friend dead early there of heroin (the one we both kissed)—all true as well.

More truth: I drugged in adolescence too, and not in an ordinary way, in a lost, many years way. Found a middlepath in my twenties I-don't-know-how.

"If your brother doesn't stop he'll die"—the emergency doctor. Shay at thirty.

the body blown, our bird breath sonic, mercy shuffle

———

One short year apart, hazel eyes veering green, our father curled/mother blond hair, our fluid boygirlness: people took us for each other. (This is childhood. This is a silky moment.)

After years disappeared, Shay at forty spots me at the courthouse, says, "Look at you, you're beautiful," his hurt teeth, his bloated face, his disbelief. Protective Services is taking his three-year-old. I'm there with my girlfriend, at Shay's plea to us, to try to adopt this Jackson we don't know. But it won't work. We live too far away. And birth

parents have visiting rights no matter how negligent.

undone churches, breast breezes, the drift abundantly

———

I landed words in teendom. He had resin-reeking dude pals, heavy metal. Our brother/sister rift full-swing. Still, once he pulled me to his room, dropped the needle on Elton John, said, "listen," hush finger raised :: and some soft thing floated us there—faint piano into wall of plucked strings (*I'd buy a big house w h e r e / we both could live . . .*). I made him play it over and over.

———

Mantras of the long-dead stepfather: "If his ass wasn't tied on he'd loose it" :: "If I could just get him in a room alone, I could beat some sense into him" :: and, moving in too close, "Why can't he be like you."

———

I can't spell certain words: *hallelujah, acquiesce, synonym* baffle me. I repeat them slow, phonetically, chanthum to raise them from my body. Yet as though the place they'd home in me is absent or smudged, they drift, like something in their root is too complicated to take in.

Sometimes we're flying, racing bikes, running feral fields, as though my writing—word velocity—far beyond the event of childhood, could retroactively swoop us out or name what was happening. It took me years to see he's my subject, the brother-sister us; that everything I write describes a leaving, and I still don't get it head on. I circle, drift back, edge in, bite hard at the blurred skein of our thenness.

And who can know what siblings know. The dense originary worlds, doubly seen: doubled. The prolonged haunt of it all afterward. Does that ubervision—split—exponentialize the loss? Does he tell these stories too? Does he need to?

———

Now, I mostly push away. Don't: offer more money, initiate calls, find out which shelter, whose sad place. (We survive the early ravages so shotgun, does any proximity again seem too dangerous, or just too exhausting?)

Shay to teen me once: "Why do you talk that way now, all fancy?"

Synonym: a word having the same or nearly the same meaning as another.

———

And when he ghosts my daughter too, what of it. His lank in her, the way her butt rests high on her legs, the slight dimpled smile that rides the right side of her face mostly, as she watches. The bone underneath. I spot it and melt. I see it and sorrow.

At seven/eight we'd lie in bed at night finger-stroking each other's backs. So light you could barely feel it. So glowy it was star prickle. We'd both want to go first, to be the one lost to small sparks, to softness given out of nothing. How did I float out and he didn't?

super-beauty, star cluster, hot gingered leaving

At my mother's pool he tries for upbeat, the good sport. And he's so close. He could almost pass. But there's another hard girlfriend on the couch, her two kids, their trashed car. All he'll need as they leave is gas money, a little rent maybe. All he'll do is disappear.

———

Letters from prison, in thick all-cap, came regularly, surprised, had poem: *I hate the count; they count us four times a day :: I envision a cabin in the woods, a firepit :: I miss showering by myself, a woman's smell.* I found a poem wedged in a mirror's corner once, in a crumbling house he lasted less than a year in with a girl (and another baby). His card to her said things like "hope," "thank you," "here," "this." I've said these things too.

Sometimes Shay at fourteen comes to me, my beauty-blissed surfer brother, young and high in the 6:00 a.m. waves, ride all ahead of him. I know the saltscalp scent of adolescent boy anywhere. And hinge words together for things I can't know.

somatized, ghost meows, the fucking comma

* Your Song

Breaking and Entering

There is nothing illegal about breaking into your own home. As long as your name is on the deed, it doesn't matter if your scuffed silver key won't unlock the back door. It's still your house, so go ahead: smash the window and let yourself in.

That's what my mother's lawyer had advised, and it's what she intended to do.

The rest of us waited while she rummaged through the garage. It was six o'clock on a late September evening, the air soft and warm, maple helicopters twirling into the gravel driveway. My brother and I stood in the small back-yard and looked at the shingled houses to the side and behind us. A month before, we'd jumped rope on that patio, swum in that above-ground pool, sauntered up these back stairs toward a jar of sugar cookies. It was the end of summer vacation then.

Now my mother emerged from the garage carrying a brick. "This'll do," she said, holding it against her shoulder as she climbed the back steps.

Uncle Marty, recently married to my mother's sister, held the screen door open, while three grown cousins stood in the driveway. It was absolutely illegal for any of them to break the window, so they kept their distance and called out encouragement. "Use the end of the brick," Andy advised.

"Be careful you don't put your hand through," added Philip.

After the first try, Timmy said, "Harder, Aunt Reet," and my mother nodded. She'd never broken a window before.

Like most adolescents, I had a keen sense of justice. "Fair is fair" and "right is right" had been credos in our home, often punctuated with the phrase "I don't care." My father might say, "Fair is fair, goddamn it, and I don't care," and my mother might retort, "*I* don't care—what's right is right." It went without saying that, in fact, they did care very much about whatever topic of argument lay between them.

When my mother told me about the plan to break into the house, I thought it seemed fair, right, reasonable. I owned things, after all, things that belonged to me, and there seemed no other way to get them. For the past month, we'd been staying in the crowded home of Maggie and Jean and Jean's three kids, but now that my mother had found a month-to-month rental apartment, we needed beds. And a couch. Pots and pans. Towels. And at twelve years old I needed—*needed*, more than clothes or furniture or even food at this point—my record albums and magazines and the posters taped to my bedroom walls.

The Bay City Rollers had come into my life the previous winter, in what had felt like divine intervention. I'd been bored and flipping through TV channels, when a circus-like concert popped on the screen, with a round stage, a studio audience, balloons and confetti raining down. The band seemed wonderfully foreign, with their eager smiles and plaid-trimmed clothing: short jackets that hung open to reveal baby-smooth chests and pants that fell to mid-shin, where striped socks and sneakers took over. The audience was filled with girls wearing similar uniforms and waving plaid scarves over their heads, faces contorted in shrieks, and now and then one of them broke through the security barrier, catching the lead singer in a headlock or pulling the guitarist to the floor. I knew about hysterical fans from footage of Beatles concerts, but I'd never seen anything like this, not with the stripes and plaids and the happy beat, not with boys who looked into the camera and sang about love as if their own hearts might break.

When the credits rolled, the words "London Weekend Television" confirmed what I'd long suspected: everything worthwhile in life came from afar. We lived in Poughkeepsie, New York, a two-hour train ride from Manhattan, but it might as well have been the Yukon. I longed to leave my provincial life for the glamorous worlds of TV: the projects of *Good Times*, the high school of *Welcome Back, Kotter*, places where people had big personalities and got lots of laughs.

Personality was on my mind that year, after I'd come across a quiz in a teen magazine. The multiple-choice answers were meant to determine whether you were (a) outgoing, (b) happy-go-lucky, (c) shy and quiet, or (d) serious yet romantic, but even after three tries, I could see no pattern to my answers. I thought hard about which adjectives applied to me, and when none did, I arrived at the dismal conclusion that in the area of personality, I was a blank slate.

This sent me to the edge of despair. For several months I holed up in my bedroom for hours at a time, listening to the radio and thinking hard about identity. I puzzled over how girls got to be "happy-go-lucky," and I felt dull, bland, not worth the attention of anyone, including Greg Larson, the boy I'd been in love with for two solid years.

Then came the Saturday afternoon in December, when the Bay City Rollers appeared. The bouncy music, the weeping girls, the spectacle of it all both attracted and repelled me, and when the program ended, I went upstairs and lay down on my bed, shaking a little. I replayed the final song, "S-A-T-U-R-D-A-Y Night," in my mind and felt the atmosphere of that stage, with the guys shaking confetti out of their hair and the girls screaming and launching themselves forward and something I couldn't see or name twisting in my stomach. Surely, I thought, that feeling offered a clue to my personality. Or, barring that, perhaps the identity of "fan" could pass for personality until a more authentic one developed.

The sound of shattering glass startled us all. "Stay here," my mother commanded, and no one moved until she'd located the broom and dustpan and cleaned up the mess. Skipper, the auburn mutt we'd left behind, was barking himself frothy in the cellar, and once we'd all stepped inside and closed the back door, my mother let him out. Skipper leapt into her arms, licking her face and peeing on the floor. His long body spun in circles, grief and gratitude rippling under his matted coat. "Okay, honey. Stop. Okay," my mother said, leading him outside and tying his leash to the clothesline.

Back inside, she told everyone to hurry. The aim was to get as much as we could before one of the neighbors called the police or, worse, my father.

I walked from the newly remodeled kitchen through the dining room with its thick, wall-to-wall carpet and into the living room. Everything seemed both familiar and strange. I couldn't help pausing to examine last year's school pictures, then to sit in an armchair and gaze toward the television. Had there always been this much space? And had I really, just a month before, belonged here? My mother and brother rushed upstairs, while two of the cousins hoisted the couch and Uncle Marty pulled knickknacks off the stereo cabinet. There was the mug painted with a map of Lake George, the bobble-head of Thurman Munson, the plaque that said, "My sister went to the Jersey Shore and all I got was this lousy souvenir." I could have drawn every inch of the room from memory.

"Go get your stuff, girl," cousin Timmy said. He was a handsome seventeen-year-old, and said "girl" with the same teasing affection he used with his sisters, so I went upstairs, eager to see my room. In the cramped house where we'd been staying, my clothes stored in a small duffel bag, I'd felt unmoored. Everything was strange, including the bus I rode to middle school and the routines that enabled eight people to share one bathroom. Three of us kids slept in one bedroom, two slept on couches in the living room, and all three of the women shared a double bed. Jean slept in the middle between my mother and Maggie, who seemed to suspect but not really to know that my mother and Jean had fallen in love. In my presence, when the other kids weren't around, my mother and Jean talked openly about wanting Maggie gone, but the house, a small duplex in the country, was owned by her parents. "We just have to be patient," they kept saying. The new apartment my mother had found was part of a larger plan, although I couldn't imagine how it was all going to work out.

I climbed the stairs, the second and fourth steps creaking as they always did, the landing bright with western sun. How tiny the hallway seemed now, with four doors radiating off it. How narrow my parents' bedroom and how dim my own, which faced east. My mother stepped out of my brother's room with a bulging black garbage bag in her hand. "Hurry," she said, before the stairs registered her weight.

The "tink" of the light switch in my bedroom was as familiar a sound as my own voice, but what followed this time felt like an electric shock. After a month away, I saw the room as a stranger might have. The narrow bed with its floral spread tucked over the pillow, the white dresser with gilded trim, the frosted glass light-fixture on the ceiling, all of these were overshadowed by a riot of images. On every wall, from the floorboards to ceiling, there were faces, bodies, plaids, stripes. Head shots, groups shots, color centerfolds, and black-and-white pinups, so close they nearly overlapped. I blinked and shook my head. This, I thought, was the room of a crazy person.

"Come on!" my brother urged from the doorway, frowning as if I didn't understand the situation of our lives.

"The police are here," I said to get rid of him, because I'd heard the single *whoop* of a squad car in the driveway. It worked. He dropped his plastic bag in the hall and fled down the stairs, but I didn't follow. The neighbors—Irene and Tony next door, who gave out little bags of candy for Halloween; Terry and Ed and their three kids, whose pool I had learned to swim in—would be out in their yards, watching. Kids across the street, on the playground of the elementary school I'd attended, would be leaning against the fence and wondering what crime had been committed in our house. I wanted nothing to do with all that.

And yet the rhythmic flashing at the window motivated me. I reached for a color centerfold, the first poster I'd affixed to the wall, back when the yellow paint was fresh. The band stood in a sunlit field, postures relaxed, looking like five of the sweetest, most promising guys in the world. They were almost feminine in their beauty, one draping an arm over another's shoulder, shirts open to the waist. Their clothes were white and red and pale denim, all trimmed in tartan, and everything about the field, the wisps of tall grass around their ankles, the sunlight falling through the trees and patting the tops of their hair, signaled romance.

I peeled the poster from the wall, corner by corner, leaving dark smudges behind. Rubbing at them with my thumb and fingernail didn't help, and if the walls looked crazy with so many posters affixed, they would look both crazy and damaged when I was done. Each time my father glanced into this room, I thought, he'd see tiny bruises.

Just then his voice rose from the driveway. "Rita! What in hell is going on here?"

Fear rippled along my skin, but I reasoned that the police would make sure no one got hurt. As daunting as all the posters now seemed, I could feel their power starting to return and with it the relief of being a girl possessed, obsessed, in love in a way that felt like salvation.

There wasn't time to take everything, so I pried the life-size head of Woody—my favorite Roller—from the wall beside the bed, where I'd kissed it before falling asleep each night. Next was a glossy poster of his long body, naked except for a strategically placed tartan scarf, those boney hips as sexy as anything I'd seen. Then on to other group shots. Some posters tore, corners clinging to the walls, while others piled up on the bed, their tape sticking to the pages above and below until everything seemed in danger of ruin.

The stairs creaked fast under my father's weight, and his wounded voice called out, "Michele!" He rushed to my doorway and stopped, out of breath. I focused on the poster in my hand, on the bright colors and carefree expressions, on rolling a piece of tape off my finger. I didn't want to look at my father's wide face and stocky build, but he stayed in the doorway until I turned toward him, defiant. His cheeks seemed sunken, etched with lines that weren't there a few weeks ago, and his normally combed-back hair flopped onto his forehead as if he'd just gotten up. I waited for him to scold me about the marks on the walls, but he didn't seem to notice. He just stared, blinking, and then he was gone again, and my mother soon took his place. "Never mind the damned posters!" she yelled. "Get your clothes."

I had planned to move faster on this mission. The girl I'd become in the past month didn't dillydally. She was mature and helpful, keeping the kitchen clean and folding baskets of laundry each night. She looked after the younger kids and sometimes made dinner, but she was also, secretly, a little weird.

She didn't shower or change her underclothes every day, and this puzzled me. Each morning I woke determined to make a change, but when evening rolled around and the bathroom rotation started, I let the shower run while standing at the sink, brushing my teeth and splashing water on my face. Once, Maggie asked whether I'd like her to buy some underpants for me, since there weren't many in the wash, and I looked at her like she was out of her mind. "I have *lots.*"

In fact, I had a week's worth in my duffel bag, and now I stuffed three more pairs into a black garbage bag filled with faces and records and a couple pairs of jeans. I dragged it downstairs, through the gaping living room and empty dining room to the doorway of the kitchen, where the two older cousins were trying to move the stove out the back door. But my father was in their way, his strength countering both of theirs.

"These are mine," my mother was telling the police officer outside. "I picked them out myself."

"How am I supposed to cook?" my father shouted from the back step, one shoulder pressed against the stove. "Where am I going to put my food?"

Timmy stood in the dining room, looking out the window at the back steps. When our eyes met, he flexed his neck as if to say, "Yikes."

The cop spoke calmly, like a judge. He understood that the appliances belonged to my mother, but since her new apartment came with appliances, and she didn't have anywhere to put these, wouldn't it be best to leave them for now? Two of the cousins jiggled the stove back to its place, and Uncle Marty plugged the refrigerator in again. "I can't believe this," my father kept saying. "You wanted me to come home from work tonight and find this? No stove or refrigerator? No way to live in this house?"

The aggrieved tone of my father's voice made my skin burn. I knew he was right, but I also knew that he had a house. He had a bathroom he didn't have to wait in line for. He had a yard and a washing machine and a dog I missed so much I couldn't go near him, tied out back, yelping his head off.

Everyone milled around while my mother explained herself to the cop. "I left him because he hit me," she said. "So of course I wasn't going to come when he was here. My lawyer advised me to do this."

"Your lawyer's a goddamned crook!" my father shouted, because it was true; he had hit her. Two punches, late at night, and we took off. No one had expected the violence, not even my father, who'd sat on the couch until dawn waiting for the police to come arrest him. But it was also true that my mother had started sneaking around with Jean before we moved out and that her denials had rattled my father to the core. He wanted to believe she wouldn't betray him, but the stories didn't add up. Why was she grocery shopping on

Sunday all of a sudden and taking forever at it? The answer, which I knew and he did not, was that Maggie took her parents to church each Sunday, leaving Jean free to talk. While my mother huddled against the pay phone by the courtesy desk, I pushed a cart through the aisles, pretending to shop for my Scottish husband.

Now, standing beside cousin Timmy in the dining room, it occurred to me that I was the only person who could see the whole situation for what it was, because of something that had to be a personality trait. I watched. I paid attention. I tucked information away and kept quiet about it, trying to make sense of the story in my head. Happy-go-lucky I was not, but observant? Good at keeping secrets? A spy, even?

It was dark by the time everything got sorted out. The living room chairs would go with us, but the couch would stay. ("The man needs a place to sit," the police officer said with authority.) We could take the stereo and the dining room table and, of course, the kids' beds, but not the pots and pans, not the dishes, not the sheets for the double bed. ("You'll have to start over a little bit, too, ma'am.") Finally, with the truck full, my uncle and cousins squeezed into the cab and headed for our new apartment, where they would unload everything so that, the next afternoon, my mother and brother and I could begin to set up our home.

Meanwhile, the police officer stood in the driveway, scribbling notes on a pad. The dog continued to bark, competing with voices until my father put him in the house, where he lunged against the dining room window. My father told the cop he had to get back to work, but the window on the back door was smashed so he couldn't lock the house. "My God almighty, what was she thinking?"

While he searched the garage for extra glass, my mother told my brother and me to get in the car. And we would have, if Skipper hadn't continued barking so loudly in the house, calling my brother to him. Just for one hug. Just to say good-bye. Of course, the moment the door opened, Skipper flew out, my brother's thin legs and hands no match for a dog's desire to join his pack. He raced to my mother, dancing and barking and howling, the fur of his face wet with what looked like tears.

"Please, take the dog!" my father yelled over the noise. "He's heartbroken! He shits all over the house, and I have to keep him in the cellar. He doesn't understand!"

"I can't," my mother repeated, shaking her head and backing up as if she'd seen a ghost. The apartment complex didn't allow pets.

In the car my brother scrunched beside bags in the backseat while I sat up front, pressing my forehead against the cool window. I watched Skipper wriggle against my father's grasp as we backed out of the driveway, watched as the dog broke free and began chasing us, determination pressing his ears flat against his head, and if this were a short story, I'd be tempted to let him catch up, to move him under the back wheel and enhance the tragedy. But Skipper didn't catch up, and he lived mostly in the cellar for the next couple of months, until one weekend morning when my father let him out and the dog, with no one around as his witness, ran straight into the path of a semi.

"Come back! Come back here right now!" my father yelled, chasing until we'd turned the corner.

The car's silence was broken by the flick of a cigarette lighter and my mother's long exhale. I rolled the window down and stared at the passing streetlights, feeling the soft September night against my face. I wasn't thinking that fair is fair and right is right but rather that it's a terrible thing to break into someone's home, legal or not. And I was thinking, too, of how easily I could have prevented the fiasco, could have convinced my mother it was a bad idea or threatened to tell my father. But I hadn't, and now I wasn't sure whether the possibility had even crossed my mind. I wanted to believe it had, but all I knew from the days leading up to this night was that I would soon be reunited with the things that mattered most. My things. Things that gave me shape and depth, that pointed toward the future. I'd wanted, and the force of that wanting had been bigger than anything around it.

All the way back to Maggie and Jean's house, I vacillated between feeling terrible for my father and impressed by the changes taking place in me, even over the past couple of hours. Once I'd been a girl who taped posters to the walls, a couple at first and then more and more as the months passed and the tensions grew, papering herself into a kind of cocoon. Now I was someone else, someone who understood that she knew things and that her silence was a kind of power. I would keep quiet, guarding secrets, becoming a repository of stories. But not forever. One day, I knew that very night, as I planned the bubble bath I would soak in for so long my skin would wrinkle, regardless of how many people banged on the door, one day I would tell on us all.

Cat Stories

The moment he heard my father's footsteps every night, my mother's cat, Neko-chan, left her side and fled to the nursery. Takako would check on me after serving Hiroshi tea, or dinner if he was inclined to eat, and find her cat sleeping in my crib, his big gray head next to mine. The fear of cats suffocating babies—sucking their breath, as it is ominously phrased—must not have been prevalent in Japan in 1957. My mother recalled the cat with great affection. Seeing us together, our heads about the same size but the rest of the cat sprawled longer across the crib, had amused her. The nursery was upstairs and my parents' bedroom was on the first floor. My father came home after midnight and left before seven. Neko-chan snuck downstairs after Hiroshi was gone and Takako was alone.

I first heard about Neko-chan at five or six, just old enough to understand that I had a past about which stories could be told. Like all the grownups, who used to be younger than they were now, I was once someone very different: a baby smaller than a cat, living in an old house in Kobe. Our family had moved to a modern apartment complex in a suburb when I was four and my brother was one, but Takako had grown up in the old house. One of her brothers occupied it after us and another settled nearby, so she took Jumpei and me for visits. Year after year, in photographs of us with our cousins, the house looked the same, though we didn't.

That house was proof that my mother had a life before she was my mother, when she and my uncles were the children standing in front of its gate in their school uniforms, but I could not recall the cat who slept with me. Neko-chan came and went through an open window. When I was two, he left in the late afternoon as usual but didn't return at night to keep my mother company while she waited up for my father. My mother and uncles searched for days in vain. Neko-chan had been with Takako for ten years. Even though he had appeared healthy, she concluded he had gone off to die. She never got another cat.

My memories start after Neko-chan was gone and I could walk: the red patent leather purse I carried everywhere, the wobbly bottom of the sandbox in a neighbor's yard, the whoosh of a bicycle passing by on the street. The interior scenes I recall are of Takako taking care of the new baby: singing to him in his crib, securing his blanket with blue-tipped safety pins, making the mobile spin above him. I was no longer the baby in the crib but a bystander, like a cat.

Neko-chan hated the camera even though it was almost always Takako—only occasionally one of my uncles and never Hiroshi—standing behind it. Maybe he was afraid of the shutter noise or the flash bulb. Being photographed was the one thing he wouldn't do for Takako, so all I know about his appearance is his big gray head next to mine in the crib. He might have been a completely gray cat, like a shadow, or a tabby with gray and black stripes. His name, Neko-chan, meant Kitty, a form of endearment appropriate for cats of any age and either gender. I never thought to ask my mother what he looked like, why she didn't give him a better name, how he came to be her cat, or if he was a kitten when she got him. I didn't wonder about these details because the most important part of the story was clear: the cat who loved my mother couldn't stand my father. Why that was, I didn't have to ask.

My parents met at the Kobe office of the manufacturing conglomerate Kawasaki Steel, where my mother worked as a secretary and my father as an engineer. Her parents didn't trust his easy charm from the beginning, but Takako said she would rather die than marry anyone else. In 1954, when most couples had arranged marriages, theirs was a rare love match. Three years later, when I was born, my father was seeing a woman who worked as a bar hostess. He came home after drinking with his coworkers and visiting his girlfriend at her bar.

I didn't know the details of their affair until 1994, after Hiroshi had died from cancer and the former bar hostess, who hadn't been invited to the funeral, called my aunt's house, where I was staying. The woman told us that Hiroshi had called her from the hospital every day until the afternoon of his death, when he was finally too sick to talk. At thirty-seven—older than my parents had been at my birth—I was surprised only by Hiroshi's faithfulness to her, the first of his many girlfriends. After our family moved to the suburbs, away from my mother's relatives, my father stopped coming home every night. While he disappeared with one girlfriend, others called our house looking for him. Long before I knew about sex, I understood that all these women were Hiroshi's girlfriends. Although my mother talked about

Neko-chan with amusement, I could hardly miss the sad truth at the heart of her story—I was born after my parents had stopped loving each other—or its corollary: Neko-chan hid out in the nursery, knowing my father wouldn't set foot there. I was not important to my father. Even a cat could tell he was a liar and a cheat.

My mother killed herself a week after my twelfth birthday in March 1969, in the house that my parents had bought two years prior. My father, by then, had been promoted to be part of the upper management. He worked till late and traveled often, supposedly on business. In the last winter of her life, Takako still waited up for him. I started doing my homework in the kitchen to keep her company. Most nights, he called with some excuse for not coming home, and she cried, saying she was worried about my brother and me growing up and leaving her because without us, her life would be nothing. She wondered what she had done to drive Hiroshi away; she berated herself for having been a failure as a wife. "Promise you won't be like me," she kept asking me. "You are smart and strong. You can't end up like me."

She meant that I should never count on anyone—on my father, on my future husband if I ever married, and, most important, on her—to take care of me. On the morning before her suicide, Takako asked Hiroshi to take my brother and me on a rare Sunday outing. When we came home and found her on the floor with the gas pipe in her hand and all the windows sealed shut, I knew she had planned the whole thing to make sure Jumpei and I wouldn't be alone at the scene.

My father should have called an ambulance instead of an old friend of his who was a surgeon. The police, summoned afterward, must have noticed that, but they allowed Hiroshi to report the death as an accident. My mother wouldn't have lived no matter what anyone did. She had stopped breathing long before we came home; her skin was cold when I touched her. Still, if Hiroshi had been more concerned about saving her than about protecting himself from blame or gossip, I might not, now, be presenting my mother's cat story as my origin story.

Because I didn't have children, I was slow to notice the difference between the parenting practices of the 1950s and 1960s, when I was a child, and the 1980s and 1990s, when I might have become a parent. My mother had been informed that the commercial formula was healthier than breast milk and that babies should be fed with a bottle on a strict predetermined schedule rather than when they decided they were hungry.

The maternal-separation experiments that I would learn about in college— in which baby rhesus monkeys overwhelmingly preferred "cloth mothers" to "wire mothers" and proved that infants needed to be held and touched—were just starting when I was born. The result wouldn't be widely available until my younger brother, too, was too old to be nursed or picked up and comforted when he cried. My mother had been taught that she shouldn't encourage babies to think they could get their mother's attention by throwing a fit. You had to train your children from an early age so they wouldn't become a burden to other people. The emphasis on discipline must have resonated especially strongly in Japan, where *gaman*, stoic forbearance, was the utmost virtue.

One of my memories of the house in Kobe is hearing my brother cry in the nursery while I slept in my new room across the hallway. Some nights Jumpei fussed for so long that our father got up and left. Over the baby's wails, I could hear Hiroshi banging out the door. My mother would then come up the stairs, but she didn't stay in the nursery very long. Her footsteps retreated down the steps while the baby continued to cry. Takako must have touched my brother's forehead to make sure he didn't have a fever, adjusted the covers, and steeled herself to walk away. I fell back asleep while Jumpei wailed on.

I didn't comprehend how difficult it must have been for Takako to let my brother cry himself to sleep until I was in my early forties and staying with friends who had just had a baby. Every time her daughter cried in the small hours of the morning, my friend came running up the stairs. She picked her up, nursed her, and walked around the house carrying her. Soon, her husband, too, was up, trying to comfort her and the baby. My friends might have been particularly anxious because they had waited into their forties to have just one child. My mother was thirty-three, but she'd had miscarriages before my birth and between mine and my brother's. She, too, knew that Jumpei was the last child for her.

Takako must have stayed awake, fretting, for hours in her bedroom. Her son refused to sleep and her husband was gone. At least she didn't have to worry about me.

"You were such a good baby," my mother always said to conclude the story of Neko-chan. "You didn't cry like your brother later did. When I snuck in to check on you, you were sleeping peacefully with Neko-chan. You didn't even know I was there."

Takako's cat story wasn't simply an exposé about my father's betrayal and neglect. It was a parable to prepare me for a future without her. Over and over, my mother was praising me for being strong and independent; she was implying that I wouldn't notice her absence and might be better off without her. She said the same things on those nights I stayed up with her at our new house and in the note she composed before she taped the windows and turned on the gas. The girl who slept soundly with a big gray cat didn't need a mother.

Although I never forgot this story, I wasn't planning to get a cat when I finally moved into a room that wasn't in my father's house or in a college dormitory. I had left Japan at twenty to finish my bachelor's degree at a college in Illinois. Two years later I was admitted into a graduate creative writing program in Milwaukee. I went there during spring break to look for a place to live.

One of the "roommate wanted" ads on the student union bulletin board read, "Top floor of a four-story brownstone. No elevator. The room, the smallest of three, has its own bathroom, with a tub large enough for a midget." At five feet two and barely a hundred pounds, I almost was a midget. The bathroom I didn't have to share was a real draw. If the roommates turned out not to be as forthright and likeable as the ad promised, I could stay in my room and avoid them altogether.

Doug and John were childhood friends from a small town near Milwaukee. Doug was a graduate student in zoology; John was a counselor at a "home for wayward boys." Their third roommate had gotten married and moved out. The living room in which Doug and John interviewed me had a low-slung couch, a battered coffee table, and spindly philodendrons and spider plants hanging from the ceiling, like in the lounges in the dormitory. The room for rent was in fact the size of my dorm room and set up in the same way, with a daybed against one wall, a dresser against the other, and a desk by the window. The attached bathroom resembled the ones given to students who served as resident hall assistants, but I wouldn't have to write up my peers for breaking visitation rules and drinking beer without obtaining a party permit, to earn my privacy.

I moved in the day after graduation and found a job waiting tables, to tide me over till my teaching assistantship started in September. Except when I was working or running, I spent the summer reading and writing in my room and seldom ventured into the living room, where the coffee table was piled with Doug's zoology books and John's Hunter S. Thompson books. The stereo was usually playing Frank Zappa, Captain Beefheart, or some jazz album I felt vaguely stupid for not recognizing. One wall was covered with religious paintings from secondhand stores, with Jesus holding out his bleeding heart and the Virgin Mary kneeling before the archangel. On the shelves under these holy tableaux, Doug had placed two aquariums full of toads, to which he fed live crickets.

Doug had red hair that kept falling into his green eyes. John had long black hair and a beard. They were only a few years older than I was, but they had an impressive air of world-weariness. On Sunday mornings, after their weekend parties, the living room was crowded with a dozen men and women who had spent the night.

Although the kitchen was outside my door, I dashed in only to make coffee and hurried back to my room with my cup. Half the space in the fridge was taken by a keg of beer, so I kept my food in the dorm-size refrigerator I bought with my waitressing tips and lived on peanut butter, apple sauce, and cottage cheese. I stopped opening the pantry drawers after I found bags of pot and also three plastic bags, vacuum-sealed, containing fetal pigs. The guys and I fell into the same "live and let live" relationship I'd had with my classmates. Although my college had fewer than six hundred students, I had been close friends with only four women, three English majors and one art major. Spending hours running or swimming or cycling and then staying shut up in my room was how I was used to living ever since my mother died and my father married one of his girlfriends (not the bar hostess, whose job was too scandalous).

I might have remained for years in that self-contained room if it hadn't been for the two cats who stayed with us in September while their owner, John's sister, was packing to move from one apartment to another. Mabel was a large calico who sat on the couch all day. She was sweet, but it was Angus, the skinny all-black male, whom I adored. His favorite trick was to bump my arm with his head just as I was raising my cup to my lips and cause me to spill my coffee so I would yell out his name, put down the cup, and chase him around the apartment. He was incredibly fast. Though I was a decent sprinter for a human, I could never catch Angus. But eventually, he'd stop, flop on his back, and pump his legs and purr like crazy while I scratched his stomach. When he'd had enough, he twisted his neck and bit my hand—not hard, just closing his mouth on the skin he pinched between his teeth and immediately letting go. The next moment, he was streaking across the apartment again with me in pursuit.

I started reading in the living room so I could get up periodically to chase Angus up and down the long hallway between the guys' bedrooms and the kitchen. At night I left my door ajar. Mabel roused herself from the couch around three in the morning. She and Angus raced around my room, batting at each other and using the bed, and my body in it, as a fort. Because John often worked the night shift at the troubled teens' group home, I took over feeding the cats and cleaning their litter boxes.

When I petted Angus till he jumped up and started running, it was as though sparks of electricity had flowed out of my fingertips into his fur and animated him. Or maybe it was the other way around. Angus drew the energy out of me, or the current flowed back and forth between us and spread into the space around us. Whatever was between us made me feel that the whole apartment was lit up brighter than the sun and filled with pure oxygen. I stopped sneaking around like a squatter, and if the TV or the stereo was too loud, I asked the guys to turn it down. John and Doug had been friends since kindergarten. To them, I would always be an awkward near-stranger. Still, I was their equal, with my own rights to the common space: the kitchen with an oven that actually worked, the living room with large windows overlooking the city, the long hallway where Angus and I ran. Finally, I started to feel at home in my first apartment. But one October afternoon I returned from school and found a note from John's sister. Her new apartment was ready, and she was taking her cats home.

I put the note back on the plant stand by the door and walked into the living room. The air in the apartment felt not just quiet but dead.

A week later, when I couldn't stand the dead air anymore, I told my roommates I planned to get my own cat.

"Cool," John said. "You should get a Siamese. They're affectionate and playful. My sister thinks Angus might be part Siamese."

In the *Milwaukee Sentinel* the guys had left on the coffee table, I found an ad: "Purebred Siamese kittens. Fifty dollars. First come, first served." I called the number, got the address, and, the following afternoon, skipped a mandatory seminar for all teaching assistants and hopped on a bus headed to the south side. The breeder lived so far away that my bus transfer ran out. At dusk, I arrived at a bungalow in a modest but tidy neighborhood, where a woman my mother's age greeted me at the door and led me to a room where four pale gray kittens were piled together inside a large pen whose door was open.

One of them came out and rubbed his mouth up and down my index finger as though my finger were a harmonica. He was smaller than my shoe, and his hair was short and thin. When he turned over on his back, I could see the pink skin of his stomach. At my touch, he purred and pumped his legs, as Angus had done. Then he righted himself and rubbed his mouth against my finger some more, his lips parted to reveal tiny teeth like dressmakers' pins. With his long tail and big ears, he resembled a rat. He was possibly the ugliest kitten I had ever seen. Fifty dollars was a lot of money for a graduate teaching assistant. But I already couldn't imagine the rest of my life without him.

The breeder, Mrs. Pookay ("like bouquet," she had told me on the phone), said, "The girls are spoken for, but that one's a boy. You can have him in a few weeks when he's weaned."

"I live on the east side," I said. "I took four buses to get here. Would the kitten be able to travel that far?"

"I can bring him to you when he's ready," she offered. "My husband can drive us."

The kitten arrived on the first day of December, in time for the holiday season. I named him Dorian for his color. Two weeks before Christmas, Dorian batted down the glass ornaments from the tree John put up in the living room. I should have been more contrite on my new pet's behalf, but I'd assumed that the tree had been a joke like the secondhand Jesus and Virgin Mary. The dozen broken glass balls, as it turned out, had belonged to John's grandparents.

After John said I should take Dorian back to the breeder, I found an efficiency studio where Dorian and I could live alone and moved out. The guys and I didn't stay in touch, so I never told John that he had changed my life. If his sister hadn't boarded her cats with us and he hadn't mentioned Siamese cats, I wouldn't have skipped my seminar and taken that epic bus ride to a stranger's house. Without Angus, then Dorian, I wouldn't be the same person I am now.

Before Angus drew me out, I was hiding from my roommates as I had from my father, stepmother, and dorm floormates, trying to make myself so small and quiet that no one would notice me. My father hadn't been home often enough during my mother's life to care what I did. Afterward, though, everything became my fault. The woman he married, Michiko, packed her bags and threatened to leave whenever Hiroshi started spending too much time with his other girlfriends. Instead of confronting him, Michiko claimed that I had made her miserable by failing to show her proper respect, so Hiroshi beat me to prove his love to her and threatened to kill me if I drove her away.

I didn't leave their house only to get into trouble on my own. At college I steered clear of people who drank excessively or smoked pot on campus—for which we could be expelled, and in my case sent back to Japan. In Milwaukee I avoided my roommates' parties by stocking my room with everything I might possibly need, as though I were preparing for a natural disaster. When I had to go anywhere, I snuck out through the kitchen and down the back steps, to avoid the strangers who had spent the night in the living room. "Hi," I said too cheerfully when I ran into some guy sauntering into the kitchen in his boxer shorts (or worse). "I'm the third roommate. I live here. But I'm going out now."

I was used to being alone, but my solitude was fearful and pathetic. Angus showed me how an animal companion could strengthen our sense of self. As he led me from room to room, he was the part of me that moved freely, claiming a larger territory than I had allowed myself. Though Angus was one-tenth my size, I was a satellite orbiting around him in an expanding universe.

My roommates were inconsiderate but not malicious. They hadn't asked me to apologize for being the small, plain, and studious person I was. It was time I stopped being so timid.

All the same, I was tired of the loud music and the dirty dishes left in the sink for days. I needed a quiet place to concentrate on my writing. Getting an apartment turned out to be even easier than finding a cat. I went through the newspaper ads and, within an hour, located one I could afford. By the end of the month, Dorian and I were occupying our first independent apartment.

I didn't walk until I was two years old because my hips had been dislocated at birth. A breech baby whose mother had already suffered two miscarriages, I didn't breathe for an alarming number of seconds after being born. The hip injury wasn't noticed until a few months later, and I spent the next year in a series of casts and braces that immobilized my legs. Neko-chan disappeared shortly after I could finally move around the house without holding my mother's hand. Perhaps he was waiting for me to become fully ambulatory before he could leave us.

Later, I wondered how I could have been such a good baby—who slept so well—with dislocated hips, but I have no memory of the injury or my recovery from it. I only know this whole episode from the other story my mother told about my childhood, which started with, "You almost died when you were born. You didn't cry right away, so the doctor had to give you a shot," and ended with, "Once you learned to walk, your uncles helped you exercise and strengthen your legs. If they hadn't, you might be walking with a limp now instead of winning medals at school for running."

The immediate moral was that my uncles—who were single when I was born—had devoted themselves to my care, taking the place of an absent father, but the story also introduced me to the concepts of irony and paradox before I learned what to call them. I almost died when I was born. Because I couldn't move until I was two, I was encouraged to exercise, which led to my becoming a runner. The plot of anyone's life is full of twists, and the truth is often the opposite of what we expect.

Dorian, for example, was exactly like his namesake, though his fur turned beige instead of gray and his face and markings, when he was full grown, were nearly black. His personality, on the other hand, was the same from the start. The day after his arrival, he whirled around and bit my friend Jane, who made the mistake of sitting on the bed he already considered his. She visited us later in our new apartment, but she knew not to approach the refrigerator after Dorian leapt to its top to growl at her, puffing up his tail and dangling his paw, hooked at a menacing angle. "You'd better come and get me that soda," she called to me. "I'm not touching Dorian's fridge." Jane was the first on the long list of people—all my friends, pretty much—to be terrorized by Dorian. Everybody made jokes about how I kept a portrait of him in the attic.

The paradox was that he let me do anything I wanted with him: hold him by his hind legs and dangle him upside down like a bat, stand him upright and walk him across the room ("let's walk like a person"), lift him over my head and pretend he was flying, trim his nails and brush his teeth. I leash-trained him so we could picnic on the lawn and spend the afternoon reading. Indoors or out, he sat on my lap, perched on my shoulder, or slept in my arms. When I returned from class or an outing with friends, he was waiting at the door. Maybe he loved me so much that he couldn't stand anyone else, but it could have been that he devoted himself to me to spite the rest of the known universe. Our relationship resembled one of those Escher etchings in which the lines tangled and wound into endless staircases going nowhere and everywhere. There was nothing simple or convenient about it. I missed him and worried about him whenever I was more than a few hours away from home. People who assume that pets are easy substitutes for "real relation-ships" never had their own.

I lived alone with Dorian for two years before I moved in with a boyfriend I eventually married. Chuck, who was finishing his degree in elementary edu-cation, was three years older than I was. He was a skinny, long-haired guy who played bass in a wedding band and told funny stories about the drunken family fights he witnessed at every reception. He shared an apartment with four roommates, one of whom was in a poetry class with me. We met when I went to watch the lunar eclipse from their balcony and ran together for sev-eral months before we went out on a date. The first time Chuck came into my apartment after our run, Dorian sprang on to the couch Chuck was standing next to and sank his teeth into his hand.

"Your cat bit me," Chuck said.

"Oh yeah," I responded from the kitchen, where I was making coffee. "He does that. Take a few steps back and ignore him. He goes nuts only if you keep invading his space."

My apartment wasn't large enough for two people, so Chuck and I moved to a new place when we decided to live together. Dorian spent the first week hiding in the closet where I'd put my clothes. When he finally came out, he stayed in the spare room, which I had set up as my writing studio with the furniture from our old apartment. A few more days later, he ventured out to the living room, where he hopped from our old rug to armchair to plant stand, assiduously avoiding anything that was Chuck's. I made Chuck throw out his relatively new mattress because Dorian was never going to sleep on it with us, and reinstated mine, which had been propped against a wall in the garage awaiting disposal.

Dorian eventually accepted Chuck and his furniture. He attacked Chuck only once at that apartment, a few months after our move-in, when Chuck and I left together to visit his family, and, two days later, Chuck came back while I flew to New York to spend the weekend with a friend. Seconds after Chuck stepped into the foyer, Dorian latched onto his leg and bit hard enough to puncture Chuck's skin through his jeans. Then he retreated to my—our—studio and didn't emerge till my return. I was upset that Chuck hadn't called me. "I would have gotten on the next plane and come home if you'd told me," I said. We both understood that it was Dorian, not Chuck, for whom I would have been willing, even eager, to cut my trip short.

Eventually, Dorian and Chuck became close enough that, if I wasn't around, Dorian would sit on Chuck's lap. But as soon as I returned, Dorian ran to the door to greet me. "He recognizes the sound of your car turning into the driveway," Chuck said. "He doesn't go to the door for any other car." On nights I came home especially late, Dorian might be sleeping in Chuck's arms, but the moment I got under the covers, he walked across the bed to settle into mine and put his head on my pillow.

After we finished our degrees in Milwaukee, Chuck and I moved to Green Bay, where I found a tenure-track job at a Catholic college and he taught at an alternative elementary school. We bought a house with a basement office I used as my writing studio. Dorian sat on the desk there and napped while I worked. If Chuck came downstairs—which he had to do to use the washer or dryer or to get something out of storage—Dorian woke up, sprang to his feet, huffed, yowled, and paced around swishing his tail until Chuck left. The studio was the only place where Dorian got so territorial. He was guarding my privacy. I didn't tell Chuck what I was writing till I was finished, leaving him to read my books when they were published, like anyone else. Dorian was the only one who saw my work in progress day after day.

When Chuck and I separated, Dorian was fifteen. He spent the last two years of his life in a small apartment I rented. Though Chuck was surprised and hurt when I told him that I was moving out, our divorce, a year later, was amicable. The two of us got along better once we didn't have to be married to each other. We played tennis once a week and had coffee, not so different from what we used to do before we went out on our first date in Milwaukee. Because Chuck was the only person who could take care of him, Dorian stayed at the old house when I went out of town. Dorian was the keeper of our friendship, the reminder and remainder of our history together. I was ready to leave Wisconsin only after Dorian died and I knew, for certain, that the first half of my adult life was over.

When Chuck and I were first married, I could sit at my desk any morning or afternoon I had a few hours to myself. I wrote my first three books—two novels and a memoir—in the countless small slivers of time I managed to carve out. In my thirties, though, I started needing several uninterrupted hours to concentrate and, in addition, began craving quiet time when I was NOT writing. I walked in the woods for hours with binoculars to watch migratory birds, wandered through museums all day looking at paintings, and went on long runs and bike rides by myself.

Halfway through the last full decade of my mother's life, I had become her opposite. While she had cried because she was lonely, I couldn't be alone enough. She had worried about my brother and me growing up and leaving her; I didn't have children because I was sure I would kill myself over the loss of my privacy. I required two kinds of solitude. The solitude of work was exhausting and exhilarating in turn, absolute clarity one moment and utter confusion the next as I pulled words out of my head on to the page, read them, erased them, and started over again. For several hours before and after, I had no desire to talk or listen to anyone. Because Chuck was home on weekends and in the summers, too, I had to go away to be alone in the woods on the edge of town or in museums in another city. I couldn't fathom being married for the rest of my life when I spent so much of my time and energy planning how not to have to talk to my husband, a low-key, reasonable, and undemanding person.

I might have found the right balance between solitude and companionship all the same, if I had absolutely loved my outings and trips. I enjoyed seeing birds and paintings, but what I wanted, more than anything, was to be alone at home, in my own private space. After Dorian and I moved into our apartment above a storefront, I felt relieved and grateful every minute I could spend reading, knitting, listening to music, cooking and baking, or simply staring out the window with Dorian on my lap. My day started with a run and ended with an evening at home, with work—and sometimes excursions alone or with friends—in between. I couldn't have asked for anything more.

Dorian followed me around the apartment, which had two small rooms— one for writing and the other for sleeping—besides the kitchen and the bathroom. He sat on my lap at the desk, on my shoulder at the kitchen counter, in my arms under the covers, on the bathmat while I showered. We didn't have guests because he hated everyone. His presence fortified my solitude. He wasn't aloof and independent: I was.

When he died, a few weeks before his eighteenth birthday, I was forty. During our time together, I had finished graduate school, gotten a teaching job, become a U.S. citizen, married and divorced, bought a house and left it, and published three books. I didn't know who I was without Dorian. Suddenly, my job at the small Catholic college, my cramped apartment above a framing store, the thirty miles I had to drive to have lunch with the one close friend in the area who was also a writer—none of it made sense.

I moved to Boston at forty-two, a year older than my mother had been at her death. I was giving up a tenured job at the Catholic school for a lectureship at Harvard. It was a scary gambit, my own version of throwing my life away, but after finishing the five-year term at Harvard, I found a tenured job on the East Coast. I now live in a co-op apartment in Washington, DC.

The picture Chuck took of Dorian hangs in the foyer, above the matching stainless food bowls—"snack bowls" meant for humans—for my two feline companions: Miles, the blue-point Siamese (named for "Kinds of Blue," but actually more gray, the color Dorian should have been for his name), and Jackson Brown-e, the sable Burmese (almost black). Sitting on a quilt with designs of roaring lions, Dorian opens his mouth to proclaim his supremacy, a true king among kings. He was yawning, but he looks fierce with his fangs bared. "That's Dorian," I tell my friends. "He's my Household God."

Dorian shared my solitude in Green Bay, where I could recall my Japanese childhood from a safe distance and write about it. In the small towns and rural areas in the Midwest, no one looked remotely like me or my family. My solitude was bracketed by the extra silence of isolation, as though muffled by the snow that covered the ground from October to April. I needed that silence to find my stories first. Then I moved east, one thousand miles farther away from Japan, and ended up in a city where half the people sitting in a café downtown could be, if not Japanese, then Asian. I no longer look or feel like a foreigner or an exile. It's been an odd, partial homecoming, but my mother's stories have prepared me for this paradox. I almost died when I was born. I settled in my adopted country's capital and made a home, alone with cats.

The first thing Dorian and I did together, the afternoon Mrs. Pookay and her husband dropped him off, was to fall asleep. I had put him on my bed and sat down to pet him. The daybed—inherited from the former occupant of the room—was tilted to the side and sagged in the middle. It was impossible to sit on it without slouching into a semirecumbent position.

When I woke up, a few hours later, I was lying aslant across the mattress with my legs and arms twisted, trying to hold my head up because Dorian had nestled under my chin. While I struggled to reposition myself without crushing him or rolling off the bed, he woke up and clung to my neck with his paws. I pictured us on a raft crossing a lake I couldn't see to the other side.

I had skipped twenty years and gone from sleeping with one gray cat to another. I assumed that the lake I pictured was the past, but it might have been the future.

These nights, I sleep with Miles under the covers, the two of us clinging to each other with his paws wrapped around my neck and his head tucked under my chin. Jackson curls up on my legs, serene and smooth as a stone in a Zen garden. I'm crossing the lake with one cat to keep me afloat and another to anchor me. That's my cat story, still in progress.

Notes toward a Partial Definition of Home

I almost always arrive a stranger. I drive up with what I can carry and carve out a space for myself. Austin. Rockville. Phoenix. Laramie. Sheridan. Hamilton.

There is an attempt to establish ties. Then, there is somewhere else. I say that it's my work, my calling, my spirit. But really, no place has held me so close that I couldn't walk away. No place has come for me after I decided to go. It is, perhaps, to much to ask of a place.

Most towns are designed with liminal spaces, and those that aren't acquire them over time. These spaces are the looser boundaries that edge the more civilized centers of neighborhoods and cities. The shaded path around the golf course, the "greenbelt," the farthest rows of the rose garden, the copse by the buggy lake, the reclaimed river walk. Streets and shops and intersections are too loud, busy, and fast for any initial insights, so it can be a slower entry to study a town's borderlands. One learns little in the middle of the action, except how to dodge and deflect, because in their bustling hearts towns most resemble one another.

Nature is obdurate in these half-wild places. Much can be learned of the blind desire to thrive despite less than ideal conditions that can be seen where what has been made or built begins to unravel. Weeds exploit cracks; vines climb any post driven. Wildflowers curl from under the edges of boards. Beetles, bees, snakes, spiders seek out whatever we've left behind and make their homes there. This growing-despite can look like freedom.

When I told my husband that we were done, I remember saying, "This isn't working. We aren't, I mean, and I'm tired of trying." It came out faster than I'd meant for it to, and he didn't believe me. Not at first. He asked, "What now?" and also, "Can't we just buy something to make this better?" (We had a lot of debt.) He said, "We could plan some trip somewhere." (We had tried that, too.) And he said, "Is this about," but he didn't finish, because he didn't know what it could be about. (There was a woman once, and I'd always wondered, but it wasn't about her, or his drinking, exactly.)

In my mind's eye, I can see us moving from the bedroom through the living room and into the kitchen, the full length of our small space, but I don't remember what I said, how he responded. I know I'd been practicing the moment for weeks.

These in-betweens, these microgeographies, can be a welcomed respite from the hassles and small sorrows that accompany frequent moves: connecting the utilities; registering your body, your car, your rights; the favorite cup, now broken; the lost box of ornaments. Though the terrain might be steep and slatey, or red-clayed and rolling like the waves that once overlaid it, and the landscape may sprout ferns as big as a vw bug or sticky cholla or fluted and waxy canna blooms, there is always something reliable, something gentle and untended about the curve of the walkways. You can walk at a pace of your choosing, and it is difficult to get lost or stray too far from landmarks you might recently have learned.

We'd been in Santa Fe only a year. I'd hoped the desert air might dry out something that had grown damp in us, but like a water stain, the mark of dissatisfaction remained. I walked out of the house after I told him. I'd only ever left the house like that once before, back in Portland, when I thought for a moment that I wouldn't marry him at all. That night, I waited at a park nearby for an hour, in the dark and the rain, sobbing dramatically on the rubber seat of a playground swing set. I dug two deep ruts with my heels in the sodden chipped wood. I was waiting for him to come find me. He never did. It was a childish game, but the only one I knew at the time.

So now, walking down the hill away from our half of the 150-year-old adobe we rented, I knew I could walk in peace; I knew he would not come for me. I felt something give in my hips, a shift with each step. I felt the precise way my feet planted themselves on the uneven stone sidewalk, then peeled up and away from it. I felt how the steps made my spine twist back and forth like a chain might, in a light wind. My arms swept heavy from my shoulders, propelling me forward. By concentrating on just that act of walking, I kept something else from happening. I walked past xeriscaped gardens and villas behind stucco walls, past spent agaves. Past clumps of prickly pear. I was not crying, but gulping at the air, like a fish. I remember the way the dust motes held still in the air while I tried while I tried to be sure. At the bottom of the hill, I called a friend, who met me at the only bar in town worth anything. She and I often played pool there, and it felt like a safe place to be torn in half.

So then I was: I wept on the couch for hours and the bartenders bought my beers. It felt very grown-up, very battered-by-life, at the time.

As I walk the edges of a new place, I try to learn the names of its trees, but I often fail after one or two. It's easier for me to learn the habits of its birds.

- In Phoenix, the mockingbirds would direct traffic; sparrows would shyly follow me down the block, in case I was in a generous mood.
- In New Orleans, all I remember hearing were starlings, screaming like car alarms in the middle of the night, and the one morning when the first cardinal I'd ever seen surprised me with his unmistakable red hood in the small tree in front of my house.
- In Portland, there were robins and house sparrows everywhere in the city; in the marshy spaces on the edge of town, red-winged black birds, herons, ducks; while deep in the woods, there were owls, woodpeckers.

Only certain birds can be at home in our landscape of cement, iron, and fiberglass. Pigeons are especially resilient, bedding down in the S-curves of neon signs or the joints of tin-shingled overhangs. Some swallows, long drawn by the gnats and midges our trash breeds, make mud nests under freeway overpasses or high arching entranceways, where once they favored tall river banks and barns. These birds can teach a person how to make the best of things.

Other birds give a different lesson entirely: to follow the pull of migration, to move or perish.

And then, when he thought he understood, there in the kitchen, his shoulders bowed but his face hidden, my husband agreed to go. Many days later, when he thought he understood better, he refused.

He insisted then, angry and full of his own practiced speech, that if I wanted to be alone so badly, I should go somewhere and be alone, then. I don't know if that was his way of asking me to stay, but maybe it was. He knew I hated to be alone. For once, I did not hold his anger against him. For once, I felt a small tenderness toward his weaknesses.

Walking around the overgrown hedgerows of a new town, you can get a picture of the people who live nearby, your new, as-yet unmet neighbors, through their trash or their fastidiousness, through the well-worn or neglected nature of their paths. It's not a fair judgment, but it is nonetheless an easy first one to make. It's a sidelong glance you can take without being caught.

He will always look the same in my memory: he's dancing terribly at a Cherry Poppin' Daddies show in jeans cut off and cuffed at the knee, black boots, and a flannel shirt, and for this (and maybe also his ridiculous wide-toothed grin), I pick him out from the other thrashing bodies in the pit.

When each song ends, I make sure I am nearby, even though his long hair is on the way out of style. Even though he is too tall and too skinny. Over and over again, I pick him out.

New Orleans is slowly being overtaken by kudzu, one fence and one doorway at a time. The flowers there are decadent and whorish, overflowing their hanging baskets and window boxes like the Quarter itself.

Oak trees tower over Mid-City, gnarled and indefatigable, like the great old barons and baronesses of yore. But the joke's on history, because the barons are dead, their power finally being eroded like the delta they tried to master, while the trees abide.

The great Mississippi flows full of stinking rot and massive steel hulls past the city's reinforced flanks. Sometimes, the river climbs the banks, wild and unimpressed with our constructs, reminding everyone whose land they live on.

At night, the smells of cayenne, cheap beer, and vomit on Decatur Street mingle in the humid air, while cicadas and brass bands keep time.

Who, who wasn't born up out of the damp loam here, like a cypress or morning glory, could imagine building a home on its uneven, sinking, sliding surfaces?

Or, what was I ever thinking? My shoes grew mold. My drawings rotted in my portfolio case. There were fleas and mosquitoes everywhere. I was cruel and petty in response to cruelty and pettiness.

I did not know what I was doing.

The more a person moves, the easier moving becomes. Leaving, however, is not the same as moving.

It was never perfect, not even at first. I hold no illusions. We fought badly and never apologized. We took everything that we built or drew toward us for granted. For my part, I lost respect for his ability to lead us. He lost faith in my ability to make a home for us.

So to be clear, it was not the loss of perfection that I mourned as I walked down the hill, gasping last or first breaths. It was something else, something that I haven't quite reached yet. It feels like a thing waiting around the next bend, a kind of understanding that might bring me some peace.

There is a release in the air on paths that mark the space between homes and not-homes, a kind of collective human exhale. These spaces are not exactly our spaces, and any people walking these paths are visitors, even if they come every day. The trees, the moving water, and the still, the hidden, calling birds—have little need of us. I can be released here of the burden of my intractable nature.

In Portland, in 1995, the waitlist for a summer wedding in Shakespeare's rose garden was nearly two years long. If we'd waited that long, what might have happened? We picked the rhododendron garden instead, because there was no wait. The flowers weren't even in bloom. I walked across a short lawn to meet him and a justice of the peace by a park bench. A few of our friends and family stood around squinting in the late summer light, their cheeks sun-reddened and balled up with smiles.

Not too many months later, we packed our shared belongings and moved to New Orleans. It took us over a year to get there, but that's a story about the middle of a thing. I'm talking here about its outer edges.

The American Rhododendron Society describes rhododendrons as shallow-rooted. They do not tolerate soils that are allowed to grow stagnant with moisture.

Maybe what I've lost isn't a place or time at all, but a belief in the integrity of the moment *before any real loss was imaginable* (of respect, of faith), that moment when a long, imperfect history lay before us because we'd sworn it would be so.

I said we were done in June, two months before our five-year anniversary. He stood at the sink with his back to me and washed his cooks' knives. It was not an intimidating act on his part, but a defensive one: washing knives was a thing he knew how to do well, arguing with me was not. He was so tall that he had to lean over to reach the water. I don't know if his shoulders were curved down in defeat or in diligence.

I remember nothing else of the month that followed, except walking down the hill with its paused motes, and an old friend coming to town from far away, to spend the last few nights with me in the house my husband and I had shared.

Was I cruel? If I was, it was unintentional. I got drunk at the bar over a game of pool with my local friend and my out-of-town friend, and I cried great choking sobs that turned into laughter. I shouted drunkenly about the irony of my hating my husband's drinking. I put my head on the green felt and thought I might die. It was my way of asking them not to go. I didn't want anyone to go, ever again. I remind myself, now, that I was still very young then. I remind myself that I was the one leaving. Who leaves.

Birds have their own ideas about what makes a marriage successful or useful. Song birds, for example, are rarely monogamous for more than a single season.

I'm not trying to say I'm anything like a song bird. I'm not trying to say anything about the institution of marriage, or my disposition for it. I'm trying to say that sometimes it's easier to describe one's arc far from the heart of things.

New Mexico is rich with yellow and red sandstones, sage, and twisted, spiked mesquite. The cactus there blooms after rain. The desert scrub is full of thrashers and quail and roadrunners. Rotten wood and quartz-streaked stones hide a menagerie of venomous creatures. As you climb the great highway from Albuquerque to Santa Fe, the hills darken with puffed and pointed foliage, until the tree line demarcates the start of ski slopes. Hawks circle overhead. There are small pines and lavish pink bougainvillea climbing pueblo walls.

It would be disingenuous to be even a little vague about the burden my unhappiness was to us both. Though he might have stayed from habit or duty, there was not much worth staying for by the time we'd reached Santa Fe.

Some cities hold onto me for a few years. Then I can learn the rhythm of their seasons:

- Bulbs push their green swan-necked stems up from under last autumn's rot.
- Flower heads wither to wispy seeds which drift, gather, set.
- Leaves pucker, darken, let go of their stems.
- Grasses yellow, lie down, wait for the snow.

I'd tried to make a home for us in New Orleans, but I couldn't pay the high cost of bars that stayed open all night for him. By Santa Fe, I'd lost all desire to dig root-deep into that hard clay. He would take the car out in to the emptiest desert, alone, and take handfuls of mushrooms. He said he was trying to find God. God had never been a part of our vows. It was his way of pulling away, too.

You can watch a plant grow more easily than you can watch a person grow. A person gets bigger, then older, then smaller—but if you know them well, something about their face always looks the same as it did when you first felt close to them. In the case of plants then, or even cities, perhaps one never knows them so well.

My out-of-town friend—let's call him the guy friend, to differentiate him from my local girlfriend, and because that's what he was—surely complicated things in ways that are difficult to piece together now, my husband having no similar support, no equivalent retort to my need for him, which is surely, in part, what that friend was (there was after all that woman, recall, but she had long moved on herself).

On my guy friend's last night in Santa Fe, we had Indian food and scoped out my new apartment. It was fully furnished, because I was taking little, besides clothes and my books. My husband was angry about the books. Perhaps he was also angry about my friend (don't forget, we stayed one night together in a hotel), but at that time I couldn't imagine sleeping with someone else ever again (which is to say, nothing happened, nor had I thought it would). Marriage can do that to a certain kind of person, I suspect. I never thought I was that kind of person.

At Christmastime, the walkways and windowsills all over New Mexico are lined with small brown paper bags, each holding some sand and a lit candle. Luminaria, or *farolitos*, they are called. They are said either to light a path to your home for the Christ child or to memorialize the dead.

By winter, my solitude and my resolve were showing new growth. I would be gone from Santa Fe by February. But on Christmas Day, my first ever alone, I left my small, furnished apartment and walked through the empty streets, where a fresh, postcard-perfect snow had fallen, and was falling. A large cross overlooks Old Town, called the Cross of the Martyrs. I climbed its hill, not thinking at all about martyrs or redemption. It wasn't for the grace of the cross, but for the grace of my own exertion, that I climbed: the curling puffs of my breath before me, the crunch and slip of the ground under my feet.

When I got to the top, I looked down on the snow-stippled pines, the low walls, the glowing arcs of lighted paths, and I picked out the orange window of my apartment and, on the other side of town, the dark mass of trees under which my husband slept. I found the curving road that led to my job. I looked for the lights of my girlfriend's house. I stood there and I sucked the cold, dry air in and I pushed it out. And then I walked back down to the road.

We'd left Portland together, in love; we left New Orleans together too, but troubled. When it came time to leave Santa Fe, we each left on our own. He tried to stay on for a while after I'd gone, but eventually he returned to the colder mountains he knew as home. We never spoke again. I moved and moved and moved and am still moving. Home for me as a place had eroded; it continues to slip past me as if on some great river.

Where I live now, great blankets of snow fall, thicker than in the desert mountains, thicker even than in the Rocky Mountains, where I've also spent some time. The snow here covers everything, softening edges and camouflaging trail hazards. And yet: chickadees and jays scratch out a winter living, and, overnight, raccoons leave their pecked footprints across my neighbor's driveway.

I snap on snowshoes, pack some water, and head out into it. I breathe easily in the relative silence and through the work of moving my arms and legs. I keep my own pace with the long-limbed bodies of blackberry and tansy, the bare-limbed trees, the thickly furred winter deer, and always birds, alongside the impressions left by hikers faster and earlier than me. My tracks are almost never the first on the trail, which I find a comfort.

Dumb Show

The hand. Exploratory, intrepid organ. Reaching far from its trunk. Instrument of the fifth sense: touch.

We touch something to know it. We make contact. In the dark, the hand knows what the eyes cannot. It eases around corners. It reaches the top shelf. It sorts, arranges, classifies.

There is a story, one sentence long, of an American slave, who, about to be sold away from her family, cut off her hand and flung it in her master's face.[1]

Shakespeare's Lavinia enters *Titus Andronicus* with two hands, a tongue, and, perhaps, as a virgin. In a political alliance she is married off by her father to a man she doesn't love. Her wedding occurs offstage. In the first act, she speaks only twice.

In the second act:

Enter . . . Lavinia her hands cut off, and her tongue cut out, and ravished.[2]

Painful stage directions in perfect nanometer. The "and" does it. The commas. Wait for it. There is more. Her hands, her tongue. And ravished. Shakespeare grieves for his character as only a writer can—through punctuation and a groomed sentence.

The violence done to Lavinia's body is committed offstage. We see her postmutilation. The audience is asked to bear witness to the true abomination of rape—the aftermath. The gruesomeness of the shocked, changed self. Remembering, remembering impotence and the expiration of choice.

Lavinia is chopped, fashioned, into a fantasy. She cannot speak. She cannot scratch. She is three holes. But she still has teeth. They forgot to knock those out.

She is silenced.

I feel this danger. In my bellybutton, that once connected me to my mother. In my snatch, trim, hollow (Shakespeare's words, not mine). I feel it. Me, of 2013. Me, woman, writer, of two hands and tongue.

How different are we, Lavinia?

Rape begins with the hand.

Hands grab you. Take hold of your throat. Clamp your mouth. Tie your wrists above your head. Pry open your legs.

The horror of other people's hands.

The woods, a site of desire. For the newly married sex of Lavinia and Bassianus. For the adulterous, interracial love of Tamora and Aaron and the genesis of their half-Goth, half-Moor babe. I think of him as brother, the only one I have in all of Shakespeare, for Othello and Desdemona never did conceive.

The woods, the site of Lavinia's rape. On her back, she looked up at the pine trees of Rome, their needled branches. Alive and chlorophyllic, bristling in the wind. She looked at the trees standing straight above the humped shoulders of the brothers, Chiron and Demetrius. When the brothers turned her over, she nestled in the dirt. It took the shape of her mangled form. It accepted her blood as if it was water.

Act 4, scene 1. Lavinia's nephew, Young Lucius, runs onstage with books under his arms, Lavinia racing after him. She takes a book from Lucius— Ovid's *Metamorphosis*. She turns pages with her stumps, thudding them against the tale of Philomel and her rape in the woods. Her father, uncle, nephew watch as she takes a wooden staff in her mouth and writes in the sand, "Stuprum [rape in Latin]—Chiron—Demetrius."

Act 5, scene 3, lines 35–36. Lavinia enters with a veil over her face. Her father has baked her rapists in a pie that their mother, Tamora, is unwittingly eating. Titus unveils Lavinia. Titus kills Lavinia. His final words to her, a command: "Die, Die, Lavinia, and thy shame with thee and with thy shame thy father's sorrows die."

January 1594: the first staged performance of *Titus Andronicus*.[3] During Shakespeare's lifetime, it was the most popular of his plays. In 1597 a new English law was passed that redefined rape as a "crime against the person of the woman rather than against the property of her family."[4]

How many lawmakers' daughters, wives, sisters, mothers, lovers, sat in the seats of the Globe and wept for Lavinia?

Shakespeare had two daughters. His eldest, Susanna, born six months after his marriage to her mother. In his will he left the bulk of his estate to Susanna. To his wife he left the "second-best bed."[5] Something difficult to interpret. Something possibly cruel.

The only thing known about Shakespeare's daughters: the dates of their births, marriages, and deaths. And that neither could read or write.

Lavinia was literate.

The staging of Lavinia's maimed entrance is the dramatic focus of *Titus Andronicus*. In 1951 director Peter Brook opted for a highly stylized rendering. Lavinia, played by Vivian Leigh, had scarlet ribbons trailing from her wrists and mouth. She entered to the "slow plucking of harp-strings, like drops of blood falling from a pool."[6]

In Elizabethan times Lavinia was played by a boy or man. (A man or a boy can also be raped. Do not forget that.) A fringe of dough mixed with blood gave a severed look to Lavinia's stumps. The actor concealed a pig's bladder filled with pig's blood in his mouth. He bit down on cue. A sixteenth-century squib.

I wonder if, in playing the part of Lavinia, there is an element of relief. One has no hands for most of the play. Hands, the part of the body an actor most commonly struggles with. Flighty, awkward, when empty of prop. The last part of the body to give itself over to a character.

I knew a director who, in rehearsal, tied the hands of an actress at her sides. She fell into her character, suddenly, like something dropped. She began to act.

Lavinia is text. She is the words of her author. She is made of language. And it was language that was taken from her.

No. Stop. Don't. Please.

Words of command, of action. Words that govern. Words that fly through the air like darts.

Throughout the play, the words that precede Lavinia's name are orders: Come, Speak, Kneel, Die.

In Louisiana and Texas, days before Hurricane Rita, people boarded up their windows and wrote messages on them. GO AWAY RITA. WE DON'T WANT YOU RITA. LEAVE US ALONE RITA.

How human a thing: to write a note to a hurricane.

No. Stop. Don't. Please.

Pleasure. That, too, taken from Lavinia.

What is love, sex, without hands and tongue? How to stroke, lick, quarrel, promise? Lavinia's mutilation represents a never-ending rape. Her truncated ability to give pleasure as well as receive. The ruination of her sense of touch, of haptic curiosity.

Love is in the senses. It is not just the sight of the beloved, his smell, the timbre of his voice, his taste. It is touch, prehension. The cup, press, spread of your hands against his body. Lavinia can take her lover in her mouth. Arouse with her stumps. But she cannot memorize his face with her fingers. She cannot make a fist inside a boxing glove. She cannot slap a raw chapati from palm to palm. She cannot form calluses hoeing beans under a Lenten moon.

She cannot lift a thumb, while scuba diving, to initiate a rapid ascent. She cannot feel the green skin of a tree. She cannot lace herself, finger to finger, to a wide-hipped woman on a wooden dance floor. She cannot braid the hair of a black-haired child. She cannot grope the dark, cold walls of a cave. She cannot scratch the head of a stray dog. She cannot pick a tomato, hanging in a dash of sunlight, and feel its juice, the burst of seed, against her tongue. That, the warm taste of lust.

There are hands you do not forget the touch of.

The last hands Lavinia felt on her body were not her own and were unkind.

Once they are cut, we never again see Lavinia's hands. They are lost, off-stage, in the woods, in the wings. I think of them, separated and rotting amid the pines. I think of Lavinia writing, her stumps moving quickly over a keyboard. She is screaming in all caps.

But this is a revision. After all, Lavinia is gone. She died on the page, in an inky grave of italics. *He kills her.*[7] That is all it took. Two pronouns of differing gender flanking a verb in present tense. And, a period.

That is the end of Lavinia. A life dictated by men. A life, motherless, unprotected. A life handed from one man to another. A life mute, before and after her tongue was cut. I have read scholarship that compares the mutilated body of Lavinia to the mutilated body of Rome. To me, her mutilation embodies her gender. She was always handless, without actions of her own, without agency. She was always mute. The maiming made her condition public, manifest. She is the woman in the play without a job (unlike the Nurse), the woman who is not a mother (unlike Tamora). Once Lavinia has been cut, men react to her suffering and pain. They do not want to see it. They want her pain to end so their pain, which comes from seeing hers, will end.

I cannot revise her death. So it is written, so it is done. Still I search the text for a getaway. For an alternative.

There is always space, time, between the acts.

Lavinia, Lavinia, I have a plan.

At the end of act 4, you must part the curtain and run, Lavinia, from the theater, before your father murders you.

A man, garbed in black, will cue a scraping wind. He will point a narrow spotlight. For you are small and need no wider beam.

I see you, a basket hanging from your left stump. Inside the basket are your hands. You want to do something beautiful for them. You walk, mutely, thirty blocks, from Broadway to Chelsea. You push my buzzer with the tip of your nose and climb three flights to my apartment. When I open the door, I recognize your dress, centuries out-of-fashion and ripped near the crotch. You sit on the edge of my sofa, and I offer you a glass of water. You grip it between your stumps. I take your hands from the basket, hold them in my lap. They are rigid, blue, and flecked with forest leaves. I flick away maggots and squeeze henna from an icing tube. I draw arrows, daggers on your fingers, and feathers on your thumbs. I draw hundreds of eyes to ward off the evil to which you are prone.

We sit for twelve silent hours. The henna hardens. I crumble the black shell. Your hands—covered once more in red. The head of a peacock, a swollen lotus, vines and eyes and arrows.

Tongueless, you smile.

I place a pen between your teeth, smooth a sheet of paper on the table. Write out again the names of those who have wronged you, Lavinia. I will hold your hands in my lap and when you spit the pen from your mouth, I will say the words aloud for you.

NOTES

1. Michel Neill, *Putting History to the Question* (New York: Columbia University Press, 2000), 168.

2. William Shakespeare, *Titus Andronicus*, in *The Arden Shakespeare*, ed. Jonathan Bates (London: Thomson Learning, 2002), 266.

3. Shakespeare, *Titus Andronicus*, 98.

4. Mary White Stewart, *Ordinary Violence: Everyday Assaults against Women Worldwide*, 2nd ed. (Santa Barbara: Praeger, 2014), 213.

5. "Shakespeare's Biography," Absolute Shakespeare.com, accessed September 2005, http ://absoluteshakespeare.com/trivia/biography/shakespeare_biography.htm.

6. Paxton Hehmeyer and Liberty Stanavage, eds., *Titus Out of Joint: Reading the Fragmented Titus Andronicus* (Newcastle upon Tyne: Cambridge Scholars, 2012), 121.

7. Shakespeare, *Titus Andronicus*, 267.

Grand Unified Theory of Female Pain

The young woman on the bus with a ravaged face and the intense eyes of some
beautiful species of monkey . . . turned to me and said, "I think I'm getting a sore throat.
Can you feel it?"—Robert Hass, "Images"

We see these wounded women everywhere: Miss Havisham wears her wedding dress until it burns. *The bride within the bridal dress had withered like the
dress.* Belinda's hair gets cut—*the sacred hair dissever[ed] / From the fair head,
for ever, and for ever!*—and then ascends to heaven: *thy ravish'd hair / Which
adds new glory to the shining sphere!* Anna Karenina's spurned love hurts so
much she jumps in front of a train—freedom from one man was just another
one, and then he didn't even stick around. *La Traviata's* Violetta regards her
own pale face in the mirror: tubercular and lovely, an alabaster ghost with
fevered eyes. Mimi is dying in *La Bohème*, and Rodolfo calls her beautiful
as the dawn. *You've mistaken the image,* she tells him. *You should have said
"beautiful as the sunset."*

Women have gone pale all over *Dracula*. Mina is drained of her blood, then
made complicit in the feast: *His right hand gripped her by the back of the neck,
forcing her face down on his bosom. Her white nightdress was smeared with
blood. . . . The attitude of the two had a terrible resemblance to a child forcing a
kitten's nose into a saucer of milk.* Maria in the mountains confesses her rape
to an American soldier—*things were done to me I fought until I could not
see*—then submits herself to his protection. "No one has touched thee, little
rabbit," the soldier says. His touch purges every touch that came before it. She
is another kitten under male hands. How does it go, again? Freedom from one
man is just another one. Maria gets her hair cut too.

Sylvia Plath's agony delivers her to a private Holocaust: *An engine, an
engine / Chuffing me off like a Jew.* And her father's ghost plays train conduc-
tor: *Every woman adores a Fascist / The boot in the face, the brute / Brute heart
of a brute like you.* Every woman adores a Fascist, or else a guerrilla killer

of Fascists, or else a boot in the face from anyone. Blanche DuBois wears a dirty ball gown and depends on the kindness of strangers. *The bride within the dress had withered like the dress.* Men have raped her and gone gay on her and died on her. Her closing stage directions turn her luminescent: "She has a tragic radiance in her red satin robe allowing the sculptural lines of her body." Her body is *allowed.* Meaning: granted permission to exist by tragedy, permitted its soiled portion of radiance.

The pain of women turns them into kittens and rabbits and sunsets and sordid red satin goddesses, pales them and bloodies them and starves them, delivers them to death camps and sends locks of their hair to the stars. Men put them on trains and under them. Violence turns them celestial. Age turns them old. We can't look away. We can't stop imagining new ways for them to hurt.

Susan Sontag has described the heyday of a "nihilistic and sentimental" nineteenth-century logic that found appeal in female suffering: "Sadness made one 'interesting.' It was a mark of refinement, of sensibility, to be sad. That is, to be powerless." This appeal mapped largely onto illness: "Sadness and tuberculosis became synonymous," she writes, and both were coveted. Sadness was interesting and sickness was its handmaiden, providing not only cause but also symptoms and metaphors: a racking cough, a wan pallor, an emaciated body. "The melancholy creature was a superior one: sensitive, creative, a being apart," she writes. Sickness was a "becoming frailty . . . symbolized an appealing vulnerability, a superior sensitivity, [and] became more and more the ideal look for women."

I was once called a wound dweller. It was a boyfriend who called me that. I didn't like how it sounded. It was a few years ago, and I'm still not over it. (It was a wound; I dwell.) I wrote to a friend:

> I've got this double-edged shame and indignation about my bodily ills and
> ailments—jaw, punched nose, fast heart, broken foot, etc. etc. etc. On the one
> hand, I'm like, Why does this shit happen to me? And on the other hand, I'm
> like, Why the fuck am I talking about this so much?

I guess I'm talking about it because it happened. Which is the tricky flip side of Sontag's critique. We may have turned the wounded woman into a kind of goddess, romanticized her illness and idealized her suffering, but that doesn't mean she doesn't happen. Women still have wounds: broken hearts and broken bones and broken lungs. How do we talk about these wounds without glamorizing them? Without corroborating an old mythos that turns female trauma into celestial constellations worthy of worship—*thy ravish'd hair / Which adds new glory to the shining sphere!*—and rubbernecks to peer at every lady breakdown? *Lady Breakdown*: a flavor of aristocracy, a gaunt figure lurking lovely in the shadows.

The moment we start talking about wounded women, we risk transforming their suffering from an aspect of the female experience into an element of the female constitution—perhaps its finest, frailest consummation. The old Greek Menander once said, "*Woman is a pain that never goes away.*" He probably just meant women were trouble. But his words work sideways to summon the possibility that being a woman *requires* being in pain, that pain is the unending glue and prerequisite of female consciousness. This is a notion as old as the Bible: *I will greatly increase your pains in child-birthing; with pain you will give birth to children.*

A 2001 study called "The Girl Who Cried Pain" tries to make sense of the fact that men are more likely than women to be given medication when they report pain to their doctors. Women are more likely to be given sedatives. This trend is particularly unfortunate given the evidence that women might actually experience pain more acutely; theories attribute this asymmetry to hormonal differences between genders or potentially to the fact that "women more often experience pain that is part of their normal biological processes (e.g., menstruation and childbirth)" and so may become more sensitive to pain because they have "to sort normal biological pain out from potentially pathological pain"; men don't have to do this sorting. Despite these reports that "women are biologically more sensitive to pain than men, [their] pain reports are taken less seriously than men's." *Less seriously* meaning, more specifically, "they are more likely to have their pain reports discounted as 'emotional' or 'psychogenic' and, therefore, 'not real.'"

A friend of mine once dreamed a car crash that left all the broken pieces of her Pontiac coated in bright orange pollen. *My analyst pushed and pushed for me to make sense of the image*, she wrote to me, *and finally, I blurted, My wounds are fertile! And that has become one of the touchstones and rallying cries of my life.*

What's fertile in a wound? Why dwell in one? Wounds promise authenticity and profundity; beauty and singularity, desirability. They summon sympathy. They bleed enough light to write by. They yield scats full of stories and slights that become rallying cries. They break upon the fuming fruits of damaged engines and dust these engines with color.

And yet—beyond and beneath their fruits—they still hurt. The boons of a wound never get rid of it; they just bloom from it. It's perilous to think of them as chosen. Perhaps a better phrase to use is *wound appeal*, which is to say: the ways a wound can seduce, how it can promise what it rarely gives. As my friend Harriet once told me, "Pain that gets performed is still pain."

After all I've said, how can I tell you about my scars? I've got a puckered white blister of tissue on my ankle where a doctor pulled out a maggot. I've got faint lines farther up, at the base of my leg, where I used to cut myself with a razor. I've got a nose that was broken by a guy on the street, but you can't tell what he did because money was paid so you couldn't. Now my nose just has a little seam where it was cut and pulled away from my face then stitched back together again. I have screws in my upper jaw that only dentists ever see in x-rays. The surgeon said metal detectors might start going off for me—he probably said *at* me though I heard *for* me, like the chiming of bells—but they never did, never do. I have a patch of tissue near my aorta that sends electrical signals it shouldn't. I had a terrible broken heart when I was twenty-two years old and I wanted to wear a T-shirt announcing it to everyone. Instead, I got so drunk I fell in the middle of Sixth Avenue and scraped all the skin off my knee. Then you could see it, no T-shirt necessary—see *something*, that bloody bulb under torn jeans, though you couldn't have known what it meant. I have the faint bruise of tire tracks on the arch of my foot from the time it got run over by a car. For a little while I had a scar on my upper arm, a lovely raised purple crescent, and one time a stranger asked me about it. I told him the truth: I'd accidentally knocked into a sheet tray at the bakery where I worked. The sheet tray was hot, I explained. Just out of the oven. The man shook his head. He said, "You gotta come up with a better story than that."

Wound #1

My friend Molly always wanted scars:

> I was obsessed with Jem and the Holograms' rival band the Misfits when I was five and wanted to have a cool scar like the Misfits, which I guess was just makeup, but my mom caught me looking in the bathroom mirror . . . trying to cut my face with a sharp stick to get a cool diagonal wound on my face. . . .

Eventually, she got them:

> I have two mouth scars from my bro's Labrador (Stonewall Jackson, or Stoney for short) who bit me six years apart, first when I was six and he was a puppy, and then more seriously when I was twelve. I needed stitches both times, first two and then twenty-something. . . . I was very much aware that I was no longer ever going to be a beautiful girl in the traditional sense, that there was

some real violence marking its territory on my face now, and I was going to have to somehow start high school by adapting my personality to fit this new girl with a prominent scar twisting up from her mouth.

She wrote a poem about that dog: "it was like he could smell the blood / in my mouth. Neither of us / could help it." As if the violence was her destiny and also something ultimately shared, nothing that could be helped, the twisting of intimacy into scar. The dog was sensing a wound that was already there—a mouth full of blood—and was drawn to it; his harm released what was already latent. "He has been at my itching," the poem goes, "and cleaned out the rot. Left me / mouthfull of love."

Wound #2

A Google search for the phrase "I hate cutters" yields hundreds of results, most of them from informal chat boards: *I'm like wtf? why do they do it and they say they cant stop im like damn the balde isnt controlling u*. There's even a Facebook group called "I hate cutters": *this is for people who hate those emo kids who show off there cuts and thinks it is fun to cut them selves*. Hating cutters crystallizes a broader disdain for pain that is understood as performed rather than legitimately felt. It's usually cutters that are hated (wound dwellers!) rather than simply the act of cutting itself. People are dismissed, not just the verbs of what they've done. Apologists for cutting—*Look beyond the cuts and to the soul, then you can see whom we really are*—actually corroborate this sense of cutting as personality type rather than mere dysfunction. Cutting becomes part of identity, part of the self.

A Google search for the phrase "Stop hating on cutters" yields only one result, a posting on a message board called "Things You Wish People Would Stop Hating On." *Seriously the least they need is some idiotic troll calling them emo for cutting/burning etc.* "Emo" being code for affect as performance: the sad show. People say cutters are just doing it for the attention, but why does "just" apply? A cry for attention is positioned as the ultimate crime, clutching or trivial—as if "attention" were inherently a selfish thing to want. But isn't wanting attention one of the most fundamental traits of being human—and isn't granting it one of the most important gifts we can ever give?

There's an online quiz titled "Are you a real cutter or do you cut for fun?" full of statements to be agreed or disagreed with: *I don't know what it really feels like inside when you have problems, I just love to be the center of attention*. Gradations grow finer inside the taboo: some cut from pain, others for show. Hating on cutters—or at least these cutter-performers—tries to draw a boundary between authentic and fabricated pain, as if we weren't all some complicated mix of wounds we can't let go of and wounds we can't help, as if choice itself weren't always some blend of character and agency. How much do we choose to feel anything? The answer, I think, is nothing satisfying—we do, and we don't. But hating on cutters insists desperately upon our capacity for choice. People want to believe in self-improvement—it's an American ethos, pulling oneself up by one's bootstraps—and here we have the equivalent of affective downward mobility: cutting as a failure to feel better, as deliberately going on a kind of sympathetic welfare—taking some shortcut to the street cred of pain without actually feeling it.

I used to cut. It embarrasses me to admit now because it feels less like a demonstration of some pain I've suffered and more like an admission that I've wanted to hurt. But I'm also irritated by my own embarrassment. There was nothing false about my cutting. It was what it was, neither horrifying nor productive. I felt like I wanted to cut my skin, and my cutting was an expression of that desire. There is no lie in that, only a tautology and a question: what made me want to cut at all? Cutting was query and response at once. I cut because my unhappiness felt nebulous and elusive, and I thought it could perhaps hold the shape of a line across my ankle. I cut because I was curious what it would feel like to cut. I cut because I needed very badly to ratify a shaky sense of self, and embodied unhappiness felt like an architectural plan.

I wish we lived in a world where no one wanted to cut. But I also wish that instead of disdaining cutting or the people who do it—or else shrugging it off, *just youthful angst*—we might direct our attention to the unmet needs beneath its appeal. Cutting is an attempt to speak and an attempt to learn. The ways we court bleeding or psychic pain—hurting ourselves with razors or hunger or sex—are also seductions of knowledge. Blood comes before the scar, hunger before the apple. *I hurt myself to feel* is the cutter's cliché, but it's also true. Bleeding is experiment and demonstration, excavation, interior turned out—and the scar remains as residue, pain turned to proof. I don't think of cutting as romantic or articulate, but I do think it manifests yearning, a desire to testify, and it makes me wonder if we could come to a place where proof wasn't necessary at all.

Wound #3

Recounting a low point in the course of her anorexia, Caroline Knapp describes standing in a kitchen and taking off her shirt, on the pretext of changing outfits, so her mother could see her bones more clearly:

I wanted her to see how the bones in my chest and shoulders stuck out, and how skeletal my arms were, and I wanted the sight of this to tell her something I couldn't have begun to communicate myself: something about pain . . . an amalgam of buried wishes and unspoken fears.

Whenever I read accounts of the anorexic body as a semiotic system (as Knapp says, "describing in flesh a pain I could not communicate in words") or an aesthetic creation ("the inner life . . . as a sculpture in bone"), I feel a familiar wariness. Not just at the familiarity of these metaphors—bone as hieroglyph, clavicle as cry—but at the way they risk performing the same valorization they claim to refute: ascribing eloquence to the starving body, a kind of lyric grace. I feel like I've heard it before: the author is still nostalgic for the belief that starving could render angst articulate. I used to write lyrically about my own eating disorder in this way, taking recourse in bone-as-language, documenting the gradual dumb show of my emergent parts—knobs and spurs and ribs. A friend calls these "rituals of surveying"; she describes what it feels like to love "seeing veins and tendons becoming visible."

But underneath this wariness—*must we stylize?*—I remember that starvation is pain, beyond and beneath any stylized expression: there is an ache at its root and an obsession attending every moment of its realization. The desire to speak about that obsession can be symptom as much as cure; everything ultimately points back to pain—even and especially these clutches at nostalgia or abstraction.

What I appreciate about Knapp's kitchen bone-show, in the end, is that it doesn't work. Her mom doesn't remark on the skeleton in her camisole. The subject only comes up later, at the dinner table, when Knapp drinks too much wine and tells her parents she has a problem. The soulful silent cry of bones in kitchen sunlight—that elegiac, faintly mythic anorexia—is trumped by Merlot and messy confession.

If substituting body for speech betrays a fraught relationship to pain—hurting yourself but also keeping quiet about the hurt, implying it without saying it—then having it "work" (mother noticing the bones) would somehow corroborate the logic: let your body say it for you. But here it doesn't. We want our wounds to speak for themselves, Knapp seems to be saying, but usually we end up having to speak for them: *Look here.* Each of us must live with a mouth full of request, and full of hurt. How did it go again? *Mouthfull of love.*

Interlude: Outward

Different kinds of pain summon different terms of art: hurt, suffering, ache, trauma, angst, wounds, damage. *Pain* is general and holds the others under its wings; *hurt* connotes something mild and often emotional; *angst* is the most diffuse and the most conducive to dismissal as something nebulous, sourceless, self-indulgent, affected. *Suffering* is epic and serious; *trauma* implies a specific devastating event and often links to *damage*, its residue. While wounds open to the surface, damage happens to the infrastructure— often invisibly, often irreversibly—and damage also carries the implication of lowered value. *Wound* implies in medias res: the cause of injury is past but the healing isn't done; we are seeing this situation in the present tense of its immediate aftermath. Wounds suggest sex and aperture: a wound marks the threshold between interior and exterior; it marks where a body has been penetrated. Wounds suggest that the skin has been opened—that privacy has been violated in the making of the wound, a rift in the skin, and by the act of peering into it.

Wound #4

In a poem called "The Glass Essay," about the end of a love affair, Anne Carson describes a series of visitations:

> Each morning a vision came to me.
> Gradually I understood that these were naked glimpses of my soul.
>
> I called them Nudes.
> Nude #1. Woman alone on a hill.
> She stands into the wind.
>
> It is a hard wind slanting from the north.
> Long flaps and shreds of flesh rip off the woman's body and lift
> And blow away on the wind, leaving
>
> An exposed column of nerve and blood and muscle
> Calling mutely through lipless mouth.
> It pains me to record this,
>
> I am not a melodramatic person.

This closing motion—*It pains me to record this, / I am not a melodramatic person*—performs a simultaneous announcement and disavowal of pain: this hurts; I hate saying that. The act of admitting one wound creates another: *It pains me to record this.* And yet, the poet must record, because the wounded self can't express anything audible: *Calling mutely through lip-less mouth.*

If a wound is where interior becomes exterior, here is a woman who is almost entirely wound—*an exposed column of nerve and blood and muscle.* Over the course of the poem, she is followed by twelve more wounded visions: a woman in a cage of thorns, a woman pierced by blades of grass, a deck of flesh cards pierced by a silver needle: *The living cards are days of a woman's life.* A woman's flesh can be played like a game of bridge or drawn like pulled pork from her body in the aftermath of a broken heart. Each Nude is a strange, surprising, devastating tableau of pain. We aren't allowed to rest on any single image; we move itinerant from one to the next.

Carson gives us a fourteenth nude in "Teresa of God." "Teresa lived in a personal black cube, / I saw her hit the wall each way she moved." Teresa dies when her heart is "rent," and her death is a response to the constant rebellion and anguish of her living: "To her heart God sent answer." The poem doesn't close with her death, however, but with the impossibility of representing it: "Photographs of the event / had to be faked . . . when the lens kept melting." The melting lens means Teresa can't be immortalized into any single frame, any single Nude, any single wounded posture. Instead, her suffering demands our imagination—our invention and necessary acknowledgment of "fakery" and fabrication—each time we try to picture how she hurt.

Wound #5

Here's the CliffsNotes version: girl gets her period; girl gets scared; girl gets mocked. Girl's mother never told her she was going to bleed. Girl gets elected prom queen and gets a bucket of pig's blood dumped on her head just when things start looking up. *Girl gets; girl gets; girl gets.* Not that she is granted things but that things keep happening to her, until they don't—until she starts doing unto others as they have done, hurting everyone who ever hurt her, moving the world with her mind, conducting its objects like an orchestra.

Stephen King's *Carrie* frames menstruation itself as possible wound: a natural bleeding that Carrie misunderstands as trauma. Carrie crouches in a corner of the locker-room shower while the other girls pelt her with tampons, chanting *Plug it up! Plug it up!* Even the gym teacher reprimands Carrie for being so upset about the simple fact of her period: *Grow up,* she says, *stand up.* The implicit imperative: own this bleeding as inevitable blood. A real woman takes it for granted. Carrie's mother, on the other hand, takes the "curse of blood" as direct evidence of original sin. She slaps Carrie in the head with a tract called *The Sins of Women* while making Carrie repeat, "Eve was weak, Eve was weak, Eve was weak."

I think *Carrie* has something useful to teach us about anorexia. The disease never shows up in its plot, but we see the plausible roots of an anorexic logic—to take the shame of that bleeding and make it disappear, to deny the curse of Eve and the intrinsic vulnerability of wanting—of wanting knowledge, wanting men, wanting anything. Getting your period is one kind of wound; not getting it is another. A friend calls it "the absence of blood where blood should be." Starvation is an act of self-wounding that preempts other wounds, that scrubs away the blood from the shower. But Carrie responds to the shame of fertility by turning it into a weapon. She doesn't get rid of the bleeding; she gets baptized by it. She doesn't wound herself. She wounds everyone else.

The premise of *Carrie* is like porn for female angst: what if you could take how hard it is to be a girl—the cattiness of frenemies, betrayals of your own body, the terror of a public gaze—and turn all that hardship into a superpower? Carrie's telekinesis reaches the apex of its power at the moment she is drenched in red, the moment she becomes a living wound—as if she's just gotten her period all over herself, in front of everyone, as if she's saying, *fuck you*, saying, *now I know how to handle the blood.*

Wound #6

Rosa Dartle is a shrew with a scar. "An old scar," says David Copperfield, protagonist of her novel. "I should rather call it a seam."

When Rosa was young, the boy she loved—sinister and selfish Steerforth, who didn't love her back—eventually grew so irritated by her that he threw a hammer at her face. It slashed open her mouth. "She has borne the mark ever since," Steerforth admits, but she does not bear it quietly. "She brings everything to the grindstone," he says. "She is all edge."

Rosa literally speaks through an open wound: the scar is closed, but her mouth is almost always open. The scar itself is a piece of language. As David describes it,

> the most susceptible part of her face . . . when she turned pale, that mark
> altered first . . . lengthening out to its full extent, like a mark in invisible ink
> brought to the fire . . . now showing the whole extent of the wound inflicted by
> the hammer, as I had seen it when she was passionate.

I should rather call it a seam: the ugliness holds her together, knits her skin like it was fabric, gives her shape. It speaks the hurt underneath: she was spurned by the first man she loved (spurned by hammer!) and now means nothing more to him than a "mere disfigured piece of furniture . . . having no eyes, no ears, no feelings, no remembrances." *No eyes, no ears, no feelings.* Just a scar, She still has that: "its white track cutting through her lips, quivering and throbbing as she spoke."

Her scar doesn't make her compassionate or sympathetic, however, only bitter and vindictive. It grants her the sensitivity of keen awareness but not of human warmth. When Steerforth spurns another woman, Rosa takes a rapturous, almost sexual pleasure in the fact of this woman's grief. When someone tells Rosa about the woman's plight—"she'd have beaten her head against the marble floor"—we see Rosa "leaning back upon the seat, with a light of exultation in her face, she seemed almost to caress the sounds." Rosa wants a companion in her damage: "I would have this girl whipped to death," she says. She can't summon sympathy for Steerforth's mother, either—another woman he's abandoned. David is shocked: "if you can be so obdurate as not to feel for this afflicted mother"—Rosa cuts him off to say, "Who feels for me?"

Wound #7

Now we have a TV show called *Girls*, about girls who hurt but constantly disclaim their hurting. They fight about rent and boys and betrayal, stolen yogurt and the ways self-pity structures their lives. "You're a big, ugly wound!" one yells. The other yells back, "No, you're the wound!" And so they volley, back and forth: *You're the wound; you're the wound.* They know women like to claim monopolies on woundedness, and they call each other out on it.

These girls aren't wounded so much as postwounded, and I see their sisters everywhere. They're over it. *I am not a melodramatic person.* God help the woman who is. What I'll call "postwounded" isn't a shift in deep feeling (we understand these women still hurt) but a shift away from wounded affect—these women are aware that "woundedness" is overdone and overrated. They are wary of melodrama, so they stay numb or clever instead. Postwounded women make jokes about being wounded or get impatient with women who hurt too much. The postwounded woman conducts herself as if preempting certain accusations: don't cry too loud, don't play victim, don't act the old role all over again. Don't ask for pain meds you don't need; don't give those doctors another reason to doubt the other women on their examination tables. Postwounded women fuck men who don't love them, and then they feel mildly sad about it or just blasé about it; more than anything they refuse to care about it, refuse to hurt about it—or else they are endlessly self-aware about the posture they have adopted if they allow themselves this hurting.

The postwounded posture is claustrophobic. It's full of jadedness, aching gone implicit, sarcasm quick on the heels of anything that might look like self-pity. I see it in female writers and their female narrators, troves of stories about vaguely dissatisfied women who no longer fully own their feelings. Pain is everywhere and nowhere. Postwounded women know that postures of pain play into limited and outmoded conceptions of womanhood. Their hurt has a new native language spoken in several dialects: sarcastic, apathetic, opaque; cool and clever. They guard against those moments when melodrama or self-pity might split their careful seams of intellect. *I should rather call it a seam.* We have sewn ourselves up. We bring everything to the grindstone.

Wound #8

In a review of Louise Glück's *Collected Poems*, Michael Robbins calls her "a major poet with a minor range." He specifies this range to pain: "Every poem is The Passion of Louise Glück, starring the grief and suffering of Louise Glück. But someone involved in the production knows how to write very well indeed." I could take issue with Robbins's "every," or the condescension embedded in "starring," but in the end I'm most interested in his conjunction. "But" implies that Glück can be a poet who matters only *despite* her fixation on suffering, that this "minor range" is what her intelligence and skill must constantly overcome.

Robbins frustrates me and speaks for me at once. I find myself in a bind. I'm tired of female pain and also tired of people who are tired of it. I know the hurting woman is a cliché, but I also know lots of women still hurt. I don't like the proposition that female wounds have gotten old; I feel wounded by it.

I felt particularly wounded by the brilliant and powerful female poet who visibly flinched during a writing workshop at Harvard when I started reciting Sylvia Plath. She'd asked us each to memorize a poem, and I'd chosen "Ariel," which felt like its own thirteenth line, *black sweet blood mouthfuls,* fierce and surprising and hurting and free.

"Please," this brilliant and powerful woman said, as if herself in pain. "I'm just so tired of Sylvia Plath."

I had this terrible feeling that every woman who knew anything about anything was tired of Sylvia Plath, tired of her blood and bees and the level of narcissistic self-pity required to compare her father to Hitler—but I'd been left behind. I hadn't gotten the highbrow girl-memo: Don't Read the Girls

Who Cried Pain. I was still staring at Plath while she stared at her own bleeding skin, skin she'd sliced with a knife: *What a thrill—my thumb instead of an onion.* Sylvia and I were still obsessed with the density of a wound—*thumb stump, pulp of heart*—thrilled and shamed by it.

Wound #9

Listen to this dream:

> The room was small, but it held all the women you could think of and all the men you were ever scared of in your whole life, passing on the street or just imagining, and all the men you loved the most. . . . There were knives and girls skinned alive and kept alive, and one woman screaming but trying to laugh it off to another: "Look what they did to my face!"—and there were amputations performed right there, the limbs cut off . . . and all the things that can be done to a person, including the pulling and ripping of everything that we didn't even know we love about a person.

Here's how the dream ends: eventually the girls are skinned to the point of interchangeability—"just bloodiness, like animals turned inside out," like Carson's nude—and tossed from the building while onlookers throw paint onto their falling bodies. They turn all the colors of the rainbow. They turn into art.

They turn, specifically, into a book called *How Should a Person Be?* Its narrator, Sheila, is one of the onlookers and also one of the girls. (She also shares her name with the author, Sheila Heti.) She is in pain but also making fun of how we distort every pain into the worst pain—*the very worst possible pain*—the worst circle of hell. Superlatives are just another way of proving hurt—an abstraction instead of a cut line on the skin. The dream offers a woman who is aware of how girls try to turn pain into a joke. She makes a joke of this tendency. She is standing in front of you—all shivering and bloody, like a freak on a stage—and cranking up the volume on the pain stereo, pushing on your eyeballs with the force of her mind. Raw bodies turn into painted artifacts. The superlative vocabulary of suffering keeps extending its wingspan.

In college I took a self-defense class with a bunch of other girls. We had to go around in a circle and tell the group our worst fear. These instructions created a weird incentive structure. When you've got a lot of Harvard girls in a circle, everyone wants to say something better than the girl before her. So the first girl said, "Getting raped, I guess," which is what we were all thinking. The next one upped the ante: "Getting raped—and then killed." The third paused to think, then said, "Maybe getting gang-raped?" The fourth had had time to think, had already anticipated the third one's answer. She said, "Getting gang-raped and mutilated."

I can't remember what the rest of us managed to come up with (white slavery? snuff films?) but I remember thinking how odd it was—how we were all sitting there trying to be the best kid in class, the worst rape fantasizer, in this all-girl impersonation of a misogynistic hate-crime brainstorming session. We were giggling. Our giggling—of course—was also about our fear: *One woman screaming and trying to laugh it off to another.*

Whenever I tell that story as an anecdote, I think about the other girls in that circle. I wonder if anything terrible ever happened to any of them. We left that shitty gym to start the rest of our lives, to go forth into the world and meet all the men we were ever going to be scared of, passing on the street or just imagining.

Wound #10

I grew up under the spell of damaged sirens: Tori Amos and Ani DiFranco, Björk, Kate Bush, Mazzy Star. They sang about all the ways a woman could hurt: *I'm a fountain of blood in the shape of a girl. When they're out for blood I always give. We are made to bleed and scab and heal and bleed again and turn every scar into a joke. Boy you best pray that I bleed real soon. Bluffing your way into my mouth, behind my teeth, reaching for my scars. Did I ever tell you how I stopped eating, when you stopped calling? You're only popular with anorexia. Sometimes you're nothing but meat, girl. I've come home. I'm so cold.*

I called my favorites by their first names: Tori and Ani. Tori sang "blood roses" over and over again, and I had no idea what this phrase meant except that pain and beauty were somehow connected. Every once in a while her songs posed questions: *Why did she crawl down in the deep ravine? Why do we crucify ourselves?* The songs themselves were answers. She crawled into the deep ravine so we'd wonder why she crawled into the deep ravine. We crucify ourselves so we can sing about it.

Kate Bush's "Experiment IV" describes a secret military plan to design a "sound that could kill someone." *From the painful cries of mothers to the terrifying screams we recorded it and put it into our machine.* The song would be lethal, but also a lullaby: *It could feel like falling in love / It could feel so bad / But it could feel so good / It could put you to sleep.* Of course the song played just like the song it described. Listening felt so bad and so good. It felt like falling in love. I'd never fallen in love. I was a voyeur and a vandal—flexing the hurt muscles in my heart by imagining myself into aches I'd never felt.

I invented terrible daydreams to saddle those songs with the gravity of melodrama: someone I loved died; I was summoned to car accident deathbed; I had a famous boyfriend and he cheated on me and I had to raise our child—better yet, our many children—on my own. Those songs gave me scars to try on like costumes. I wanted to be sung to sleep by them; I wanted to be killed and resurrected.

More than anything, I wanted to be killed by Ani's "Swan Dive": *I'm gonna do my best swan dive / in the shark-infested waters / gonna pull out my tampon / and start splashing around.* If being a woman is all about bleeding, then she'll bleed. She'll get hurt. Carrie knew how it was done; she never plugged it up. She splashed around. *I don't care if they eat me alive*, Ani sings, *I've got better things to do than survive*. Better things like martyrdom, having the last laugh, choosing the end, singing a song about blood.

I was listening to "Swan Dive" years before I got my period, but I was already ready to jump. I was ready to weaponize my menarche. I was waiting for the day when I could throw my womanhood to the sharks because I finally had some womanhood to call my own. I couldn't wait to be inducted into the ranks of this female frustration—the period as albatross, lunar burden, exit ticket from Eden, keys to the authenticity kingdom. Bleeding among the sharks meant being eligible for men, which meant being eligible for hope, loss, degradation, objectification, desire and being desired—a whole world of ways to get broken.

Years later I worked at a bakery where my boss liked putting on a playlist she called our "Wounded Mix." We hummed along with Sade and Phil Collins; we mixed red velvet batter the color of cartoon hearts. My boss said that when she listened to these songs, she imagined being abandoned by some cruel lover on the shoulder of a dusty highway—"with just my backpack and my sunglasses," she told me, "and my big hair."

I started hunting for more ladies singing about wounds. I asked my boyfriend for suggestions. He texted instructions: *Google "you cut me open and I keep bleeding." Best bathos on the air.* I found Leona Lewis: *You cut me open and I / Keep bleeding, keep, keep bleeding love / I keep bleeding, I keep, keep bleeding love / Keep bleeding, keep, keep bleeding love.* Each chorus returns, at its close, to the main gist: *You cut me open.* The lyrics could be lamenting love or affirming it, trusting the possibility of falling for someone in the aftermath of hurt, or else suggesting that love dwells in the hurting itself—that sentiment clots and coagulates in bled blood, another version of the cutter's logic: *I bleed to feel.* Bleeding is the proof and home of passion, its residence and protectorate. This kind of bloody heartbreak isn't feeling gone wrong; it's feeling gone right—emotion distilled to its purest, most magnificent form. *Best bathos on the air.* Well, yes, it is. *Turn every scar into a joke.* We already did.

But what if some of us want to take our scars seriously? Maybe some of us haven't gotten the memo—haven't gotten the text message from our boy-friends—about what counts as bathos. One man's joke is another girl's diary entry. One woman's heartbreak is another woman's essay. Maybe this bleeding ad nauseam is mass-produced and sounds ridiculous—*Plug it up! Plug it up!*—but maybe its business isn't done. *Woman is a pain that never goes away.* Keep cutting me open; I'll keep bleeding it out. Saving Leona Lewis means insisting that we never have the right to dismiss the trite or poorly worded or plainly ridiculous, the overused or overstated or strategically performed.

In the reader's group guide to my first novel, I confessed, "I often felt like a DJ mixing various lyrics of female teenage angst." I got so sick of synopsizing the plot, whenever people asked what it was about, I started saying simply: *women and their feelings.* When I called myself a DJ mixing angst, it was a preemptive strike. I felt like I had to defend myself against some hypothetical accusation that would be lobbed against my book by the world at large. I was trying to agree with Ani: We shouldn't have to turn every scar into a joke. We shouldn't have to be witty or backtrack or second-guess ourselves when we say, *this shit hurt.* We shouldn't have to disclaim—*I know, I know, pain is old, other girls hurt*—to defend ourselves from the old litany of charges: perfor-mative, pitiful, self-pitying, pity hoarding, pity mongering. The pain is what you make of it. You have to find something in it that yields. I understood my guiding imperative as keep bleeding, but find some love in the blood.

Wound #11

Once I wrote a story from that open wound Yeats calls "the rag and bone shop of the heart." In this particular case, my rag-and-bone shop had been looted by a poet. He and I had a few glorious autumn months in Iowa—there were cold beers on an old bridge, wine in a graveyard, poems left on pillows—and I thought I was in love with him, and maybe would marry him, and then sud-denly we were done. He was done. I knew this wasn't an unusual occurrence in the world, but it hadn't ever happened to me. I kept trying to figure it out. A few nights before the end, feeling him pull away, I'd talked with him for a long time about the eating disorder I'd had when I was younger. I honestly can't remember why I did this—whether I wanted to feel close to him, wanted him to demonstrate his care by sympathizing, or whether I just wanted to will myself into trusting him by saying something that seemed to imply that I already did.

After he was gone, I decided maybe this conversation had something to do with why he'd left. Perhaps he'd been repulsed—not necessarily by the eating disorder itself but by my naked attempt to secure his attention by narrating it. I was desperate for a *why*—at first because I wanted to understand our breakup and eventually because I realized any story I wrote about us would feel flimsy if our breakup had no motivating catalyst. Pain without a cause is pain we can't trust. We assume it's been chosen or fabricated.

I was afraid to write a story about us because heartbreak seemed like a story that had already been told too many times, and my version of heartbreak felt horribly banal: getting blackout drunk and sharing my feelings in fleeting pockets of lucidity, sleeping with guys and crying in their bathrooms afterward. Falling on Sixth Avenue in the middle of the night and then showing my scarred knee to anyone who'd look. I made people tell me I was more attractive than my ex. I made people tell me he was an asshole, even though he wasn't.

This kind of thing, I told myself, wasn't what I'd come to the Iowa Writers' Workshop to write about. Maybe sadness could be "interesting," but not when it looked like this. The female narrator I'd be depicting in my story—a woman consumed by self-pity, drowning her sorrows in drink; engaged in reckless sexual self-destruction; obsessed with the man who'd left her—didn't seem like a particularly appealing or empowered sort of woman to think about or be. Yet she was me.

Maybe drunken heartbreak was the lamest thing I could possibly write about, but this was precisely why I wanted to write about it. I wanted to write against my own feelings of shame at my premise—its banality and waft of self-pity, the way in which its very structure suggested a protagonist defined almost exclusively in terms of her harmful relationships to men. The story wouldn't just *seem* to be about letting men usurp a woman's identity; it would in fact be about this. My own squeamishness goaded me forward: perhaps self-destruction in the aftermath of heartbreak was a trite pain, but it was *my* trite pain, and I wanted to find a language for it. I wanted to write a story so good that my hypothetical future readers would acknowledge as profound a kind of female sadness they'd otherwise dismiss as performative, overplayed, or self-indulgent. There were also practical concerns. I had a deadline for workshop. Seeing as how the breakup was all I thought about, I didn't see how I could write a story about anything else.

I wrote the ending first. It was an assertion: *I had a heart. It remained.* I liked it because it felt true and optimistic (my heart's still here!) but also sad (my still-here heart hurts constantly!). I put the eating disorder conversation into the story so that readers could point to it—if they needed to point to something—and say, *Oh, maybe that's why he got out.* I also meant the eating disorder to clarify that my protagonist's impulse toward self-destruction wasn't caused so much as activated by the breakup, which had resurrected the corpse of an older pain: an abiding sense of inadequacy that could attach itself to the body, or a man, an impulse that—like a heat-seeking missile—always sniffed out ways it could hurt even more.

I realized that this causeless pain—inexplicable and seemingly intractable—was my true subject. It was frustrating. It couldn't be pinned to any trauma; no one could be blamed for it. Because this nebulous sadness seemed to attach to female anxieties (anorexia and cutting and obsession with male attention), I began to understand it as inherently feminine, and because it was so unjustified by circumstance, it began to feel inherently shameful. Each of its self-destructive manifestations felt half-chosen, half-cursed.

In this sense, I was aware that the breakup was giving me a hook on which I could hang a disquiet much more amoebic—and not so easily parsed. Part of me knew my story had imposed a causal logic on the breakup that hadn't been there. My ex had been pulling away before I'd ever confessed anything to him. But I recognized a certain tendency in myself—a desire to compel men by describing things that had been hard for me—and wanted to punish this tendency. Punishment involved imagining the ways my confessions might repulse the men they were supposed to beckon closer. When I punished myself with this causality, I also restored the comforting framework of emotional order—*because I did this, this happened; because this happened, I hurt.*

In the meantime, I was nervous about workshop. Would I be lauded as a genius? Quietly understood as pathetic? I chose my outfit carefully. I still remember one of the first comments. "Does this character have a job?" one guy asked, sounding annoyed, and said she might have been a little easier to sympathize with if she did.

Interlude: Outward

As it happened, that story was the first one I ever published. Sometimes I get notes about it from strangers. One woman in Arizona even got part of it tattooed on her back. Men say it helps them sympathize more with certain female tendencies. These men write to me about their relationships: women who once seemed like reckless bitches, they say, start to seem like something else. A frat guy wrote to say that now he "got" girls better. I trusted he meant: understood. Another guy said, *I have always been curious of the psychology of women who tend toward a want to be dominated.*

A Hawaiian real estate agent wrote about his little sister. He'd never been compassionate about her painful relationships with men. *I'm sure that your goal was not to educate men on the psychological nuances of women,* he said, but he felt he could relate to his sister's self-destructive tendencies better after reading the story—*a little wisp of understanding,* he said. I was thrilled. My pain had flown beyond the confines of its bone shop. Now it had a summer home in the Pacific.

I wouldn't say writing that story helped me get over my breakup any faster; it probably did just the opposite. I ended up consigning that ex into the realm of legend—a sort of mythic prop around which I'd constructed this suffering version of myself. But the story helped me weave the breakup into my sense of self in a way that ultimately felt outward, directed toward the lives and pain of others. And yet—do I still wonder if my ex ever read that story? Of course I do.

Wound #12

The summer after my freshman year of college, my mouth was wired shut for two months while my jaw healed from an operation. The joint hinge had been damaged in an accident—I'd fallen off a vine in Costa Rica, twenty feet to cloud forest floor—and certain bones had been drilled into new shapes and then screwed back together again. The wires held everything in place. I couldn't talk or eat. I squirted geriatric energy drinks into the small opening between my teeth and the back of my mouth. I wrote notes on little yellow pads. I read a lot. Already, then, I thought of documenting my experience for posterity. And I already had the title of my memoir in mind: *Autobiography of a Face.*

That's how I discovered Lucy Grealy. Her memoir, *Autobiography of a Face,* is the story of her childhood cancer and enduring facial disfigurement. I read it in an afternoon and then I read it all over again. Its central drama, for me, wasn't Grealy's recovery from illness; it was the story of her attempt to forge an identity that wasn't entirely defined by the wound of her face. At first she couldn't see her face as anything but a locus of damage to which everything else referred:

> This singularity of meaning—I was my face, I was ugliness—though sometimes unbearable, also . . . became the launching pad from which to lift off. . . . Everything led to it, everything receded from it—my face as personal vanishing point.

These are the dangers of a wound: that the self will be subsumed by it ("personal vanishing point") or unable to see outside its gravity ("everything led to it"). The wound can sculpt selfhood in a way that limits identity rather than expanding it, that obstructs vision (of other people's suffering, say) rather than sharpening empathic acuity. Carrie doesn't do anyone any favors. Rosa Dartle is all edge.

Grealy had been craving the identity-locus of damage even before it happened to her, and was happy, as a little girl, when trauma first arrived: "I was excited by the idea that something really was wrong with me"—like Molly with a razor at her cheek, trying to make herself a Misfit. Years later, Grealy still took a certain comfort in her surgeries. These were the times when she was cared for most directly, and when her pain was given a structure beyond the nebulous petty torture of feeling ugly to the world. "It wasn't without a certain amount of shame that I took this kind of emotional comfort from surgery," she writes. "Did it mean I liked having operations and thus that I deserved them?"

In Grealy's shame I see the residue of certain cultural imperatives: to be stoic, to have a relationship to pain defined by the single note of resistance. These imperatives make it shameful to feel any attachment to pain or any sensitivity to its offerings. What I love about Grealy is that she's not afraid to be honest about every part of her pain: how she takes some comfort in her surgeries and feels discomfort at this comfort, how she tries to feel better about her face— over and over again—and just can't. She can't make ugliness productive. She can't make the wound fertile. She can only take solace in how much it hurts and in how this hurting elicits the care of others. In this confession, of course, the wound does become fertile. It yields honesty. Her book is beautiful.

As a little girl, Grealy learned to be what she calls a "good patient," but the book itself refuses this posture: she offers no false resurrections of the spirit. She insists on the tyranny of the body and its damage. Her situation was an extreme one, but it gave form and justification to how I was living then, silently: my own existence defined by injury.

Most of the negative Amazon reviews of *Autobiography of a Face* focus on the idea of self-pity: "She was a sad woman who never got beyond her own personal pain"; "I found this book extremely sorrowful and drowning in self-pity"; "it seems like she could only think of herself, her complete misery and pain at being 'ugly.'"

A man named "Tom" writes,

> In all of the books I've read, I've never encountered such terribly [*sic*] moaning and wallowing in self-pity. I can easily sum up the entire 240-page book in 3 words: Woe is me.... In addition to a mess of crying, the author cannot seem

to make up her mind on anything. First she says she does not want to be felt sorry for by anyone, then she proceeds to scorn others about their inability to feel an ounce of sympathy.

The woman Tom describes as "wallowing in self-pity" and unable to decide what the world should do about it, is exactly the woman I grew up afraid of becoming. I knew better—we all, it seems, knew better—than to become one of *those* women who plays victim, lurks around the sickbed, hands her pain out like a business card. What I'm trying to say is, I don't think this was just me. An entire generation, the next wave, grew up doing everything we could to avoid this identity: we take refuge in self-awareness, self-deprecation, jadedness, sarcasm. The Girl Who Cried Pain: she doesn't need meds; she needs a sedative.

And now we find ourselves torn. We don't want anyone to feel sorry for us, but we miss the sympathy when it doesn't come. Feeling sorry for ourselves has become a secret crime—a kind of shameful masturbation—that would chase away the sympathy of others if we ever let it show. "Because I had grown up denying myself any feeling that even hinted at self-pity," Grealy writes, "I now had to find a way to reshape it."

Reshape it into what? Into faith, sexual promiscuity, intellectual ambition. At the pinnacle: into art. Grealy offers this last alchemy, pain-to-art, as possibility but not redemption. It seems likely that for all her wound has given her—perspective, the grit of survival, an insightful meditation on beauty—Grealy would still trade back these wound boons for a pretty face. This confession of willingness is her greatest gift of honesty, not arguing that beauty was more important than profundity, just admitting that she might have chosen it—that beauty was more difficult to live without.

Interlude: Outward

When I started writing this essay, I decided to crowdsource. I wrote a message to some of my favorite women, asking them to tell me about their thoughts on female pain. "Please don't not-respond," I wrote; "it would make me feel totally alone in my obsession with gendered woundedness." They responded.

"Perhaps too obvious," wrote a friend in divinity school, "but the fall?" She pointed out that Eve is defined by the pain of childbirth. Another friend suggested that perhaps childbirth shapes women as a horizon of anticipation. Women come into consciousness, she speculated, imagining a future pain toward which their bodies inevitably propel them.

A friend described an upbringing "thoroughly, thoroughly obsessed with not being a victim." She typed *not being a victim* in italics. Another friend described her young devotion to the oeuvre of Lurlene McDaniel, an author who writes about sick girls—cancer-ridden, heart-transplanted, bulimic—who make friends with even sicker girls, girls turned angelic by illness, and always eventually watch these sicker girls die. These books offered an opportunity for two-pronged empathy: the chance to identify with martyr and survivor, to die and live at once, to feel simultaneously the glory of tragedy and the reassurance of continuance.

I got confessions. One friend admitted that female pain often felt, to her, like "a failure of an ethic of care" and that her ideal of feminine pain might be the grieving Madonna: "the pain of care whose object of care has been removed." She was afraid this ideal made her a secret misogynist. Another friend—Taryn, a poet—confessed that her greatest fear was that her poems would come across as solipsistic transcriptions of private suffering and that in this self-concern they would also register as somehow "feminine." She too was afraid that this first fear made her a secret misogynist.

One friend got so worked up by my e-mail that she waited until the next morning to reply. She was tired of an abiding societal fascination, she wrote, with women who identified themselves by their pain—women who hurt themselves, or got too drunk, or slept with the wrong men. She was more than *tired of*. She was angry.

I think her anger is asking a question, and I think that question demands an answer. How do we represent female pain without producing a culture in which this pain has been fetishized to the point of fantasy or imperative? *Fetishize*: to be excessively or irrationally devoted to. Here is the danger of wounded womanhood: that its invocation will corroborate a pain cult that keeps legitimating, almost legislating, more of itself.

The hard part is that underneath this obscene fascination with women who hurt themselves and have bad sex and drink too much, there are actual women who hurt themselves and have bad sex and drink too much. Female pain is prior to its representation, even if its manifestations are shaped and bent by cultural models.

Relying too much on the image of the wounded woman is reductive, but so is rejecting it—being unwilling to look at the varieties of need and suffering that yield it. We don't want to *be* wounds ("No, you're the wound!") but we should be allowed to have them, to speak about having them, to be something more than just another girl who has one. We should be able to do these things without failing the feminism of our mothers, and we should be able to represent women who hurt without walking backward into a voyeuristic hashing of the old cultural models: another emo cutter under bleachers, another hurt-seeking missile of womanhood, a body gone drunk or bruised or barren, another archetype sunk into blackout under the sheets.

We've got a Janus-faced relationship to female pain. We're attracted to it and revolted by it; proud and ashamed of it. So we've developed a post-wounded voice, a stance of numbness or crutch of sarcasm that implies pain without claiming it, that seems to stave off certain accusations it can see on the horizon: melodrama, triviality, wallowing—an ethical and aesthetic commandment: don't valorize suffering women.

You court a certain disdain by choosing to write about hurting women. You get your period with sharks around—*exposed column of nerve and blood*—but everyone thinks it's a stupid show. You want to cry, *I am not a melodramatic person!* But everyone thinks you are. You're willing to bleed, but it looks, instead, like you're trying to get bloody. When you bleed like that—all over everything, tempting the sharks—you get told you're corroborating the wrong mythology. You should be ashamed of yourself. *Plug it up.*

In 1844 a woman named Harriet Martineau wrote a book called *Life in the Sick Room.* Ten years later she published an autobiography. In this second book she compresses her illness to a footnote, explaining, "There is no point of which I am more sure than it is unwise in sick people to keep a diary." She knew better than to yoke her identity as an author to her status as a sick woman, especially in a culture eager to see women as invalids-in-waiting. Perhaps she was justifiably afraid that her sickness would be understood as limiting the scope of her vision, that it might quarantine her into category. *A major poet with a minor range*: The Passion of the Invalid.

Lucy Grealy learned to be a good patient when she learned that it was possible to fail at being sick. "My feelings of shame and guilt or failing not to suffer," she writes, "became more unbearable. The physical pain seemed almost easy in comparison." Sometimes we call *failing not to suffer* something else: we call it wallowing. Wallow, intr. v.: to roll the body about indolently or clumsily, as if in snow, water, or mud; to luxuriate, to revel. This is the fear: that we will turn our bodies clumsy if we spend too much time mourning what has happened to them; if we revel in our pain like a shark-infested sea; if we wear the mud like paint across our skin-stripped bodies.

Wound #13

When Misfit Molly was twenty-four, a stranger broke into her Brooklyn apartment and tried to rape her at knifepoint. She was able to get away—fleeing her studio naked, after a ten-minute struggle—but of course that didn't release her from years of fear, years of trying to make sense of what had happened. "Imposing a truly sensible narrative on my attack," she writes, "proved impossible in its aftermath." She moved in with a good friend, and they watched films to help them fall asleep at night:

We turned to what we wanted to watch, and that happened, reflexively, to be stories about women in peril, women without autonomy, girls who disappear, dark ladies hurting within and without. On the subway, I found myself obsessively listening to old-time murder ballads like "Pretty Polly," fascinated by the perverse beauty of lyrics like "He stabbed her through the heart and her heart's blood did flow."

Dark ladies hurting within and without. It doesn't surprise me that Molly was drawn to them. Maybe they gave her visions of pain worse than her own, or made her feel less alone, or simply granted her permission to inhabit her own pain by offering a world in which the logic of pain held court.

This essay isn't fighting for that world. It isn't simply criticizing the post-wounded voice or dismissing the ways in which female pain gets dismissed. I do believe there is nothing shameful about being in pain, and I do mean for this essay to be a manifesto against the accusation of wallowing. But the essay isn't a double negative, a dismissal of dismissal, so much as a search for possibility—the possibility of representing female suffering without reifying its mythos. Lucy Grealy describes much of her artistic life as an attempt "to grant myself the complicated and necessary right to suffer."

I'm looking for the thirteenth nude, who arrives at the close of Carson's poem:

Very much like Nude #1.
And yet utterly different.
. . . .
I saw it was a human body
trying to stand against winds so terrible that the flesh was blowing off the bones.
And there was no pain. The wind
was cleansing the bones.
They stood forth silver and necessary.
It was not my body, not a woman's body, it was the body of us all.
It walked out of the light.

This Nude is like the first Nude because she is nothing but ragged flesh, but here the "flesh [is] blowing off" and her nakedness signals strength. Her exposure is clean and necessary. There is no pain. The nerves are gone. The move away from pain requires a movement into commonality: "out of the light" of human particularity and gender ("It was not my body, not a woman's body") and into the Universal ("it was the body of us all"). Walking out of the light simultaneously suggests being constituted by this light—walking forth from the substance of origin—and leaving it behind, abandoning the state of visible representation. Once pain is cleansed into something silver and necessary, it no longer needs to be illuminated. Pain only reaches beyond itself when its damage shifts from private to public, from solipsistic to collective.

One friend sent me a letter about pain, written on a piece of nearly translucent paper. She suggested we could see our wounds as "places of conductivity where the pain hits your experience and lights something up." Her translucent paper mattered. I could see the world beyond her words: the table, my own fingers. Perhaps this visibility—this invitation to see parts in relation—is what pain makes possible.

We shouldn't forget how this thirteenth Nude recalls the first one, that primal artifact of pain, whose bloody ghost limns these silver bones like an aura, reminding us that the cleansing cannot happen without some loss: *cleaned out the rot, left me mouthfull of love.* Like Stevens and his thirteen blackbirds, we see pain from every angle; no single posture of suffering is allowed any measure of perceptual tyranny. We can't see suffering one way; we have to look at it from thirteen directions, and that is only the beginning—then we are called to follow this figure striding out of the light.

We follow this figure into contradiction, into a confession that wounds are desired and despised; that they grant power and come at a price; that suffering yields virtue and selfishness; that victimhood is a mix of situation and agency; that pain is the object of representation and also its product; that culture transcribes genuine suffering while naturalizing its symptoms. We follow this thirteenth nude back to the bleachers, where some girl is putting on a passion play with her razor. We should watch. She's hurting, but that doesn't mean she'll hurt forever—or that hurt is the only identity she can own. There is a way of representing female consciousness that can witness pain but also witness a larger self around that pain—a self who grows larger than its scars without disowning them, who is neither wound-dwelling nor jaded, who is actually healing.

We can watch what happens when the girl under the bleachers puts down the blade. Suffering is interesting but so is getting better. The aftermath of wounds—the strain and struggle of stitching the skin, the stride of silver bones—contours women alongside the wounds themselves. Glück dreams of "a harp, its string cutting / deep into my palm. In the dream, / it both makes the wound and seals the wound."

When I read Taryn's poems, I see imagination twining like a vine out of injury. You can see bits of her life—a major surgery to remove a tumor wrapped around her liver—but the prone body of her female subject ("she is laid out supplicant") is never the only body in view. This female voice is never allowed any monopoly on hurt. The poems are thick with damage—a gardener's birds with their thin bones snapped, a dead fat doe ("Her delicious odor!")—and butchering instructions: "Spread the ribs with a stick . . . accordion of bone glows beneath. Reveal the leg meat. This is like opening a set of French doors." These verbs are verbs of opening, slicing, parting, exploring, excavating, and extracting. Damage isn't for its own sake. It's for epistemology or else it's for dinner. *Sometimes you're nothing but meat, girl.* Where others might navel-gaze, Taryn is opening the navels of animals—*not my body, not a woman's body*—but her gaze feels personal in its vulnerability. She offers a sense of the violence intrinsic to the feat of living in a body—any body, among other bodies—an awareness necessarily embedded in the body of us all, that body made of light and departing from it.

I want to honor what happens when confession collides with butchering instructions: how we find an admission of wounds but also a vision of manipulating bloody bodies, arranging and opening their parts. I want to insist that female pain is still news. It's always news. We've never already heard it.

It's news when a girl loses her virginity or gets an ache in the rag-and-bone shop of her heart. It's news when she starts getting her period or when she does something to make herself stop. It's news if a woman feels terrible about herself in the world—anywhere, anytime, ever. It's news whenever a girl has an abortion because her abortion has never been had before and won't ever be had again. I'm saying this as someone who's had an abortion but hasn't had anyone else's.

Sure, some news is bigger news than other news. War is bigger news than a girl having mixed feelings about the way some guy fucked her and didn't call. But I don't believe in a finite economy of empathy; I happen to think that paying attention yields as much as it taxes. You learn to start seeing.

I think dismissing female pain as overly familiar or somehow out-of-date—twice-told, thrice-told, 1,001-nights-told—masks deeper accusations: that suffering women are playing victim, going weak, or choosing self-indulgence over bravery. I think dismissing wounds offers a convenient excuse: no need to struggle with the listening or telling anymore. *Plug it up.* Like somehow our task is to inhabit the jaded aftermath of terminal self-awareness once the story of all pain has already been told.

For a long time I have hesitated to write a book on woman, is how de Beauvoir starts one of the most famous books on women ever written. *The subject is irritating, especially to women; and it is not new.* Sometimes I feel like I'm beating a dead wound. But I say, keep bleeding. Just write toward something beyond blood.

The wounded woman gets called a stereotype and sometimes she is. But sometimes she's just true. I think the possibility of fetishizing pain is no reason to stop representing it. Pain that gets performed is still pain. Pain turned trite is still pain. I think the charges of cliché and performance offer our closed hearts too many alibis, and I want our hearts to be open. I just wrote that. I want our hearts to be open. I mean it.

Gun Shy

A pistol is a great morale booster.—Bruce Quarrie, Waffen-ss soldier, 1940–45

In the beginning there was the Waffen-ss Walther P.38 that my stepfather, Kirdy, found on a battlefield in Italy. A Nazi officer's pistol, meant for up-close execution and fighting to the end, customized with a hand-etched swastika and ss double lightning bolts. Evading capture was supposed to mean shooting Americans, allies, or yourself. But sometimes in retreat, bravery failed, and officers dropped pistols, medals, and insignia, disguising themselves as common grunts less likely to be pursued by their enemy.

If Kirdy's business hadn't been robbed twenty-five years later, my mother might never have known about the gun. He kept it stashed in our cellar behind the fake wall he'd built to conceal a horde of cash and single malt scotch. If civilization fell—and with the Cuban Missile Crisis and weekly bomb drills in school, we thought any day it might—we wouldn't need banks, bars, or cops.

After the break-in Kirdy vowed to use the gun on the sonofabitch who'd broken a side window at his nightclub, demolished the cash register, and cleaned him out of cash and expensive booze. Since it involved several nights away from home, he had to tell my mother his plan: lock up the nightclub and leave as usual but, halfway home, circle back; stash his car behind a friend's auto-repair shop; jog through alleys in his dark suit, gun in hand; creep in through the back door; and lie in wait behind the bar.

My mother told him it was crazy. He told her it was legal as long as he dragged the body inside if the guy fell backward in the doorway. The cop on the beat had said so. My mother lost the argument. For a week Kirdy slept behind the bar cradling that gun. Each night my mother concealed her terror, reading to me at bedtime as usual, my favorite Hardy Boys series, kids facing criminals on their own. As she read, her husband might be shooting someone or getting shot himself. At eight years old, I didn't know enough about guns to share her anxiety. To me, Kirdy was just working later than usual, as if lying in wait with a gun were an ordinary aspect of business, like doing inventory or taxes.

The thief never showed up, but the P.38 was no longer a secret Kirdy could conceal in the cellar. My mother had never objected to the shotgun he kept in the living room closet, leaning against the wall just inside the door. Pull the chain to turn on the light, and your hand might brush the barrel. But with children in the house—their toddler and me—she wouldn't stand for a pistol. He could keep the shotgun, too unwieldy for children, but the pistol had to go.

For Kirdy, the Waffen-ss Walther P.38 was never just a gun. It lay on the battlefield because his unit beat the Germans. It was a hard-earned trophy, a symbol of a time when both he and America were strong. What's more, he'd served his country while also protecting the Old Country, the beloved Italy his parents had fled but never left behind in spirit. A gun like that couldn't be sold, pawned, or even given to one of the men he drank with nightly at his bar. So Kirdy followed the letter of my mother's law and got rid of the gun by giving it to her ex-husband, my father, whose house I visited every Sunday.

My father fell in love with that P.38. He'd tried to join the marines at the height of World War II when he was only fifteen, requiring parental permission his mother wouldn't grant. She hadn't fled war-torn Eastern Europe with him and his sister—waiting three years for her husband to make enough money for them to cross the Atlantic in steerage—to have her son die in a war. Three years later, at the age of majority, he became a marine, but the war was nearly over, and instead of seeing battle he served on a submarine tender and sailed through minefields to Le Havre to pick up prisoners, American GI's charged with crimes like shooting an officer, looting, and trading in war booty. The kind of trading my stepfather had excelled at, but with impunity, encouraged by officers who looked the other way for a cut of the action, happy to have a soldier fluent in Italian out on the streets collecting fine Italian leather and family heirlooms traded in the desperation of war-torn towns. By the grace of his commanding officers, my stepfather wasn't locked up on a ship like my father's. By the grace of my stepfather, my father got a little piece of the Great War.

Every Sunday evening, my father oiled and polished the P.38 in his living room while I watched TV or played Barbies. It took pride of place in his gun cabinet, along with a shotgun he wielded one night as his girlfriend's daughters and I danced to Sam the Sham's "Woolly Bully." It was unlike my father to allow loud rock and roll, but for once it suited his mood. As we blasted the song over and over, he dimmed the lights, opened the curtains, and stood beside the picture window holding his shotgun high, as if aiming for the stars, so that jerk of a neighbor next door would know whom he was dealing with.

I didn't care what the neighbor had said or done. I was in thrall of Sam the Sham's gruff voice, the wild motions of our bodies, the open aggression of my father, the guns out, and the power and glory of the guns and the music, everything that was not allowed at my mother's house.

The next year my father sold his house and bought a hundred acres of fields and forests with a cluster of sheds, the remnants of a house destroyed in a fire, and a run-down cattle barn, silo rotted half away. He lived in a hand-hewn log cabin on the edge of the property. There he took up arms against the creatures he considered a nuisance. He lay on the side of the hill like a sniper, shotgun raised, waiting for woodchucks to creep out of their burrows. He left their corpses in the field for hawks to retrieve. He took a pitchfork to snakes, left poison pellets for mice, sprayed DDT in the cabin and on the horses he soon purchased. He peered behind sliding barn doors and into the eaves, BB gun raised against sleeping bats.

At the farm, with the Waffen-ss Walther P.38, my shooting lessons began.

My father was fifteen years old when he got his first gun, a .38 with no Nazi etchings. He'd lied about his age to get hired as a night security guard for the railroad. Without offering shooting practice or instructions on firing a weapon, the boss told him to shoot anyone prying open freight cars or otherwise threatening property and profits. My father was hatching a plot to drop out of high school and run away from home—which he found oppressively Catholic, immigrant, and hostile—and was in need of cash for the cross-country bus trip that would take him to a forestry job in the Northwest. He readily carried that gun, prowling Bridgeport Railroad Station for a month of nights. He was prepared to shoot, but no thieves came in the night.

That experience as an armed child, I suppose, along with having no sons, made him think it was a good idea to teach his ten-year-old daughter to shoot a .38. I'd proven myself as a bona fide tomboy by taking readily to the wild hundred-acre farm and two stubborn, hard-mouthed horses he stocked it with. Behind the log cabin he set up a tree stump, and on the stump an empty beer can, Schaeffer, which he drank in moderation and let me sip after we worked together clearing paths through the woods. He set me up with the Walther P.38 my mother was relieved to have gotten out of her house and taught me the fine points of holding the gun, taking aim, and firing.

My father's approach to lessons at his makeshift outdoor gun range was intimate and tactile, yet my memory of learning to shoot is disembodied and technical, centered on the visual and on my quiet struggle with my father.

We stand together in the field behind his log cabin, in the shade of an ancient oak. The tree stump and Schaeffer can are twenty yards away. My father kneels just behind me, peers over my right shoulder, wraps his arms around me and positions my hands on the pistol grip, cradles them in his own. Our right hands clutch the grip, my index finger on the trigger. Our left hands steady our right hands, assuring that the grip won't swing left or up or down when we pull that trigger and the bullet blasts out of the barrel. We kneel, hands clasped as in prayer.

We raise the gun to eye level, close our left eyes, site with the right. We position the little nib at the end of the barrel smack in the middle of the beer can. We adjust the barrel—keeping the nib on the can—until the nib is centered in the site. It's like working a carpenter's level, small adjustments centering the pistol. My father says to squeeze the trigger slowly, not with a jerk, and he tightens my hold on the barrel as I pull. My father holds the pistol steady against the kickback, and the can falls off the stump.

We place the gun down—carefully, gently, it's loaded—and walk over to the can, examine the entrance wound, smooth and clean, and the exit wound, jagged and sharp. My father sets up a new can, and we shoot again, miss, and again, hit. He reloads and tells me I'm on my own, that the trick is holding the gun steady when it fires, countering its kick. Hard as I squeeze, the gun goes feral when I fire, jerking left and up. My father stands to the side observing me, chastising me for shutting my right eye, siting off the left. "Why do you keep doing that?" he says. I tell him it feels right. He tells me it's wrong, and we are back to when I first learned to write, and he would remove the pencil from my left hand and place it in my right. I aim his way when he kneels beside me. My way when he steps back.

I aim slowly, methodically, lining up the site as he has shown me. I press my hands together, squeezing the barrel as hard as I can; focus on my index finger, a gently paced pull; and the can falls. My shooting is slow and methodical, a child on training wheels, nothing like the movies where cowboys blast away, right hand gripping the pistol, left hand holding the horse's reins, slaughtering bad guys and Indians in mere seconds.

My father kept the Walther P.38 close by over the next eight years. He wore it holstered when we rode the horses through the woods and into town. He carried it at his hip when we walked the perimeter of his land. He slipped it under the driver's seat of the Chevy pickup when he drove me back to my mother's house, and one night reached for it when a man emerged from the car blocking us on the highway entrance ramp. But the car was stalled, and he was coming to explain, not attack us, so my father put the gun away. When he slept, my father kept the gun on his night table, and on one harrowing winter night he disappeared alone with it into the dark when screams awakened us. "It's a woman," my father said and set out with the gun to rescue her. I took cover in the guest bedroom, pulling a blanket over my head, terrified that he'd be shot, leaving me alone to fend for myself against the attacker. But my father returned, shaking his head, and told me what we heard was a cat, not a woman. He headed back to his room, gun in hand.

Like my stepfather after his business was robbed, my father was ready to use that P.38 to defend life and property. I never stopped to wonder if the Nazi who etched the swastika and ss symbol into the gun had used it to kill Americans or allies or to execute any number of people the Nazis wanted dead. It never occurred to me that my stepfather might have fired it during the war. To me it was just an object, inanimate and inert, and if my father's relish for the power it granted made me a bit uneasy, its constant presence at his side lulled us into thinking of it as necessary to farm life, like our cowboy boots, saddles, work gloves, and scythe. Like the arsenic we left in the grain shed for the mice, and the DDT in pneumatic tubes to keep the horses botfly free.

We all kept the secret, my father, stepfather, and I, and my mother never knew where the P.38 ended up, only that it wasn't in her home. Her daughters, she believed, were safe from guns. She didn't know about target practice with the pistol or shooting bats with a BB gun, even after I brought home two dead bats securely snapped into a little plastic case meant for a medal. They were two of dozens of bats we killed out of ignorance, not bothering to learn how they cleared the air of mosquitos and other bugs, that they were gentle, not vampiric hunters of human necks. They lived in the rafters of my father's barn, hundreds of them—you could watch them fly out of the damaged silo at dusk, spinning out through the top, then deploying in separate patterns of dipping and curling. We shot them by day as they slept. Open the sliding shed door and find one hanging upside down, wings folded in like a shroud, ugly pug face at rest, and they were an easy target. Raise the BB rifle, aim, and fire. Each bat hit the ground with a thud.

The bats I'd brought home were a wonder to my father and me, a mother with a baby clinging to her, which we noticed only after we shot the mother and she fell to the ground. My father pierced them with a pitchfork to put the baby out of its misery, and his girlfriend snapped a picture of the two of us, my father holding the pitchfork up, looks of wonder mixed with disgust on our faces, like some macabre reenactment of Grant Wood's *American Gothic*.

My father idled the truck in our driveway as I walked to the door and rang the bell—the door was always locked, and my mother saw no need for me to have a key. It's hard to imagine that my father thought she'd be pleased and let me keep the tiny corpses in her home. The porch light went on, and my mother came to the door in her bathrobe. I held up the plastic case so she could admire the bats. She told me to take that goddamn thing back to the truck and never do anything like that again.

My mother didn't ask how the bats had died, and I didn't say. If I wanted my life on the farm to remain the kind of wild, unrestricted life forbidden at home, I couldn't tell my mother about the guns. My father with his rifle picking off woodchucks. The two of us hunting down bats. The P.38 raised against Schaeffer cans.

After I went away to college, my father sold the horses and farm, and I saw that Waffen-ss Walther P.38 only two more times. Once, as he slipped it into his waistband before walking me into Bridgeport Railroad Station—where he'd wielded his first pistol as a teenaged night watchman—because, he claimed, Bridgeport had gone downhill and was a dangerous city, the station no doubt swarming with criminals ready to rob him or jump me. "Jump," his euphemism for rape.

Oh Jesus, I said, when I saw the gun. He insisted on carrying my heavy suitcases too and had to stop twice to adjust his Sansabelt slacks—he'd lost a little weight and the gun was slipping down his hip. You're going to shoot your foot off, I told him. The station platform was elevated, and down below we watched a meter maid ticketing cars parked near my father's truck. Take her out, Dad, I said. He smiled.

He was seeing me off to Iowa, where I'd begun graduate school. My little childhood rebellions—siting with my left eye instead of my right; sewing a peace sign to his Marine Corps jacket, which I appropriated and frequently wore; flashing him the peace sign to say good-bye (to which he'd respond with a fist in the air and say, "war"!) had become, in adulthood, petty jabs. I no longer fired pistols. I was appalled that we'd once shot bats. Until I saw the P.38 at the railroad station, I'd forgotten about it. My father had moved into a ranch-style house near the factory where he worked, a neighborhood thick with squirrels, which he shot methodically in his backyard, bent on total eradication.

I lived too far away to see my parents often, and rarely considered what their lives were like without me. I was shocked each annual visit to discover how much the three of them had aged. The man who stood beside me packing the Waffen-ss Walther P.38 as we waited for my train seemed frailer than the cowboy who'd taught me to shoot and had ridden horseback packing that pistol on his hip.

The last time I saw the gun was at my apartment in Iowa, where my father had come to visit. By then I'd completed classes and split my time between languishing in despair over my dissertation and teaching tae kwon do, a skill I'd picked up during grad school in pursuit of self defense because there had been a stalker, and I was by then antigun. I'd studied the real thing, under two different Korean masters, and our training was as much spiritual and metaphysical as athletic. For every board we broke, every sparring match we competed in, every violent move we learned to make by instinct, we were taught to avoid confrontation, understand our flash points, keep ourselves and unforeseen situations under control.

On the third day of my father's visit, I was driving to the Fieldhouse for an evening of teaching tae kwon do, when a flash news bulletin interrupted the radio program I was listening to: there had been shootings in the physics building, and it was under lockdown. Later the full story would unfold, that a disgruntled doctoral student had shot a rival, three professors, an administrator, and her assistant. But on that Friday evening my immediate concern was the children's class that by then should have been under way, a class taught by another black belt, Andy, a doctoral student in physics. I never feared that Andy had been shot—or was a shooter—because things like that didn't happen in 1991. My big worry was that he was stuck in the locked-down building, and that some two-dozen children were wandering around the Fieldhouse unsupervised. I was the head teacher, and the students' safety was up to me.

Instead of loose children, I found Andy leading them in drills. I watched through the window as he called out a desultory series of roundhouse, front snap, and side kicks. He'd been in the physics building during the shooting, he'd tell me later, but managed to leave before lockdown. He stayed to assist me with the adult beginners' class and to work out in the advanced class. I watched him, fascinated by how unaffected he seemed. Shots had been fired in his building. People he knew were murdered. But there he was, going through the motions as if it were an ordinary Friday night.

At the end of class I asked if he wanted to talk. No, he said, and walked home alone, as usual.

I returned home to my father, who'd been mesmerized in front of the TV for the three hours I'd been gone. He'd watched the unfolding news story and briefed me on the details. How many shot, how many dead, the extent of the injuries, the severely injured young woman who'd been called in as a temporary secretary in the administration office, the rottenest possible rotten luck.

What my father locked onto was the choice of weapon—a P.38—and he disappeared upstairs to the guest bedroom, returning with the Waffen-ss Walther P.38 I didn't know he'd carried cross-country into Iowa. I didn't want a gun in my house, let alone the ordeal of watching him dissect it in front of me and describe—in technical terms—what happened to each bullet when someone pulled the trigger and, worst of all, what happened to human flesh and bone and organs and brain when one such bullet hit and entered, the churning exploding destruction of heart and mind and essence. But he was driven, compelled, speaking not to me but to the very air. I let him talk. We sat in my sparsely furnished living room in a pair of mismatched armchairs, the news of the dead still broadcasting before us.

It never occurred to me to question his fascination, to ask whether he'd ever shot someone or looked down the barrel of a gun himself. I believed he'd been willing, like my stepfather, to shoot—and maybe kill—to save his property or someone's life. Maybe that was part of going to war and their training as marksman, their willingness to step up and save Europe from Nazis, to kill to do it, affected their lives forever after. My father held the Waffen-ss Walther P.38, unloaded and open before me, as the TV news displayed photos of the dead.

By the time I graduated and got a job offer at a university in central Florida, my father was already taking refuge there each winter, having retired and bought a pool house in a golf community a little over an hour away from where I'd be teaching. When I told him about the new job, he didn't say congratulations, or how nice it will be to have you nearby. He said, "You'll get a gun."

I said no. Over the years I'd learned to dodge arguing about politics with him, and guns were political, as political as Florida in those years, back when the orange juice maven, Anita Bryant, was spouting homophobia, and gun laws there made it sound like the Wild West, not the "concrete heaven" of retirement communities my mother labeled it. She and my stepfather had purchased their own piece of concrete heaven, a one-bedroom condominium near Palm Beach, but the next year my stepfather died of lung cancer. She visited once more and then, in despair, rented it out.

"You'll get a gun," my father repeated. I turned the conversation to the several feet of snow Iowa had, how I'd taken ridiculous pictures: my Toyota buried in snow, the front steps of the house where my apartment was, freshly shoveled. It was the beginning of my months-long process of saying goodbye to Iowa and to the northern climate I'd lived in all my life.

He wasn't taking the weather bait and started in on the various threats Florida had to offer, especially to a "vulnerable" woman living alone. A man impersonating a police officer had pulled women drivers over and raped them. An alligator as big as a boat blocked the "only" highway to my university from his house, where I would stay temporarily while looking for a rental.

How a gun would protect me from such hazards was a matter my father side-stepped. If he pictured my new life as a professor to be a series of Wild West–style pistol-wielding encounters—me drawing on the fake cop, shooting the alligator in the head and then kicking it off the road—he didn't say so. When I was in high school, our political disagreements were largely a joke. My peace signs sewn onto his old marine jackets, my flashing him the two-fingered peace sign and his response, a fist raised in the air and "war" shouted out. I didn't know that after World War II two fingers held up meant victory in war, not peace. My idle protests made a mockery of what he valued most.

He persisted, mailing me news clippings about violent crime in Florida, rapes especially, variations on a theme of a woman alone, sometimes in her car, sometimes on the street. Phone calls became arguments, the most heated, whether or not you should get in the car if someone ordered you to at gunpoint, as one of the Florida rapists had done. I said no. Better to get shot on a public sidewalk where there might be a witness than tortured and raped, body abandoned and lost forever in a marsh. He argued yes. A gun was a power so absolute that there was no saying no. Only the immediate moment of looking down that barrel.

We never spoke about the day my shooting lessons ended because I had occasion to look down the barrel of the Walther P.38. I was twelve, and one of my father's girlfriend's daughters, two years older than I, was about to learn to shoot. As my father set up the target, she turned the loaded gun on me. I remember her slow turn, the gun aimed high, at my face, a few seconds of stunned silence. I could barely breathe. And then my father lunged, grabbed her arms, and snatched the gun away.

"You never, *ever* point any gun at a person," he said.

She claimed it was a joke, that she would never shoot, but my father and I both had our doubts. His girlfriend's daughters were prone to fits of rage and screaming, and their mother's only intervention was to grab them by the wrists, lead them to the car, and make them sit in the backseat until they calmed down. I'd see the wary look on my father's face as he passed the car where one girl or the other sat fuming. Maybe aiming the gun at me was the impulsive, naive, but stupid, joke she said it was. Or maybe there was something more. The land and horses were ours, not theirs. If the sisters were going to ride, it was one at a time, borrowing my father's horse and accompanying me as I rode a horse of my very own. But in the end, motive didn't matter, and shooting lessons, even for me, ended that day.

I moved to Florida—without a gun—one miserable, steamy August, having faced bands of tropical storms on my drive from Iowa, cat mewling in her crate, bike on a roof rack, boxes shipped ahead. My father's house was empty—he was a snowbird, migrating north to a condominium each summer. I encountered neither alligators nor rapists on my drives to the university. But during one evening out running I noticed vultures circling above. A pair of nonmigrating sandhill cranes also lived in the neighborhood, and they'd stand in the street on spiky legs, staring down cars. I feared for them and my ability to withstand the heat, neither of which I could fix with a gun.

My father returned in December, and one night he walked as I rollerbladed, and when we met up again he was eyeing a slow-paced, forty-something man in a Windbreaker, an odd sight in that golf-course retirement community, especially on my father's street, a cul-de-sac. When we returned to the house together, my father brought out his gun.

He no longer had the Waffen-ss Walther P.38. He'd sold it to his girlfriend's brother, also a veteran—and ex-cop—in that sense keeping the gun in the family, while whittling his collection down to one modern pistol he could carry on those long drives between Connecticut and Florida. The new pistol was also a .38, but sleeker, more modern. A gun with no history. Just a weapon. He gazed out the frosted window on his front door, but the man wasn't lurking on the lawn.

"Maybe we should leave the gun on the dining room table," my father said, and he placed it there. "Then if he comes around later and looks in the window, he'll know this is a house with guns, and he won't break in." I told him I didn't think that was a good idea. Without speaking, he returned the gun to his bedroom, presumably the top drawer of his bedside table.

It was the last I saw or heard of his guns. In his new golf-course home there was no struggle against woodchucks and bats. Instead, he worked to cultivate a thick grassy lawn, artificially imposed on Florida's sandy soil. He put on old work gloves to spray poisons around the perimeter of his house. He hired a crew to mow and fertilize the yard. But when he found a fire ant mound in his front yard, he asked me to get rid of it using something he called "ant medicine."

The spring before I'd argued with Janna, my Iowa landlady, about her handyman's use of herbicides and pesticides on the lawn, worried about my cat playing in the poisons. She called him over to join the conversation, and while Janna stood with us he argued that everything he applied around the house was harmless. But when Janna walked away, he shook his head. I'll show you how to get rid of weeds, he said, and bent down to pull some up. That's when we noticed, on the sidewalk out front, a dead snake with a live frog impaled on is fangs and locked in its jaws. The frog blinked, forlornly, I thought. Flies circled above, waiting for the second death. I asked Ron to do something, by which I meant free the frog, but he picked up the snake with the frog snugly attached and threw it into the bushes. My theory was that pesticides had killed the snake. Ron lost interest and didn't propose a theory.

That was the last in a quick succession of animal encounters that marked my last days in Iowa. There had been barred owls on the electrical wires outside my porch every night. There had been a squirrel hit but not killed by a car, writhing in the street, and after my frantic calls to the Humane Society and animal services had been laughed at, I took him to a sympathetic vet who donned elbow-length leather gloves, lifted him out of the box, looked into his face, and when the squirrel barred his teeth, said, to the squirrel, not me, "It's hard to be a squirrel." He diagnosed a chipped tooth and concussion, gave the squirrel a few shots, and sent him home with me to feed. Each day the squirrel became healthier he also became more aggressive, lunging at my hand when I lowered fresh bowls of water, bananas, blueberries, and sunflower seeds into the box.

"That's funny," my father had said when I told him about the squirrel. "I shoot squirrels and you save them."

My landlady, an elderly Bohemian sometimes-counselor asked me to consider the psychic significance of all those animal encounters. I didn't know if she thought I'd brought the animals on myself or if the earth had brought them to me. But I was also just superstitious enough—a legacy of my stepfather, whose great terror of shoes left up on tables or chairs, anywhere but the floor, still haunted me to that day—to consider that they'd been some kind of sign, something related to leaving Iowa for the South.

Now my father was asking me to do something I found repellent: kill and spread poisons on the earth. "Ant medicine," he called it. But not for curing ants of some disease. "Ant medicine." But not like the small coyote bone I'd bought at a powwow in Iowa, "coyote medicine" that—if you believed—protected you from harm. Ant medicine, a potent powder my father kept in his garage, was there not to cure sick ants but to cure us of the annoyance of ants. I gritted my teeth, held my breath, and sprinkled it onto the ant mound. My father and I watched as the little red bodies writhed and spun and then lay still.

All the little deaths, I thought, we build our lives on.

The first time I wanted a gun was seven years later, when my mother died suddenly and young of a fast-moving cancer she didn't know she had. By then my stepfather's shotgun was packed away in the cellar, but she'd gotten a gun of her own, a little pearl-handled .22-caliber pistol. It didn't occur to me then how incongruent, how utterly odd it was that my mother had a pistol, how far she'd come from ordering my stepfather to get rid of his P.38.

She talked about the pistol as if it were a lark. It was never "my gun," always "my pearl-handled pistol." It went with her new mahogany desk, ornate and curvy-legged, decorated with hand-painted vines. She admired Mae West, tough film noir heroines, and old movies about the West where a woman was as likely to be packing as a man. In her closet was a pearl-colored sequined top, a mink coat, and a leopard jacket with beaver collar. She once said, when I was sweating out the final stages of my graduate degree and job search, "That's funny, I was taught to spend money making myself look pretty so someone *else* would pay the bills." The pearl-handled pistol was an accessory like the clothing, one of the accoutrements a woman might use to snag herself a man.

For a while after my stepfather's death, she'd dated an ex-detective, who'd procured the gun, but she never spoke of it as a means of self-defense. Instead, she joked about it in an unconvincing imitation of a southern drawl. When my mother died, I wanted the desk and the pearl-handled pistol that went with it. My half sister and I had already distributed what counted as the most valuable and sentimental items, the jewelry and crystal. She'd picked all the serving platters, and I chose the wine and champagne glasses, proving my mother's theory right: I took after the woman she had been in the 1970s, unconventional, Bohemian, and my sister was what my mother became in the 1980s, conventional, a homebody. Add the two of us together and you'd have one normal person. Separate, we were caricatures of my mother, stuck in separate moments of her past.

Like my mother, my sister spent her money on shoes and clothes and makeup and hairstyles and lived as a homemaker a few miles from where we grew up. I'd gone off and become the kind of person my mother had always hoped I'd marry, a professor and writer. I wanted the desk and the pistol because my mother had wanted them. And because I wanted what I could no longer have, a connection with my mother. But months of disagreements over my mother's medical care, burial, and estate—compounded by years of sibling rivalry—trumped our previous verbal agreement that I could have the gun, and as I was driving to Connecticut for the final settling of the estate, my sister called the police, pretended she'd just discovered the pistol in our mother's things, and asked them to come and take it away.

The second time I wanted a gun was five years later at a gun show at the state fairgrounds in Tallahassee, Florida. I'd approached the trip as a kind of anthropological field study—who were these Crackers buying guns?—accompanying a friend's husband dead set on getting her a pistol for Christmas. Men walked around with rifles and shotguns. Swarms of people hovered over rows of tables loaded with pistols and a disconcerting array of shotguns, rifles, and other weapons and paraphernalia.

An antique pearl-handled .22-caliber pistol caught my eye. It was perfect for my mother's desk, which was now in my possession. I admired newer .22s with pink grips. Guns for girls. My friend bought his wife a not-so-girly .22, and we headed back to their house, where my husband and I were spending the holidays. If not for the weeks-long background checks in Florida, I might have bought a pearl-handled pistol that day. And though my friend later claimed that she'd never wanted a gun of any type, something in me had turned.

By then having earned a third-degree black belt in tae kwon do, I'd been trained that the ideal method of self-defense was to deescalate and call the police. But there was something about that pearl-handled pistol. A connection with my mother. And maybe a kind of protection I'd never considered. We'd begun spending summers in the mountains of rural New Mexico, out of range of cell phones, within range of bears, coyotes, rattlesnakes, and an alarming number of compounds where purported skinheads and survivalists lived.

At my second gun show, in Orlando, I considered an antique pearl-handled .22-caliber pistol, or maybe a newer one in pink. I was one of several women considering a pink gun that day and telling myself that it was an accessory rather than a weapon was a good way to kid myself. These were guns for women. There was nothing wrong with a little pink gun slipped into your purse. But I'd never liked pink. Pink was the fetish of my father's girlfriend, from the house she was losing when he first met her, to the Florida home where they spent winters together. My favorite color was blue. I hadn't lost the tomboy streak cultivated by all those Sundays spent with my single father.

Once you start talking seriously about buying a gun, something shifts. The vendor eases you into considering the purpose of a weapon. And a .22, you discover, just doesn't cut it. We visited several tables, and all the salesmen, after I'd admire some vintage pearl-handled pistol or newer nonpink .22, brought out the big guns and told me why. In the end I ordered—pending background check—a Smith & Wesson .38-caliber pistol. The type of gun I'd learned to shoot on, absent historical significance.

Once cleared, I picked up the gun at Shoot Straight, a gun shop and shooting range in Seminole County, Florida, the same county where four years later George Zimmerman would shoot and kill Trayvon Martin, bringing Florida's "stand your ground" law to national attention.

The selling floor was decorated with dead things. Two animals stuffed whole and perched on shelving units—a buck and some kind of climbing mammal, nailed to a tree limb. The walls were lined with heads. Moose, deer, and ram. I wasn't surprised that animal heads decorated the walls above the gun and rifle displays. But the life-size cardboard figure of then presidential candidate Barack Obama was a shock. The figure stood beside the entrance to the shooting range near a sign that read, This man will take away your right to own a gun. Walk into that range with a target in the shape of man, and Obama's is the last face you see. Out in the parking lot, ours was the only bumper with an Obama sticker. Our Toyota Tundra stood out among the Fords and Chevys with bumper stickers advocating McCain and Palin and the NRA.

Signs warned that we were being watched, that our weapons should be unloaded, that the staff was armed and happy to shoot first, ask questions later. Until I bought my gun, I walked unarmed among the armed. Men in camouflage looked over rifles and shotguns. A clerk sold me bullets to go with my gun, and paper targets—figures of a man. On Mondays "Ladies shoot free," but it was not Monday, and I paid for my range time, which came with thick headphones, required. My husband, a former Marine Corps medic, classified as a sharpshooter during the war, was there to show me how to load, handle, and fire the gun.

In the shooting range, a hall-like space with several bays, even with thick headphones the shots were loud, visceral. I flinched at each shot fired. Shells flew, hot metal pellets struck my feet. It was the last time I wore sandals and a skirt to shoot. We loaded our guns on tables beside the bulletproof window to the showroom. Standing in the narrow opening and setting up my target, I wondered what was to stop anyone from shooting me. It would be as easy as a slight turn.

Beside us, shooters with a grudge against our presidential candidate shot out the heads and hearts of paper targets featuring the outline of a man. My husband loaded the pistol, set up the target, and shot a few times himself to demonstrate technique. It was just as my father taught me, right hand on the grip, left hand cradling right hand, nub on the target, and align it between the sites. I aimed for head and heart. I hit arms and the edges of the paper, loaded again, and almost got the heart.

Once you own a gun, it's hard to resist the notion of applying for a concealed carry permit. Emphasis on carry, not concealed: no civilian is allowed to swagger down the street, as my father used to do, with a gun openly holstered at the hip. I bought a little holster that could slip inside the waistband of my pants and began a course at Shoot Straight. By then Obama had won the election, but his cardboard effigy remained at the door to the shooting range for another few months.

The concealed weapons class took place in a back room and was taught by a deputy from Seminole County. We learned to handle the gun. Load it. Respect it. We didn't learn to handle ourselves, though, and within an hour, we'd revealed ourselves as types. There was the pretty young girl in short shorts, the men eyeing her legs, who'd purchased a fat .45 for protection all those lonely nights alone in her apartment. There were a few people like me, a little wary, harboring some vague notion of a last resort—if the police didn't arrive in time, or if confronted in the New Mexico forest out of cell phone range. There was also an apparent vigilante, already asking about his right to shoot people he found, say, hassling women in the Walmart parking lot. The deputy assured us that we were not the police, but I wished he'd kick that man out of class the way our tae kwon do master would refuse lessons to anyone especially anxious to inflict punishment on the world.

After completing a written test, we shot, one by one, in the shooting range, alone with the deputy standing beside each of us to assess our skill. The pretty girl volunteered to go first, and the deputy seemed happy to be standing beside her. We watched through the bulletproof window as they talked and laughed. Her aim was accurate and quick. Most of the men went next, and then me, the only other woman in the class.

It's not easy to aim. My hands sweated as I loaded the gun under the deputy's observation. I sited up, my father in mind, using my right eye. My right hand shook. I steadied my grip and right hand with the left. I squeezed the trigger slowly and used up all my bullets, hitting the target several times near the heart, shoulder, and abdomen. My aim wasn't perfect, but that guy would have been good and dead.

"Congratulations," the deputy said. Within a month of leaving my fingerprints with the local police and sending the state a passport-size photograph, I received the permit to walk about armed.

A year later, in that same shooting range, a woman brought in her twenty-year-old son, rented two guns, and while the son aimed at the target, she aimed at the base of his skull. After she murdered him, she killed herself. It took only seconds, and neither the shooters beside her nor the staff outside the window could do a thing to prevent it. For a while, they stopped renting guns at that location.

For the next two years I stayed away from shooting ranges, and carried my .38 just once, in the mountains of New Mexico, on a walk with two women friends and, between us, six dogs. I carried because the men were off fishing, and the coyotes had been close for the past two nights. I loved the lonesome baying of the coyotes—we slept in a tent and heard them all night. In the morning, the dogs ran the perimeter, remarking the territory.

The yearling males, ready to leave the pack and start one of their own, had an eye for my friend's young unspayed setter, and they circled her and played on morning walks. The female coyotes with pups glared at us and the dogs, and we worried that one might head in our direction. But I would never shoot a coyote, and carried the gun only for the noise. I carried it concealed in my tiny holster just inside the waistband of my jeans, an echo of my father at Bridgeport Railroad Station, constant slippage of the gun and all.

Florida is shaped like a pistol, pointing west. Follow its aim and you are on Route 10, all the way to New Mexico, and every state you drive through recognizes a Florida-issued concealed weapons license. Legally, we carry our guns in our glove compartment, and, as instructed, our insurance and registration elsewhere—on the driver's side sun visor—because if the police have cause to stop you and they've run your plates, they will discover that you are legally armed. Reaching into the glove box is an aggressive act.

My friends think the very fact of having the concealed weapon license makes me aggressive. They don't believe that I never carry the gun in Florida, not even on dog walks at one in the morning. I say, if a cell phone, two dogs, and a third-degree black belt isn't enough, then fuck it. They don't laugh.

Four years after I get my concealed weapons license, George Zimmerman shoots Trayvon Martin to death, with no arrest made because, the deputies think, he was standing his ground. Standing your ground, the center of Florida's gun laws, says you don't have to turn away, as I was taught to do in martial arts, from someone picking a fight. It is what my stepfather wanted to do at his nightclub those nights he spent with the Walther P.38 behind his bar, waiting for the thief to strike a second time. It is what my father had in mind when he carried that same gun on his hip and disappeared into the night to save a woman who turned out to be a cat.

The puppy who won't roll over and show belly, the snake that won't slither away. Standing their ground is aggressive. Choosing a pet, you avoid the puppy who won't roll. In the park I take my dogs on another route if there's a snake that won't move, that raises its head and flutters its tongue. You couldn't earn a black belt, skilled as you might be at sparring competition, unless you could prove to the master instructor that you would—and could—walk away from a challenge, were brave enough to dare losing face.

In every Florida car, in every jacket, in every waistband there could be a gun. It's the law. For every gun-fearing woman like me there are dozens of people happily carrying, ready to stand their ground or someone else's.

In the beginning I thought the free magazine I could get in lieu of a fifty-dollar rebate when buying my first gun meant *Guns and Ammo* or *Field and Stream* (not an extra chamber of bullets), and no one had been shot in the range where I practiced, and no young man had been followed and shot dead in the county where I learned to shoot. In the beginning I shot bats and beer cans until the P.38 was pointed at me. Now, my partially loaded gun is tucked away near where I sleep, but without practice I've forgotten how to handle it, load or unload, how to shoot. I recall only its feral nature, how it snaps my hands left or up.

The deputy who trained us said not to hold a gun in one hand, finger on the trigger, and use your other hand for anything else, like opening a door. Hands are sympathetic. Move the fingers on the empty hand, and the fingers on the trigger will move with them. Ask our new officer, he said, whose right hand accidentally pulled the trigger and shot out a sliding glass door he was trying to pull open with his empty left hand.

What do gun owners want? My father and stepfather each wanted to stand ground, a grand piece of ground in the war, and a little piece of ground in civilian life, protect it on their own from predators and thieves, human and otherwise, they saw around them. My mother wanted a little piece of glamor, but maybe something more, a little piece of toughness, like the movie heroines she admired. What I wanted, at first, was to be as tough as my father, take part in his world. And after my mother died, to hold onto something she once cherished. Later, I wanted more, a kind of individual power and protection that, in the end, was more than I could—or wanted to—handle.

I've never witnessed a person being shot, but my imagination is sickeningly accurate. Over and over I heard my father describing what bullets do to flesh and bone and brain. I flinch at the sound of gunfire in the range where the mother executed her son. I don't own a business or a farm, don't claim enough ground to want to stand any of it, whether from woodchuck, bat, or person.

What happened to the Nazi officer who dropped the gun my stepfather found? Did he decide that though the battle was lost, the ultimate power conferred by that gun, the power to die shooting or take his life rather than be captured, was not worth the price? Or was he shot in battle, the gun either dropped as he fell or plucked from his side by Kirdy or someone else in his unit?

What I wanted at first was a small gun like my mother's, an accessory for my desk. What salesmen and my husband convinced me was that such a small gun wasn't enough. A .22 could not take down a charging man or coyote or bear. The .38 was lethal, and the point of having a gun was to possess the power to kill.

Over the years I've grown terrified of my .38, its feral power, how hard it is to aim and hold steady while firing. In the first year I owned it and practiced shooting regularly, an old man in the shooting range admired my aim. Try this, he said, and handed over his long-barrel .22. It was light and smooth, easy to aim, with no kickback.

I keep my .38 loaded, within reach of my side of the bed. But I'm afraid now even to unload it. It doesn't have a safety, and, without practice, I can't remember how to open the chamber, can't be sure I've left out one bullet so that even an accidental slip of my trigger finger won't fire a bullet into the wall. Or my foot.

My husband sometimes takes me back to Shoot Straight for practice, exposure meant to trump fear. I flinch at each gunshot when we enter the shooting gallery, ask my husband to shoot first, wipe my sweaty hands on my jeans, step in, aim, and fire. I've lost my steady hands and shoot left, then up, before hitting the target in the shoulder and ribs. The last time I shot, the woman beside me used a laser site, which I consider cheating. We went through a pack of bullets, and I was relieved when we were done. I put the gun away, unloaded, beside the bed. I set my sites on a .22.

In martial arts what I wanted at first was the ability to defend myself. But despite all the fierceness of the kicking and hand techniques, for all the power—if you don't hit, hard, you will never be able to thwart an attack—traditional martial artists value restraint. My teachers also taught me to want something more, a kind of Taoist approach not just to fighting but also to life outside the *dojang*, a way of seeking to grasp something beyond the physical world, to try to move in concert with the universe, some force, something that would knit together body and mind.

In my concealed weapons license class, responding to a perceived threat—bluntly, shooting to kill—seemed to be the central value. And there is nothing spiritual in the cold hard metal of my gun.

White Boys

Asian girls with white guys. You see them all the time. You know the stereotypes: sexualized, submissive. Old, embarrassing ideas about hyperfemininity
and control. Who would admit to such things? Yet this is how it goes: 40
percent of Asian American women marry outside their race. On dating sites
WMAF is the most common interracial pairing. I see them: the girl in tight
clothes with a skeevy-looking guy; the slatternly woman with an accent, out
with an older man who's balding and paunched; the girl geek and boy geek;
the parents at middle age with their hapa kids.

I have been a version of that Asian. Maybe am still. I've never felt comfortable
in public with a white boyfriend or even my white husband. I've never wanted
to hold a white guy's hand while walking down the street. The worst is crossing
the gaze of Asian guys. *It's not what you think*, I want to say to them. *He's not a
fetishist. It's not a fucked-up yellow fever situation.* But perhaps, on some level, it
always is, or perhaps it always begins that way. How could I say for sure?

I grew up having crushes on white boys. Even in elementary school I would
scope out the classroom, scanning the boys—almost all of them white, born
and being raised in our small, conservative town on the west side of Michigan
in the 1980s. Over the course of a year the objects of my affection would
shift. Blue-eyed Keith, so charming in the fall, would seem dull by winter,
and suddenly curly-haired Mark would look appealing. There was one boy
I liked simply because he wore a winter hat knitted with the words *ski snow
sky*, which I would repeat to myself sometimes. I usually found a new crush
just before school let out for summer because there's nothing like unrequited
longing amplified by absence.

I didn't even care if the boys knew. Often they did, because I would tell a
friend who would end up telling them. I felt safe because I knew that whatever I was feeling was a product of my own imagination. I had no expectation
of anyone liking me back. I enjoyed the feeling of thinking about someone, of

looking forward to seeing that person. At times I would daydream dialogues. We could walk around the playground together. Maybe we could even hold hands. Ski, snow, sky. It was a practice in preflirtation. And the crushes were always on white boys.

I grew up in a Vietnamese American household in a very white culture. Every image of desire I saw at school, in magazines, on television, and at the movies was white. It wasn't so much a message as it was an assumption. The few nonwhite boys I knew were family friends whom I sometimes played video games with at parties. I thought of them as distant cousins, closed off and separate from the world of whiteness—meaning access—that I had learned to want. Wanting whiteness was something conscious, unconscious, unavoidable, and necessary for survival.

In fourth grade I had a crush on Rick Springfield. He of "Jessie's Girl," smoldering and brooding in the music video. He of the guitar smashed into the bathroom mirror. *I wanna tell her that I love her but the point is probably moot.* He's the first celebrity crush I remember. I later carried a brief fondness for Johnny Depp in *21 Jump Street* and Andrew McCarthy in *Pretty in Pink*. My older sister adored Kirk Cameron, Rob Lowe, Matt Dillon, and John Stamos. We were all the time crushing on white boys. So many of them, arriving and fading on our screens.

Soon enough, they appeared in real life. They were the boys down the street, the boys at school. Boys with their fair heads of hair and frequent blue eyes. The older I got, the worse it got. I had a crush—I fell in love. Every falling was with one of them, the whiteness unattainable yet closer and closer at hand.

There was one other Vietnamese girl in my elementary class, and in high school a few South Asian kids joined the ranks. I remember two black students in my elementary grades and three in my entire high school. We didn't band together or even really associate with one another, because there weren't enough of us, and I think we had a sense that such a banding would not be profitable. If we talked, it was never about race or identity. We didn't have the language for that, or the safety. In fact, we rarely talked to one another at all.

Now, I wonder, what did they do about their crushes? Did they, too, whiten their gaze? Did everyone roam the classrooms looking for someone to love?

I had lots of these infatuations in elementary and middle school. I loved that feeling, near enough to joy, whenever I saw my chosen object, even though, eventually, I wouldn't notice when that feeling disappeared. Such is the nature of a crush: it's not supposed to last.

But it wasn't until ninth grade that I started to understand why it was called a crush. My focus: Brian. Whenever I saw him at his locker or walking into a classroom, I felt not just a tightening in my chest but a sense that I could be done in by the weight of what I felt—an unnameable jumble of nerves, pleasure, and self-hate. In such moments I wished to be invisible. I wanted a one-way mirror: the only way to be alone with my crush. There was nothing at stake and yet it felt, in all high school earnestness, like my whole life was at stake.

Brian was a sophomore, destined to be his class valedictorian. He kept company with a popular group, performed in school plays, and was a starter on the varsity soccer team. But he was more of a nerd, with a thin frame and thin glasses. He was on the debate team and the Model UN team. He was funny at no one else's expense.

Of course, he was white. Which meant, in my mind, circa 1989, that I could love him, but he could not love me. I remember clearly saying this to myself: If I were white then maybe Brian would be able to like me. If I weren't Vietnamese, then maybe I'd have a chance. I thought of this as basic fact.

Still, I felt what I felt. And I reveled in that strange desire to be crushed. I got ready for school with the thrill of it. Of course, I never talked to Brian; he didn't know who I was. The high school had about nine hundred students, so I could lurk well enough.

One spring day, he saw me. Brian and I took different buses home from school, and I'd discovered that if I sat in the right place on my bus, I could observe Brian getting onto his. There were many days he did not, when he stayed for sports or extracurriculars, but when he did, I watched. I had been watching for months. And then one day he caught me. Standing in the aisle, waiting to find a seat, he looked through our separate sets of windows and saw me watching him. It was a long moment—in my mind it seems longer than it could have been—and for the rest of the day I could think of almost nothing else.

A few days later it happened again, and this time it seemed deliberate, like he was looking for me looking for him. In the days and weeks that followed this kept happening. We didn't smile. We didn't do anything. In the hallways of our school we rarely crossed paths, and when we did I pretended not to notice him. The moment on our buses was private, wondrous. The smallest thing, which was the only thing I had of him. As the end of the school year approached I dared myself to hold Brian's gaze, and did. He held mine. I remember this—the haze of afternoon light, the sound of the bus as it idled in the drive—and all the space between this boy and me.

In the fall Brian no longer rode the bus; a friend of his with a new license and car drove him to and from school. By then I had thought enough about the past year to feel embarrassed and to be thankful that I'd never shared my secret obsession with any of my friends. The crush wasn't quite over—there was still a thrill in seeing Brian in the hallways—but it was too worn to go on. In my new classes with new seating arrangements I found new boys to think about. I accepted that this was how things would go: in my mind I would conjure relationships; they would last a while, and then I would let them go.

Late in high school I plotted to get myself a real boyfriend. Call him Evan. A white boy, of course, but someone I truly respected, and I considered it a great triumph that I'd gotten him to go out with me. I figured that, given the impediment of my race, I would have to trick a guy into a relationship. So we studied precalculus together and analyzed the books assigned for English class. We went to the library. I courted him in classic ugly-duckling fashion: I could make him like me by liking my mind.

I should say that I didn't think of myself as ugly. I thought I was nothing in particular. I had come to accept the idea of whiteness as the norm and the default. I had come to believe in the strangeness of my race.

Evan and I spent our whole senior year together. Some of our classmates called us John and Yoko, but after a while everyone got used to us. I got used to us too. I didn't know it then, but I was adapting—my days, my behavior, my body—adapting, again, to my next way of life.

It's a measure of where and when I grew up to say that I didn't learn anything about stereotypes until I got to college. I was amazed to learn, in a classroom, words that named experiences I already understood—the model minority, the perpetual foreigner, the meek Asian—and how I felt them already assigned to me, a series of expectations, based on my face.

But I remember almost laughing at the idea of the exoticized, sexualized Asian woman. I couldn't recall ever feeling that way or being seen that way. Had I grown up in a town so profoundly white that I'd never experienced such a thing?

Here's a twisted thing to say, to admit: that stereotype made me realize that boys might actually find me appealing.

I went on a few dates with Asian guys in college and had a relationship with one of them for several months. The population at the school was diverse compared to where I grew up, but not really diverse enough. I joined a couple of Asian American student groups, where I found myself feeling just as uncertain as I did in all-white groups. The usual double-culture dilemma: never truly American; never truly Asian. In truth, I wanted to settle down with a nice Asian guy. It seemed the correct and responsible thing to do. I thought, I should try to be a credit to my race. My parents would have agreed. Did I try hard enough to do this? Maybe not. Was I working against a tide of media inculcation, white-washing, even internalized racism? Surely. And so I kept dating the white boys. They weren't the obvious fetishists—the ones who dated only Asian girls or the ones who said things like, *I think Vietnamese girls are the prettiest of all the Asians.* But still I wondered what any white boy saw in me, and what I saw in any of them. Even now, married for years, the question complicates my mind: what are the politics of attraction?

Stanley Kunitz wrote, *What makes the engine go? Desire, desire, desire.* When I read that poem for the first time, I thought I understood it. But what makes the desire go? How do we know what it means to want what we want?

Where I live now, in the Bay Area, there are so many Asians that Asian is often the definition of normal. I see Asian couples everywhere, young and old, holding hands, and I wonder what it's like for them. I see Asian-white couples everywhere too and sometimes feel kinship and sometimes feel unease. My husband and I, with our hapa children, do not hold hands in public. Most of my Asian friends also have white husbands, and we can laugh at this, make fun of ourselves, even while feeling vaguely unsettled, unsure of what we are saying.

Longing doesn't form by itself; it is always informed. I see this still, every day, when all the screens return to me the images I've always known: the white boys. There they are, continuing to laugh at their own irony. They are bearded, they are tall, they are standing around, checking their phones, taking the space they know to be theirs. They look wherever they want, and when. They are surrounded by beautiful white women and men, they who make the engine go. And I am still watching, maybe crushing just a little bit. The imagination goes the way of the pale. Ski. Snow. Sky. White-hot, I think. White as desire.

Grip

Over the crib in the tiny apartment, there hung a bullet-holed paper target, the size and dark shape of a man, its heart zone, head zone, perforated where my aim had torn through: thirty-six little rips, no strays, centered on spots that would make a man die.

Beginner's luck, said the guys at the shooting range, at first. *Little lady*, they'd said, until the silhouette slid back and farther back. They'd cleared their throats, fallen silent.

A bad neighborhood. An infant child. A Ruger GP .357 with speed-loader.

It's not as morbid as it sounds, a target pinned above a crib: the place was small, the walls already plastered full with paintings, sketches, pretty leaves, hand-illuminated psychedelic broadsides of poems by my friends. I masking-taped my paper massacre to the only empty space, a door I'd closed to form a wall.

When my stepfather got out of prison, he tracked my mother down. He found the city where she'd moved. He broke a basement window and crawled in. She never saw his car, halfway up the dark block, stuffed behind a bush.

My mother lived. She wouldn't say what happened in the house that night. Cops came: that's what I know. Silent, she hung a screen between that scene and me. It's what a mother does.

She lived—as lived the violence of our years with him, knifed into us like scrimshaw cut in living bone.

Carved but alive, we learned to hold our breath, dive deep, bare our teeth to what fed us.

When I was twenty-one, my son slept under the outline of what I could do, a death I could hold in my hands.

At the time, I'd have denied its locale any meaning, called its placement coincidence, pointing to walls crowded with other kinds of dreams.

But that dark torn thing did hang there, its lower edge obscured behind the wooden slats, the flannel duck, the stuffed white bear.

It hung there like a promise, like a headboard, like a *No*, like a terrible poem, like these lines I will never show you, shielding you from the fear I carry—like a sort of oath I swore over your quiet sleep.

Portrait of a Family, Crooked and Straight

A black-and-white photo, 1976. In the foreground, two daughters in jeans and Windbreakers pluck at cotton candy. Wispy grayish clouds hover low, bad weather approaching. Behind them their parents cha-cha, arms lifted. They're hamming it up, improvising for the photographer, a family friend. After the last shutter click, the parents will kiss. This is not captured on film, but the elder daughter recalls it clearly, even years later. She must have turned from her cotton candy to see it.

It might not have been the cha-cha. Their hands might not have been raised. It's possible the parents weren't even dancing. Where is that photo? Boxed up in one of the parents' basements? Pressed in an album? Thrown away? The elder daughter can conjure clearly her pink Windbreaker and her younger sister's red sneakers. As for the parents, she believes they were standing behind their daughters and that they were gazing at each other. They are parents of two children who demand all their attention. But in this moment the children are distracted; it's their first time touching this pink gauze that turns to sugary mist in the mouth. The parents are caught on film in a gaze any adult would see is the private currency exchanged between lovers.

I thought of how the sisters that Sunday afternoon stood with sweet mist in the back of their throats. You don't even know how many reasons you have to be happy; you don't know that behind you your parents are exchanging the gaze of lovers, or that hardly anyone's parents exchange that gaze, or that there will be a time, years from now, when your parents will no longer agree to look upon each other that way.

The father in a plaid work shirt, his weekend shirt for tinkering. He fixes what breaks, rigs up schemes, makes the household chug and hum with ease.

He would get the picture hung properly.

Would he remember that lover's gaze?

Would she?

That portrait isn't one of the pictures I'm trying to hang. Where is it? It has gone the way of that family, into the unreliable archive of memory. Maybe it's also in a box somewhere. None of them, not the mother or father or either of the sisters, is going to search it down.

Still, I can't help conjuring it so that I can drive a nail into the wall and hang it for everyone to see, the mother and the father and the daughters, one of whom sees her parents kiss.

The wall over the fireplace, in the living room.

There.

They were married for twenty-nine years. From their yearbook photos, it was easy for their elder daughter, at fifteen, to slot them into categories. Gayle, nicknamed "Binky," got voted Most Popular, Best Looking, Best Teeth. Best *Teeth*. David, like his daughter, didn't win any popularity contests. Still, yearbook photographs capture him as Tom Wingfield, the male lead in the Paul D. Schreiber Class of '61 production of *The Glass Menagerie*. Back then he sported the big, black-framed glasses popularized by Buddy Holly and, in the yearbook photo, held a book open in the palm of his hand. He's skinny and bookish and earnest. A *thespian*. This member of the Thespian Society belongs to a different crowd than Binky Spanier, who in addition to the popularity and looks and teeth is head cheerleader, in a short skirt and a sweater with a bullhorn sewn on the front. The letters of her name descend diagonally along the bullhorn, BINKY.

On the inside cover of her yearbook, David writes, *I hope you get the appreciating mate you deserve.*

They married in a small ceremony at her parents' house. No one—not David's parents, British emigrants who had come to America by boat after the end of World War II; not Binky's family, New York Jews expecting their beautiful daughter to marry well to one of their own—was happy about the marriage. David and Binky ("Binks," he called her) had to carry the wedding day on their own enthusiasm, feeding each other cake with their hands and skirting around the discomfort of having a wedding in a living room, rather than in the Episcopal Church or the temple.

They got lost looking for their honeymoon motel and, when it got dark, chose one on the New Jersey Turnpike. An uncertain, inauspicious beginning for a marriage that would last almost thirty years before sliding precipitously, permanently, out of focus.

Each of my parents kept belongings in the night table on either side of the bed. In my father's, copies of *Machine Design* magazine, more than one calculator, cufflinks, spare change. In my mother's, always, a candy stash. In her childhood her father hid Mallomars and chocolate bars, and in mine she too hid her sugary vice, as if hiding and searching down sweets were traits passed on from parent to child. In her night table she kept Swedish fish, Jordan almonds, jellied fruit slices sprinkled with sugar. She ate the colors she favored first, leaving the undesirable green and yellow slices. I'd find them in a ripped plastic bag under her *Ms.* magazines and pop psychology books: *If You Meet the Buddha on the Road, Kill Him, Jonathan Livingston Seagull, Have You Checked Your Erroneous Zones?* She must have known that I was stealing from her, though I tried to be careful not to eat what she might notice missing.

One day I noticed something other than the candy. I must have been old enough, for the first time, to turn my attention away from the predictable stash, with its hoard of discarded colors and flavors. I turned from the candy and read and reread the title of a book: *Surpassing the Love of Men.*

I must have been in my mid-teens. I'd had my first boyfriend, an offbeat sophomore named Melvin who refused to be called Melvin: he answered only to Sam. At night, while my family slept, he biked to my house and left gyros from Souvlaki Place on our front stoop, offerings in wax paper and congealed grease. On the phone he acted out exchanges for me between Jeopardy contestants and the host, all the characters channels for a chaotic, underutilized intelligence. His chaos and charisma, his ability to draw out of my dry sense of humor, the petting under a sleeping bag we'd done almost every day that icy February: all this was preparing me to devote myself to loving men. Men charmed me: from Sam on, I fell always for the chaotic, the comic, the hilariously neurotic. I fell in love with the gyro on the front stoop, the pratfall, the arrow through the head. I preferred the profane to the sacred, the gangly juggler to the swaggering quarterback. My friendships with girls were solemn affairs meant for the entrusting of secrets, the confessing of fears, the forming and shifting and testing of alliances. Not so with boys. Boys meant breaking the rules, snubbing authority, swinging from the rafters. I could not, in short, comprehend the project of *surpassing* the love of men. At fifteen, I was just getting started on the project of securing their love.

My mother's book would need to be tucked under the others, forgotten about, stashed away.

"Rosie's crooked," my mother said. "So are Richard Gere and Cindy Crawford."

"People say Travolta," someone offered.

"People say Hillary," said someone else.

All the women—seven of us—shrugged and sighed and stared out at the water from our beach chairs. Ambitious women were always accused of being lesbians. My mother and Deb headed back to our room at the motel and returned with champagne and happy hour hors d'oeuvres: olives, crackers, grapes, cheese. Happy hour sent the conversation off in some other direction, away from the speculative game about who was and wasn't. I felt relieved. I wouldn't have relished admitting it, but I couldn't get used to the word "lesbian," with its buzz of consonants in the middle of it. It wouldn't slip out of the mouth in one clean syllable, like "gay." Worse, I couldn't square it with "mother," a word that held not just my affective ties, but also a definition of the world as a stable, knowable place.

"Lesbian" tipped the meaning out of the word "mother." I didn't want it to. Back in Utah, where I was living at the time and going to graduate school, I lay in my bed and tried out the sentence. "My mother is a lesbian," I said into the dark. The phrase sounded like one of the slogans printed on the buttons my mother collected: "A Woman without a Man Is Like a Fish without a Bicycle," "My Karma Ran Over My Dogma," "My Other Car Is a Broom." I knew I was supposed to be a liberal, a feminist, a person of tolerance and good will. None of this kept me from squeamishness when I pictured my mother sleeping in a king-size bed in the suburbs with her androgynous three-hundred-pound girlfriend. This was the nineties. Everywhere around me, I saw the new, prurient interest in gay people. Actors played them on TV; preachers made pronouncements to the press about Ellen "Degenerate," condemning the actress Ellen DeGeneres for coming out as a lesbian.

My sister couldn't abide it. She marked out distance and territory between herself and my mother, refusing to go to her house. The spare bedroom at my mother's became mine by default. Visiting her dropped me into a domesticity disconcertingly alien and familiar. I recognized in it my mother's fondness for framed photographs of beaches, seashells she'd gathered over decades of summers, blond wood, candles, a palate of creams and blues meant to evoke sand and sky and sea. All this reproduced the domestic scenes of my childhood. But another version of my mother asserted herself here. Look closely at the beach scene, and there's a rainbow flag flying beside the rambling Victorian bed-and-breakfast by the sea. This isn't just any beach; it's Provincetown, where my mother and Deb vacationed with the two women in the photograph on the refrigerator.

In their bathroom the impressionist painting of the woman bathing changes, takes on trappings. One evening, too much wine in me, I stand and stare at the painting, the woman's flesh benignly blurred by the painter's brush. I would not have lingered over it at a museum. But here, in the bathroom that belongs to my mother and her lover, that flesh irks me, the woman's breasts and belly suddenly taunting and lurid. I open the medicine cabinet and survey the contents. On my mother's side, the same overpriced creams and conditioners I use, the mousses and eye gels and promises of beauty in a jar. On Deb's side, a bottle of men's cologne, the Polo player eternally swinging his mallet from atop his horse. Then toothpaste and eyedrops and antibiotics, tweezers, nail scissors, flea powder for the dog.

What was I expecting? The men's cologne unnerved me a little, but the ordinariness unnerved me more. My mother, crooked now, still used the same mousse I did. Still went after the beauty in the overpriced jar. I closed the cabinet and studied my face in the mirror. I didn't know it yet, but I was beginning to search my own surface for signs. The conversation on the beach would return and echo. *Rosie's crooked. Travolta. Richard Gere.* My mother, after years of what I considered enthusiastic and successful heterosexuality, had declared herself crooked. Any day the frame of me might tilt.

My belongings arrived in Alabama a week after I did. I'd gotten a teaching job at the University of Alabama, a place I'd never given a moment's thought to until I got the job. I didn't own much: a bed frame and boxes of clothes, plates and cups wrapped in newspaper, some framed pictures I'd paid extra to have the movers wrap. I drifted through thick July heat, 102 degrees, to unpack what little I had. Two champagne flutes, miraculously intact. But several plates were broken, margarita glasses smashed. And my large, framed Georgia O'Keeffe print, when I removed the movers' cocoon of plastic, sat behind splintered spears of glass.

I brought the print to a shop to have the broken glass replaced. My pictures would have to be hung right away. This became a fixed idea for me, almost an obsession, entirely unreasonable. I didn't even have a sofa yet. I didn't have proper kitchen utensils. My apartment was large and cavernous; my voice, when I worried aloud to myself, echoed off the blank walls.

After the sun went down one day, I went for a walk to case out the neighborhood. A man sitting splay-legged on a sloping lawn called to me.

"Want to pick some nut grass?"

He had the smooth skin and lanky limbs of a preadolescent boy. He had a boy's full head of hair cut in glossy bangs he tossed out of his eyes. When nervous or excited, his right eye twitched involuntarily, a tic that I at first mistook for overly enthusiastic winking. A twelve-year-old might have been stretched and broadened to the dimensions of a grown man; this, I saw later, was what disarmed me. Only the spidery network of laugh lines around his eyes convinced me that he was six years older than me, thirty-nine.

That summer in Alabama, my first, was a languid, stifling sequence of days that shaded into night with no discernable drop in temperature. I had never experienced such unabated heat. Most of the twenty thousand students and faculty whose cars jammed the main thoroughfares in town during the school year left for the summer months. It was both the emptiness of Tuscaloosa in summer and the emptiness of my apartment, walls formidably blank, that brought me into Mark's orbit.

We would need to paint the bathroom and hallway, Mark announced. He took on the project with gusto, choosing paint with me and hauling in a ladder for the job. He wouldn't take the money I offered him, asking only that I keep him company while he worked. Soon we were trading opinions, the northerner and the southerner laughing at each other's assertions. I heard myself, appalled, recoil and scold when he used the word "nigger." When I punctuated stubbing my toe with "goddamn," he objected with a forcefulness I at first thought was a put-on. Southern Baptist meets Yankee agnostic. We managed to piss each other off at least once an hour.

He told me jokes while he painted.

"What did the two black lesbians say to each other?"

"'You da man.' 'No, YOU da man!'"

Mark and I thought it would be a big party, but it was just five of us for dinner. Linda, the hostess, served us wine. The other two young women seated at the table conversed alternately in English and German. Right away, an animated conversation began.

"A hen party!" Mark sat back, amused, arms crossed over his chest. He managed to stay quiet for half a minute or so before he was back in the conversation, as big a talker as any of us.

Linda told a story about going to an employee Halloween party dressed as Aunt Jemima. She had painted her face black, but not her arms. She had worn a kerchief on her head, and, instead of serving pancakes, she said, poured shots of whiskey into people's mouths. The week after the party, some of the employees lodged a complaint. At the meeting called to address the matter, one black woman wanted to know why Linda had painted her face black but not her arms and neck. Another asked how Linda would feel if someone dressed up on Halloween as Chandler, Linda's mildly retarded nephew. Linda felt it entirely unfair to compare an invented character to an actual person. Mark nodded in agreement: *Only thing worse than a nigger is a nigger who can't take a joke.* This ignited a discussion about race and gender that stretched into hours. More hours, more wine. Somewhere in the midst of this we ate a delicious German noodle dish. As the evening drew on, the discussion got more contentious, sharper lines drawn between us. We discussed women and men and date rape and domestic violence and patriarchy. I was the one who got us going on patriarchy. I was pontificating.

I'd had too much to drink, and I was angry. The woman beside me, Jamie, joined in, agreeing with my points and sometimes, remarkably, backing me up with statistics. I didn't know where she was getting these numbers, but they sounded marvelous. Furthermore, they flummoxed Mark. I began to enjoy seeing Mark flummoxed.

Jamie took one of my wrists and circled it with her hand. As Mark rebutted my remarks and her statistics, she worked her other hand up and down my forearm. Mark was explaining how just as many men as women got the shit kicked out of them, maybe even more, but that men never reported the violence because they feared the authorities' perception of them.

My mother worked at a domestic violence agency on Long Island. So many men attempted to threaten women being served by the agency that the offices were now housed in a building with a false storefront and an elaborate security system. I was planning to explain all this to Mark. I was planning to jump in and refute him any minute, as soon as he gave me an opening.

Mark suddenly detoured from the argument he was making and stared at Jamie. "What are you doing?"

"I'm going to be a massage therapist," Jamie said.

Mark made a face and returned to the question of men being afraid to admit their wives could whip their asses.

Jamie leaned in and whispered to me.

"Do you think he'd notice if you left for a bit?"

"No," I said.

She got up and left the table. I remained for a few minutes, then got up and excused myself. I didn't know where I was going; I hadn't seen any part of the house other than the room that led from the front door to the kitchen. She let me in the bathroom and locked the door. We sat down together on the edge of the tub.

"He's a piece of work," she said.

"He's a bastard."

We laughed.

"Is he your boyfriend?"

"God no," I said. I told her how I'd just moved to town and how he was the first person I'd met in Alabama. She listened carefully, commiserating with me about the conservatism of the locals. She'd been living in California the previous year and had only recently been transferred to Alabama.

"And that thing about Aunt Jemima," I said.

We agreed Mark was a Cro-Magnon. We agreed, and then, on the edge of the tub, we leaned in and kissed each other, as if to seal it. Something hateful had to be banished; that was how I felt in that moment. The current of sympathy that traveled between us could blot out the hate.

I'd never kissed a woman on the lips before; I'd never passed my hand over a breast. The exercise was instructive. I felt how small a woman could be in the hands of a man, how a man could bend and snap and break her. All the people I'd embraced passionately had until that moment been men, young men, dense with muscle, never frail. This woman, smaller even than me, self-possessed and lit from within, could be bashed with one blow. I saw myself bashed with one blow, though I'd never been hit.

We kissed for a stretch of time that felt like fifteen minutes. I could hear the distant, dwindling conversation in the kitchen.

"What are the two of you doing in there?"

"Talking," I said. Jamie and I pulled apart, wiped our mouths, smoothed down our hair.

When I opened the door Mark looked shaken and a little sick. "You were in there forty-five minutes! What were you doing in there for all that time?"

How could I formulate in words what had passed between us? The kiss that blotted hate, the sympathy that traveled in currents, the laugh and ease on the edge of the tub, the listening, the embrace. I couldn't explain, either, how Mark himself had been what made Jamie and I kiss each other in the first place. Already I understood that no language would ever be invented to convey this to Mark. A great drunken wash of sadness passed over me then, for all in experience that was untranslatable. Between women and men I often felt an abyss open when we talked: the way they framed the world and the way we did.

As Mark and I crossed the dark lawn toward my car, he said, "You humiliated me. The two of you in there, what were you doing?"

I focused on the road, in the overcautious way of drunks.

"Did you have each other's clothes off?"

"Jesus, Mark."

Bitterly he said, "She kiss better than me?" He was thinking aloud and didn't give me time to answer a question before he thought of another. "You had sexual feelings toward her?"

I was about to respond when he made another observation. "You're driving erratically."

"No, I'm not." I knew I was weaving.

Later that night, he called me. "I'm coming over," he said.

"No, you're not." I was sitting on my kitchen floor with the portable phone. I was eating cheese. I was having a hard time picturing Jamie's face. It was three o'clock in the morning.

"I'm coming over," he said.

In the morning we got up and went to church. To *church*. I showered and put on a flowered dress I'd worn for teaching. I had a vague memory of being told I was going to be shown what a man was, alongside an equally convincing belief that I'd merely invented that, dreamed it. I'd awakened in the morning with him in the bed beside me. When he reappeared for church, he was showered and combed and wearing a suit. At the Northport Baptist Church, we sat in the back, behind three elderly congregants who greeted us and shook our hands. They were pleased to see Mark. "Is this the next Miz Booth?" one of them asked.

An interminable karaoke-like business in which a woman accompanied by recorded instrumentation sang about Christ as the lamb whose blood healed her gave me time to assess. I'd never sat in a room full of Baptists. The preacher got up and gave a spiel from Numbers in the Old Testament. The sermon was about Spiritual Presumption—presuming that one was just waiting around in this life to be delivered into heaven. This led him, by some route, to citing Ellen DeGeneres ("from television, the outspoken lesbian"), who had claimed publicly that each person has to decide for him or herself what's right and wrong and then be responsible for one's actions. I thought this sounded like a pretty reasonable idea. The preacher, though, countered by saying that one doesn't decide. There is a right and a wrong, he said. You find it right there in the Bible.

"Ooh, I love that girl!" My mother lifted the photo of her partner and kissed it. In a little while we'd go to dinner with new colleagues of mine, two women—a couple—my mother wanted to meet. In the meantime, she was missing Deb, who'd stayed in New York for this, my mother's first visit to my new home in Alabama.

We drank wine. My mother smoked a joint, and I, feeling how palpable her homesickness was, opted not to object to her smoking pot in my living room. I knew I was objecting on the basis of some arcane principle anyway, the notion that "mother" and "smoking pot in daughter's living room" were somehow inappropriately paired. I didn't have any legitimate objection beyond that; I wasn't afraid of some vice squad showing up and arresting her. My sister, whom my mother and I had long ago nicknamed Nancy Reagan for her strident antidrug stance, would have flown off the handle had my mother lit up a joint in her living room. Impossible to imagine what she would have done in response to my mother's enthusiastic photo kissing.

Over the course of two days my mother bought and hung curtains for me, procured flatware at Walmart, hung pictures. She struggled and apologized for her clumsiness, saying Deb would be better at hanging pictures and curtains. At home Deb had a workshop in the garage, tools mounted neatly on the walls, my mother's cases of diet Snapple iced tea stacked on shelves Deb built. My mother missed that girl too much; she would, as it turned out, leave a day early to return to New York, where her girl sat in a men's T-shirt and pulled weeds on the front lawn. When I drove down University Boulevard and saw Mark pulling nut grass on his lawn, I couldn't help but superimpose Deb on his image. No, not superimpose. I put them beside each other on a lawn in some imagined suburbia, where the gay neighbors and the straight neighbors talked lawn maintenance and helped one another pull weeds.

At my sister's wedding two professional photographers documented every move we made. In a preceremony photo session on the beach, the bridal party was directed to run—in our suits and gowns and dyed-to-match shoes— down the beach. Sand sifted into our shoes, carefully coiffed hair became tangled. Then portraits of our families: the groom's family, the bride's family, the groom with the bride's family, the bride with the groom's family. Somewhere, out of the frame, Deb stood in a black suit with long tails. At the reception, she and I danced. At first I wavered clumsily, resisting her lead. But then I gave into it. She knew how to lead better than I did, and I was slender and in a gown and heels, and she was dressed like a man, and I was enjoying the dance. I didn't seek out my sister while we danced; I let the rest of the room settle into momentary anonymity, as if no one could see the maid of honor dancing with her mother's lesbian girlfriend. No one knew it, but I had kissed a girl, and I had been date-raped for it, and I had gone to a Baptist Church, and I had sat in with all the other Baptists and listened to a preacher speak out against gay people, and my mother and her girlfriend weren't allowed to dance at this wedding, and my mother and father didn't want to dance with each other at this wedding, and they wouldn't, and there would be no portrait from this wedding of the father and the mother and the two daughters together, no portrait for my wall.

When Deb looked at the photo albums from the wedding, she noticed there weren't any of her. Those she found later, in a box. There wouldn't be any photo of her and the maid of honor dancing, not even in the ones relegated to the box. The heavy woman with the black suit and tails spinning the slender woman in the midnight blue gown and dyed-to-match shoes, hair unkempt, is only in the archive of memory. I'll hang it now, on the wall in my living room.

Is it straight or crooked? Tell me.

There.

TV Time in Negroland

My sister is in our parents' bedroom, at Mother's vanity dresser. She tries on earrings and necklaces; she hazards a provocative smile; she puts her right elbow on the glass-covered dresser top and places her chin on her hand. (Her ballet-class hand, soft but alert and slightly rounded.) Before dinner, she will ask, "Who do I look more like, Lena Horne or Dorothy Dandridge?"

I am listening to records. *Guys and Dolls, The King and I, Oklahoma* . . . I perform rake bravado, soubrette whimsy, judicious womanliness. . . . In the South Pacific, the beautiful young lieutenant from Main Line Philadelphia has found himself in love with a beautiful brown-skinned girl in the South Pacific. She is Polynesian and speaks no English. (We know, though the rest of America may not, that Juanita Hall, who plays her mother, is really a Negro.)

The lieutenant has learned a lesson I already know, a lesson he sings about with the fearless, legato insistence of the wholly sheltered. "You've got to be taught to be afraid / Of people whose eyes are oddly made." Singing along, I make the *oddly* more staccato and curl my lip. His "and people whose skin is a different shade" is earnest, impassioned. I keep the passion but mute the earnestness with a raised eyebrow.

It's weekend-television time.

Sammy Davis Jr. is going to be on *The Milton Berle Show*.

Dorothy Dandridge is going to be on *The Jerry Lewis Colgate Comedy Hour*.

Lena Horne is going to be on *The Frank Sinatra Timex Show*.

These are seminal moments in the viewing mores of the whole nation.

After dinner the four of us gather in the TV room. Our parents are on the couch; Denise and I push the hassocks as near the TV as we can or stretch out on the floor till we're told to sit up.

Ladies and gentleman, please welcome . . .

Sammy Davis Jr. does a swing run onto the stage. He wears a taut, close-fitting suit and rectangular black-framed glasses.

My parents saw him live in New York.

My father: "He can do it all!"

My mother: "He certainly can. [*Pause.*] He still has too much oil in his hair." They've talked about how men in show business use either too much oil or oil that's too thick. They don't always use stocking caps, either. Stocking caps settle the hair into thin ridge waves that needn't pretend to be straight.

Sammy can dance (beautifully) and sing (very well). He enunciates crisply, with no trace of a stock Negro accent. He imitates the racially neutral vocal stylings of Nat King Cole and Billy Daniels *and* the racially white vocal stylings of Cary Grant, James Stewart, and James Cagney. This is cheeky and very satisfying. Daddy sits back on the couch. We hear him chuckle. Mother leans forward eagerly and tips her cigarette into the aquamarine glass ashtray.

Sammy isn't on his own, though—not yet. For now, he is always followed onstage by two quiet, portly, balding men. He is still tied to his father, Sammy Davis Sr., and the kind employer of his childhood, whom he still calls Uncle Will. He is still part of their Will Mastin Trio. "He's carrying them along," Mother says. The older men have the generic smiles of vaudeville second-stringers who learned many years ago how to frame the star, keep time, recede, do their specialty step, recede, and exit. They're from an age before television: before Broadway theaters like Ed Sullivan's, where cheerful white people sit, eager to be entertained; before TV rec rooms; before dens where Negro families sit waiting to be entertained and hoping not to be denigrated. Will Mastin and Sammy Davis Sr. are folk art before folk art becomes museum-worthy.

"I think it's time for them to go," my father says in a gentle but definite way.

My sister and I study pictures of Lena and Dorothy. Lena's nostrils flare; they do not spread. The bridge of her nose is thin and exact. Dorothy's nose is a little bit fuller, but it's not *full*. And she has a dimple right above her lips. Cupid-bow lips. Maidenly lips. Lena's smile is wide, but her lips are not. She has high, wide Indian cheekbones, so she needs a wide smile. Her top lip is so narrow that she probably has trouble applying lipstick properly. Like my grandmother.

Lena and Dorothy can wear their hair any way they want. Upswept with bangs and tendrils, like Jennifer Jones; shoulder-length with wave clusters, like Elizabeth Taylor; trimmed to a cap of wayward curls, like Ava Gardner, who's from the South and *may have black blood*. They look glamorous, they look comfortable, in evening gowns and fur stoles like Mother and her friends. But most people don't know we Negroes dress like that.

When a woman sings on a television show, she's supposed to be singing in her apartment or her boudoir. There's a window frame with curtains behind her. She can peer into a mirror frame and pout. She can perch on a small cushioned chair and kick her legs up. She can fling herself onto a love seat. She can even pick up a real poodle when the song ends and hug it.

Dorothy wears a pale ruffled ball gown in her "apartment." She has put her hair in a society-hostess bun with a center part. There are four strands of pearls around her neck. She looks down, as if she's misbehaved, then lifts her head and smiles. "Blow out the candle," she sings pertly,

> Blow out the candle,
> Blow out the candle so the neighbors won't see!

She cups her hands at her waist, clasps them at her throat—opera singers always do this on TV—throws her head back just a bit, and smiles again. She extends an arm, then flings it up and flicks her wrist. It's almost Spanish! Her shoulders move slightly, no more than a few measures, and off the beat. Then she sways her hips, pretending not to notice they're swaying. ("Just enough," says my mother.) She mimes snuffing out a candle like French maids do in operas.

> Won't you blow out the candle,
> So there will be no scandal?
> And no one will know
> You've been ki-is-ssing me!

"Why couldn't they give her a real song, Ellington or a show tune?" my father wants to know. He doesn't want to know, he knows, and we know, too. "She did the best she could do with that little ditty."

But Lena sings Cole Porter. She's wearing a black sheath with full-length see-through sleeves. The white curtains behind her curl and drape.

"While tearing off a game of golf . . ." Hah! My father doesn't care about golf, but plenty of his friends do. The neckline of her sheath is tulle netting. Tulle ruffles cuff her wrists. Lena doesn't move her body at all. She stands in profile the whole time she sings. Her behind is perfectly round, not big. One arm is poised at her waist. The other moves stealthily toward the fancy chair that must go with a vanity dresser that isn't on the set. She places her wrist on the chair back with extreme care. (*Hauteur* is my mother's word.) She has ballet hands, but they're a little pointed. They're show-business ballet hands. She lets two fingers touch the curve of the chair and move back and forth.

"Ah just adore his asking for more" (she makes her eyes very big and stares out), "but my heart belongs to Daddy." Now she is smiling and curling her lips at the same time. She stretches her mouth open, she makes it very wide, and we see her teeth, whiter than the curtains and gleaming in perfect formation. She turns her face away and lifts her chin. She shows only her profile as the song ends, and the audience applauds.

My parents talk about what she does with her face. Lena mugs, they agree, but she can get away with it. She's a beauty. And she used to be bland. Then she married Lennie Hayton. He was a bandleader and a big wheel at MGM. He gave her sophisticated arrangements and taught her how to put a song over with personality. Hayton is white. When you see pictures of them in *Ebony*, though, he's the one who looks grateful. He's always smiling. He's standing behind her most of the time, with his white hair and little beard.

Lena knew what she was doing. And she always knows how to carry herself.

They Didn't Come Here Cowboys

At the arena gate the young barrel racer readies her horse. Its chestnut body gleams and ripples in the sun, its muscles taut, impatient. The horse tosses its shiny brown mane. Someone has tied green ribbons in its hair and wound more green ribbons around its ankles. It is well cared for.

The rider, too, holds her body on alert, somehow both erect in the saddle and crouched with anticipation of the movement about to happen. Beneath her cowboy hat her hair is long and brown, and when the horn blasts and the horse takes off flying she throws her body forward into a low sling, clenching her thighs to keep herself steady, and her ponytail flies out behind her, the flag of her motion, the echo of the horse's tail below it. Horse and rider, the brilliant green of the horse's flying feet flashing and the light glinting off the rider's brilliant green silk shirt, they are one.

They reach the first barrel. They fly around it so smoothly the horse could be the blade of a skate, it tilts so cleanly, and the rider, she hangs on. She reaches back and slaps at the horse's flank, driving it forward—but there's no need, the horse is flying, carrying her as if she were weightless—

Then the next barrel. Women's barrel racing is the only professional event at the Angola Prison Rodeo in Louisiana, the only event in which inmates, all male, do not compete. She circles the barrel perfectly. She and her horse, they have done this before, so many times, and now they are doing it here, and the crowd in the stands are whooping them on; the inmates have climbed up on the bull chutes for a better view, their bodies hanging half off the gates as they twist into better positions to follow her flight, some of them hollering and others staring in concentrated silence at the woman and her horse in the sun who fly.

The straight stretch is over in a blink, and then there's only one more barrel, and then home. She drives into it, hard. Horse and rider lean. As close as they can, as clean as a blade—

Clank.

The rider's head against the aluminum support pole of the arena. Her body slumps, falls from the horse, hits the ground. The horse, suddenly free of her weight, bolts at its new lightness. Then it crashes to a halt. It seems confused, as though suddenly remembering her.

She lies on the hard dry dirt of the arena, twisted on her side, her eyes closed. A slow drone builds from the crowd in the stands around me, late in coming. An intake of breath, a murmur. Real fear is quiet when it comes. Next to me, a mother covers her daughter's eyes. *Oh, no. Poor girl. Don't look, baby.* Two officials in cream cowboy hats run to the young woman and kneel over her, their boot soles suddenly visible cocked against the dirt. Now a stretcher is rolled out, a backboard already strapped to it, pushed by two EMTs from the ambulance parked just outside the arena's entrance.

I watch from the stands. Already this moment is being push-pinned into my mind, the stab-through of something unknown and inarticulable and un-understood and troubling. Not the woman falling, not the tragedy we've just watched. The problem is this: the ambulance.

Angola, the Louisiana state penitentiary, has had a rodeo for almost fifty years, but in recent times it's grown. What was once a few pickup trucks backed up onto the field and a few inmates and guards come out to, in the assistant warden's words, "play with the horses," now brings in nearly $450,000 per show, packing people into a new ten thousand–seat arena. The rodeo takes place in October and April every year.

It is April 2008, the day of the rodeo, and the rodeo has not yet begun and the woman has not yet hit the pole. The day is hot and dry and dusty, the famed Louisiana humidity absent. Where I sit in the arena, there's no protection from the beating sun, and all around me mothers thumb open their rodeo programs into fans they flutter ineffectually at their sweltering children. No shade, from no tall buildings, here on the prison grounds; the penitentiary is sprawling and flat, studded with low camps and spiked with only the occasional guard tower that sticks up like a stake driven into the earth. And today—just for today, for the rodeo—a pink and purple bouncy castle, the kind found at children's fairs and rented for birthday parties, pressed up against one of the towers. The castle sways airily; the children inside it laugh and shriek. Above its gray balloon turrets, in the guard tower's perch, a gun's long neck is visible through the railing.

Around the tower the grounds stretch eighteen thousand acres. Angola is the largest prison in America, larger than the borough of Manhattan, and bordered on one side by the Mississippi. Stretches of barren dirt and lush, almost tropical, green fields of marsh grass alternate abruptly, then neat square patches of hewn rows where tufts of green rise from the dirt. The prison is a working farm. Many prisoners here still serve sentences at hard labor, working until they pay off their keep and after that for wages that range from two to twenty cents an hour. Any other day—any nonrodeo day—the visual is too familiar, like an echo across history: mostly black prisoners bent over in lines, working the land on foot. Seventy-eight percent of Angola prisoners are black. Over them a white guard on horseback, carrying a gun. Sixty-six percent of guards are white. The prison grounds were stitched together from land bought from plantation owners in the 1830s, then the prison was named for the region in Africa the slaves who once worked these fields were taken from.

The arena is sold out, full of families who now settle into their seats. They've come from all over Louisiana; maybe some, like me, from even farther. This rodeo is famous. The emcee's been brought in from the pro circuit, and as we sit in the stands and fan ourselves and the children call to one another and bite at sticky cones of cotton candy, his voice crackles out from the loudspeakers. "This here is the land, America. This here is the *land*." He draws the vowels out like a lounge singer, like a lounge lizard, and onto the sun-packed dirt of the arena, inmates walk in blue jeans and boots, their chambray shirts, "Angola blues," replaced for the day with black-and-white striped shirts that recall old prison uniforms. They squint into the sun. They wave at the stands.

From here, the rodeo unfolds. The bull riders are tossed from the bulls, their rides lasting one, two, three seconds before their bodies hang crooked from the side of the body of charging muscle or go arcing, flung through the air. To win they must reach six seconds, two seconds less than the pro standard of eight, but most won't come close. They aren't allowed to practice. Amateur bull riding doesn't make for much sport. The event ends quickly. Then more games. Halftime. Then the barrel racing. The clank. The hush. The ambulance.

I'd come to the rodeo to write about it. The spectacle of it—the bouncy castles, the capuchin monkeys trained to ride border collies with tiny saddles on their backs for the halftime show, the way the prison gates open wide so the public can drive right onto the mythical fields and later the way you see children at the New Orleans airport wearing pink-and-blue Angola Prison Rodeo T-shirts—has become part of controversial warden Burl Cain's efforts to address the problem of the public's perception of the prison, a place so historically violent that the federal government took it over after, in the early 1970s, a dozen inmates were stabbed to death each year, with dozens more injured. Burl Cain has reduced censorship of the inmate newspaper, replaced the cardboard boxes inmates were once buried in with wood coffins inmates make for their friends or themselves in the woodshop, increased the availability of Bible study, and started annual weekends for prisoners' children to visit. In newspaper interviews, he talks constantly of the new Angola, how violence is no longer an issue, how it's now a model community of model inmates.

But he hasn't succeeded entirely in shaking the mystique—and perhaps he doesn't want to, as the old Angola is Angola, *that* Angola, Angola of movies and song, so violent that one of its wardens was, famously, later imprisoned for conspiring to murder his wife. That Angola has a kind of panache to it. You can see it in the gift shop just outside the front gates of the prison, combined with a small museum devoted to Angola's past and staffed by volunteers from the local parish of West Feliciana, women of a certain age with lemon-yellow hair teased and sprayed into cotton candy bouffants and circles of peach blush on their faintly creased cheeks, women who in a different town might be volunteering with the Rotary Club or at the information desk of the local hospital. The gift shop sells T-shirts printed with a graphic of the prison gates and the words, "Angola: A Gated Community." The museum has the old electric chair, not behind glass but with just a rope in front of it, like a visitor could just hop the rope and sit in it. It has Susan Sarandon's set chair from *Dead Man Walking*, the film adaptation of Sister Helen Prejean's book about the execution of Robert Lee Willie—not a book, or a movie, that could be said to be in any way supportive of Angola's practices. It has a life-size wallpaper mock-up of the execution chamber, including the gurney on which inmates die, so that a visitor can walk up by the gurney and photograph herself posed as though to lie on it or press the buttons that will inject the fatal drugs. Angola doesn't hide from its reputation, or apologize for it. It *is* its reputation.

That was what I intended to write about. The way the rodeo intersected with this performance of what Angola is, done by Angola. Every few years newspapers seem to discover the rodeo anew and run brief stories about the oddity of inmates riding bulls and about the redemption the articles say the men find there. I thought I might write that kind of piece.

But whenever I tried, I got stuck on that detail that didn't fit into that narrative, that became outsize in my head, the horrible clank of the woman's head against the pole and then the arrival of the ambulance. I heard the clank so clearly in my memory, how it had bounced through the arena, how it had severed the chatter in the rodeo into silence. It was the problem of capturing that sound—the size of it—that tripped me up. How could I convey all that sound had meant? And why did I keep trying to? It was the thing I remembered most clearly from the day, yes, but it wasn't about the inmates.

I'd write of the flyer I was given at the gate instructing me to leave my cell phone in the car, the car windows up and the car locked. Of the booths around the arena that sold refreshments to benefit inmate clubs, and the guards some of the booths had stationed in the back, watching the inmates who interacted with the public. Of watching the rodeo.

And then I'd get to the sound and be stuck.

Because, I realized, I *hadn't* heard the sound. I had been an arena's length away, she on the other side. There was no way I could have heard the sound.

In the audio documentary *The Sound of Sport*, Peregrine Andrews explains that even televised sporting events contain, like movies do, created sounds.[1] When the viewer watches the picture of, say, a boxing match—the medium of television fooling the viewer's brain into thinking she's really there—she'll expect certain sounds to match what she's watching, without even knowing she expects them. Yet many of those sounds—the thwack of the glove against the skin, the spit of the boxer expelling the mouth guard—are impossible to capture with microphones. In real life, the boxers can't be miked. In real life, the sound of the crowd drowns out these more subtle sounds, what might be called the proofs of movement.

So the sound engineer adds them in. He or she might have previously recorded other boxers striking each other, getting in close in an empty practice ring with no crowd, no distractions, having them repeat the hit over and over again until it sounded real. Now that sound is linked to a button, and the engineer hits it each time the boxer hits his opponent, until the faked movement becomes an echo of the real movement, to make it seem more real.

When I was a kid, my family visited Disney World, where there used to be a fake soundstage where you could practice faking the sounds that sound engineers did. I remember grasping a coconut shell half in each palm and clip-clopping them along on a slate tile, trying to strike in time to match a cartoon horse as it galloped across the scene. When I got it right it was a neat trick, the way that even though I was making the sound my mind could almost believe that it came from the cartoon horse.

The horses I probably did hear that rodeo day. When I watch video clips of the rodeo from years past, I hear the horses, the crowd, the hollering. But in my memory, all that suddenly hushes and falls away. When the men had fallen from being tossed by the bulls, the sounds of the crowd hadn't paused; nothing had stopped. But in my memory when the woman hits the pole it is as though a spotlight comes on and everything silences. Then that horrible clank.

A year after the rodeo, I came back to Angola to visit the museum at its gates. I couldn't say what drew me back. Just curiosity, really. Just unease. I was still trying to write about the rodeo journalistically, and I was still stuck. And yet

I didn't feel I could let go of it. It had the same hold on me that a dream does when you don't quite remember it. The dreams you recall vividly, you can let go of. It's the ones who come back in shadow-moments, the ones whose shapes are too fuzzy to quite make out, that claw on and stay, like something perched on your back that you can't see but can't quite shake, either.

I was standing in the museum, looking up at a stuffed bull's head mounted to the wall. The mounted bull had been the most famous and fearsome in the rodeo's history, now there for its immortality, with the red chip from the event that closed out the rodeo, Guts and Glory, tied between its horns. For that game inmates were let into the center of the arena on foot, and then the bull let in. The men were to try to grab the chip, worth $500, from between the horns.

On an old television mounted next to the bull, a greatest-hits loop played from past rodeos: improbably long rides on the bull's back, crashes, a man at a time grabbing the chip from between the bull's horns and raising it high. Inmates tossed flying from the bull's horns. Below the television was a mannequin wearing the black-and-white uniform of the inmate riders, posed tall and triumphant with a wide-brimmed hat shading its eyes and a rope lasso in one hand. I recalled the announcer's voice at the rodeo: "They didn't come here cowboys," he'd said when the first bull riders took their places straddling over the chutes. That line spun out the American grandeur of what we were seeing, the possibility of bootstrap transformation, a kind of dream of what this day would be in the lives of these men, spun it out as weightless as a lasso-rope loop goes spinning through the air.

And when I had sat in the stands and listened as the bulls in the stock chutes pawed at the ground and snorted, and the crowd chattered and cheered and ate their popcorn and drank their sodas, and the announcer came over the loudspeaker, his voice the rat-tat-tat of those trained to call Western events, I could almost believe in the beauty of the scene he painted. I could almost believe in the bright flags strung up for color and the corn dogs being sold and the rah-rah spirit of the day. The first time I saw a man fall I was scared for him, and taken aback, but nothing in the rodeo stopped; the event kept going, a friend of the man's just came and dragged him off, patting his shoulder in reassurance, and so quietly was it handled, with no outward fear, that I could almost believe that the man wasn't hurt, at least not seriously so. That if he'd been bruised in a way that would last it was a rodeo kind of hurt, the kind that gets old bull riders respect for their scars, the kind that is about taking a chance against something wild and bigger than you are. I could almost believe that because the ambulance hadn't come, and the game hadn't been halted, and the announcer's voice didn't cut through the crowd in half-hour updates on his condition the way the announcements would later come for the woman, that surely that must mean he wasn't really hurt. Man after man fell, and nothing happened. I got used to it, even. I relaxed into the day.

While I was watching the rodeo video, a man came up behind me, and I turned at the noise. He was wearing the white "trusty" jumpsuit inmates who are deemed safe to be around visitors are allotted and pushing a broom around the museum. I recognized him immediately. His name was Edrick. I'd met him right after the rodeo, at the craft fair that accompanies it, where trusty inmates are allowed to sell wares they make to the public. Most of those crafts are kid-themed, a reflection of the way the day is a family day, and maybe a reflection of how many of the inmates miss their own families. Woodworking had been the dominant craft, with countless Harry Potters and Dora the Explorers burned into handcrafted toy chests, bed frames, coatracks. Biblical quotes and the Louisiana State University tiger had vied for second in decorations. There was a chain-link pen at the center of the fair, in which men who had not been deemed "trusty" but who had wares to sell shouted out prices and enticements to passersby, their crafts laid out on picnic tables that surrounded the pen like the spokes of a wheel. There, too, woodworking dominated, but the crafts were simpler: stepstools and hooks to pull a hot pan from the oven like I'd made as a child in woodshop class, countless wooden roses. And among them, on one table, made by one man, who didn't shout but just stared intently at whoever came by his table, tiny perfect wooden replicas of the electric chair, the helmet that conducts the electric current to the condemned man fashioned from leather scraps and a tiny wooden Bible affixed to the seat.

Amid all the wood, Edrick's wares had stood out. He was selling elaborate picture frames made from folding hundreds of gum wrappers into triangles and hooking one to the next so that each frame was a riot of color, a chevron pattern on it from the folded wrappers. I hadn't bought one—I liked him, but found the frames garish and couldn't imagine how one would fit into my apartment back home—and I'd regretted that later. What would it really have cost me, even if I didn't need the frame? A twenty I could spare, that he didn't have other means of making?

Now I greeted him and saw that he remembered me, too. We'd talked for a while about his frames and about the rodeo. "You were going to write about the rodeo," he said. "Did you?"

I felt caught out. How could I explain the problem that overtook me whenever I tried to write? The strange wordlessness I found myself with, hung up on a sound and an ambulance that wasn't even for the men, a detail that wasn't the right one with which to write about the day. "I've tried," I said, "but nothing's come together yet."

We stood together in front of the video and watched it silently for a minute. On the screen, a man flew weightlessly from the bull's horns. Captured on film, music playing in the background, his flight was almost beautiful, a slow arc through the air.

"Let me ask you," I said, "do inmates ever get hurt?"

Edrick turned and looked at me, the handle of the push broom still in his hand but forgotten. Then he repeated my words. "Do inmates ever get hurt. Do inmates ever get hurt. Man," he said. He looked disappointed. Something more than that. "Do inmates ever get hurt."

I understood my mistake instantly. Of course inmates got hurt. I knew that. I had seen that with my own eyes. I knew what gravity was and what the body was and that a man's body couldn't just fall like that and not be hurt.

I knew that. Yet I asked.

After the bull riding that was over so quickly, but before the barrel racing, came the games made just for Angola, known by the prison as "convict poker" and "convict pinball." In poker four inmates sit at a red plastic table in the middle of the arena, as though at a card game, their elbows on the table. Two rodeo clowns stand nearby, in blue jeans and bright, oversized shirts, their faces smeared comically in grease paint. Rodeo clowning dates back to the 1920s, when competitive rodeos started using more aggressive Brahman bulls and needed a way to distract bulls from charging thrown riders. The job of the clown is to draw the attention of the bull away from the competitor. The clown gets himself charged instead and then scrambles to hide in a barrel just when the bull charges. "Fearlessly funny," the clowns call themselves. A noble profession.

But this isn't an ordinary rodeo. And the games designed for the inmates are not about who can stay on a bull the longest, but who can stare down a bull the longest. So while the men sit four-square at the mock poker table, their legs tucked under the table, their elbows on it, and stare straight ahead, the clowns stand between the men and the bull and wave their arms and shout at the bull until the bull charges toward the table where the men are. Then the clowns dart to safety while the bull barrels at the table. Last inmate still sitting wins. For pinball five purple hula hoops are dragged onto the dirt and arranged flat. A man stands in the circle formed by each one. The clowns provoke the bull. Last man standing in his circle wins.

From the stands, I watched this inversion. The clowns incited the bull to charge. Men fell, and we watched. A man was dragged off, and we watched. The rodeo kept going.

And then the barrel racing. The clank. The hush. Finally, the ambulance.

In the stage cues my mind has assigned to that moment—the way the rest of the arena falls away into hushed dark as it couldn't have in life, the way the amplified clank ricochets—are clues to the irresolvability of what I keep failing to write about. The amplified clank is like an aural spotlight. Charles Baxter calls these moments "widowed images," the memory-images one has that seem to lose their authorship and their tie to the moment they were a part of. These images "[stick] in the memory as if glued there," he writes, but only because they have lost their original meaning, their original easy size in the narrative.[2] In the writer's mind, the image becomes something else. It swims free and lodges in the murky, grassy seafloor of the subconscious, taking on the detritus of unnameable meaning.

"My main problem, vis-à-vis journalism, is that I just don't have an instinct for what's important," the essayist Charles D'Ambrosio has written.[3] I don't know the woman's name, or what ended up happening to her, beyond the announcer's call toward the end of the rodeo, "She's going to be all right, folks." I don't know if the organizers pulled the barrel a bit farther from the pole for the next rodeo or how, if so, that affects whatever distance between the second and third barrels the professional circuit requires (105 feet—that, actually, I just looked up). I don't know who among the inmates was hurt that year or how many inmates are hurt each year—the prison won't say—and if they're ferried to the prison infirmary out of sight of the spectators (I hope they are) and what that recovery's like and whether the inmates, beyond Edrick, are bothered by the presence of the ambulance, knowing it's not for them, knowing that this symbol of courtesy and caring is, like so many other things, not for them anymore, as they serve out their time and, for most of them, their lives in a world removed from the world of the spectators. From the world I know.

Some of these facts I could dig up, but I haven't. What I want to know isn't found in those facts. It can't be. It's found in the sound of the woman's skull against the pole, the tracks the ambulance's tires left across the arena dirt, the expressions on the faces of the inmates who watched the ambulance come, watched it pick up the woman, watched the ambulance drive her off, and listened to the updates the announcer made periodically over the loudspeakers, letting us know her condition at intervals. What I want to know—no, to imagine, it's impossible to fully know with living it—is what it feels like to listen to those updates, knowing that they wouldn't be made for you, that you have left the world of all that behind and been made to live in this other world, separated, where others have come to look at you. And I want to know how we can change what a rodeo clown does and make him into a way to get the bull to charge at a man.

I had asked Edrick whether the men were ever hurt not because I didn't know the answer. But because I couldn't ask, couldn't even form, all the other questions. The questions that had no answers.

The unknowable things. The things that exist in the story, yes, but become widowed when they meet the viewer, when they become the images that will tug loose in the viewer's mind and grab hold of what is beyond comprehension. Something beyond simply articulable fact, yet something that cannot be fulfilled with only imagination. It is where the two meet, fact and imagination, and how memory joins in a triad, the glue of this fractured narrative. The spillover, the sticky irresolvability, the falling short of comprehension. The problem.

As I write this essay, we've entered the year of the fiftieth anniversary of the Angola rodeo. It will be held six times in 2015, two Sundays in April and every Sunday in October, and I know I'll go this year, as I haven't since I watched the woman fall. I'll drive from New Orleans as the sun rises, and then along the long narrow road that looks like it will dead-end nowhere but actually dead-ends at the prison gates, and then those gates will open before me and through the windshield of my car will spread the fields of Angola, where some men live out their lives and where some of us come only to visit for a day. How do you capture an inequality so plain it leaves you breathless with its starkness?

When the woman fell, she fractured something open for me, the complicated complicity of what I was seeing. I know I'm not done with the image of her falling, nor the echo right behind it of what this scene really means, of why I'm drawn to keep trying to write about it: the ambulance. The distinctions we draw about whom to care about and how, whom we gasp at the hurt of, whom we see and recognize. The stark cold irresolvability of that inequity, repeated over and over again in society. It's the strange ways we reorder the world that I'm drawn to, the corrections we add in like the sound engineer rejiggers life, and the way the vestiges remain in our subconscious to remind us of what we'd like to paper over.

This year, Warden Cain has said, there will be no pinball game, no men standing in their hula hoops and staring down the barreling bull while the rest of us watch. There will still be poker, but for it, the inmates will be given helmets and protective vests.

In their way, the helmets and the vests are the proof—added later—of what we all saw back then, the year the woman fell. What we watched. They're proofs of movement. Proofs of the harm.

NOTES

1. Peregrine Andrews, *The Sound of Sport*, 99% Invisible podcast audio, August 11, 2014, episode 127.

2. Charles Baxter, "On Defamiliarization," in *Burning Down the House: Essays on Fiction* (Saint Paul: Graywolf, 1997), 31.

3. Charles D'Ambrosio, "Loitering," in *Loitering: New and Collected Essays* (Portland: Tin House Books, 2014), 44.

We Regret to Inform You

April 12, 1970
Dear Young Artist,

Thank you for your attempt to draw a tree. We appreciate your efforts, especially the way you sat patiently on the sidewalk, gazing at that tree for an hour before setting pen to paper, the many quick strokes of charcoal executed with enthusiasm. But your drawing looks nothing like a tree. In fact, the smudges look like nothing at all, and your own pleasure and pride in said drawing are not enough to redeem it. We are pleased to offer you remedial training in the arts, but we cannot accept your "drawing" for display.

With regret and best wishes,

Art Class
Andasol Avenue Elementary School

February 12, 1974
Dear Ninth-Grade Girl,

We regret to inform you that no suitable match has been found to accompany you to the school dance. The volume of requests we receive makes individual feedback impossible, but please do feel free to attend on your own, perhaps with another rejectee, and stand awkwardly in a corner with a glass of warm punch in your sweaty hands. Watching others dance and have a good time is excellent preparation for the roles you will play in the future.

Best,

Boys Council of Patrick Henry Junior High

October 13, 1975
Dear Tenth Grader,

Thank you for your application to be a girlfriend to one of the star players on the championship basketball team. As you can imagine, we have received hundreds of similar requests and so cannot possibly respond personally to everyone. We regret to inform you that you have not been chosen for one of the coveted positions, but we do invite you to continue hanging around the lockers, acting as if you belong there. This selfless act serves the team members as they practice the art of ignoring lovesick girls.

Sincerely,

Granada Hills Highlanders

PS: Though your brother is one of the star players, we could not take this familial relationship into account. Sorry to say no! Please do try out for one of the rebound girlfriend positions in the future.

November 15, 1975

Dear Prospective Dancer,

Thank you for trying out to be a Highland Dancer. We regret to inform you that you did not make the cut into the second round of auditions. Though we know you looked forward to wearing the cute kilt and argyle kneesocks, the crisp white dress shirt and the tasseled shoes, we cannot recommend you for future dancing endeavors. Some girls are simply not coordinated enough to be a member of this elite troupe. It's not your fault; you just haven't quite "grown into" your body yet. We wish you the best of luck in finding your niche elsewhere.

Highland Dance Team, Granada Hills High School

January 15, 1977

Dear Future Thespian,

Thank you for your interest in being a drama major at Cal State, Northridge. While we are not the most elite acting school in the southland, we do take pride in a rigorous curriculum that requires all students to be fluent in diction, singing, movement arts, and a certain indefinable "something," a je ne sais quoi, which gives a young woman presence on the stage.

Unfortunately, we regret to inform you that you do not have what it takes to be a star, but will always be relegated to the "second girl" or the "waitress," with one or two lines belted out with imperfect timing. We understand that in high school you got to play Emily in *Our Town*, watching the townsfolk you loved from your perch in the afterlife, and once you had a leading role in *The Effect of Gamma Rays on Man-in-the-Moon Marigolds*, but your costume, a pink pinafore, was distracting and you delivered your lines too earnestly, eager to please.

We understand that you love turning into someone else for the space of an hour or so and that you feel exhilarated once you hit your mark. But your lisping voice and your rather spastic dance moves force us to ask you to turn your attentions elsewhere.

You might have more luck in background roles, perhaps writing? It's come to our attention that you once wrote a one-act play called *Backstage*, which consisted of two stagehands waiting for the stage manager to arrive; the stage manager never arrives, and even the play itself is an illusion! Cute.

With best wishes,

Drama Department, Cal State, Northridge

December 10, 1978

Dear College Dropout,

Thank you for the short time you spent with us. We understand that you have decided to terminate your stay, a decision that seems completely reasonable given the circumstances. After all, who knew that the semester you decided to come to UC Berkeley would be so tumultuous: that unsavory business with Jim Jones and his Bay Area followers, the mass suicide, an event that left us all reeling. After all, who among us has not mistakenly followed the wrong person, come close to swallowing poison?

And then Harvey Milk was shot. A blast reverberating across the bay. It truly did feel like the world was falling apart, we know that. We understand how you took refuge in the music of the Grateful Dead, dancing until you felt yourself leave your body behind, caught up in their brand of enlightenment. But you understand that's only an illusion, right?

And given that you were a drama major, struggling on a campus well known for histrionics and unrest: well, it's only understandable that you'd need some time to "find yourself." You're really too young to be in such a city on your own. When you had your exit interview with the dean of students, you were completely inarticulate about your reasons for leaving, perhaps because you really have no idea. You know there is a boy you might love, living in Santa Cruz. You fed him peanuts at a Dead Show. You imagine playing house with him, growing up there in the shadows of large trees.

But of course you couldn't say that to the dean, as he swiveled in his chair, so official in his gray suit. He clasped his hands on the oak desk and waited for you to explain yourself. His office looked out on the quad where you'd heard the Talking Heads playing just a week earlier. And just beyond that, the dorm where the gentleman you know as "pink cloud" provided you with LSD to experience more fully the secrets the Dead whispered in your ear. You told the dean none of this, simply shrugged your shoulders and began to cry. At which point the dean cleared his throat and wished you luck.

We regret to inform you that it will take quite a while before you grow up, and it will take some cataclysmic events of your own before you really begin to find the role that suits you. In any case, we wish you the best in all your future educational endeavors.

Sincerely,

UC Berkeley Registrar

October 26, 1979

Dear Potential Mom,

Thank you for providing a host home for us for the few weeks we stayed in residence. It was lovely but, in the end, didn't quite work for us. While we tried to be unobtrusive in our exit, the narrowness of your fallopian tubes required some damage. Sorry about that. You were too young to have children anyway, you know that, right? And you know it wasn't your fault, not really (though you could have been a *tad* more careful in your carnal acts, but no matter, water under the bridge . . .) Still, we enjoyed our brief stay in your body and wish you the best of luck in conceiving children in the future.

With gratitude,

Ira and Isabelle

November 3, 1979

Dear Patient,

We regret to inform you that due to reproductive abnormalities, you will not be able to conceive children. "Sterile" is not a word we use these days, but you may use it if you so choose. Your two miscarriages were merely symptoms of these abnormalities, which we surmise were acquired in utero. It's not your fault, but you may choose to take this misfortune as a sign of G-d's displeasure and torture yourself with guilt and self-loathing for many years to come.

All best,

Student Health Center, Humboldt State University

June 2, 1982

Dear White Girlfriend *Little Raven*,

Thank you for your three-year audition to serve as the white girlfriend/savior/martyr to a Native American alcoholic man twelve years your senior. Your persistence has been admirable, but we regret to inform you that we can no longer use your services.

Yes, we appreciate the fact that you smoked tobacco in a cherrywood pipe and that you wore a turquoise eagle around your neck. You listened to drums and chanting for hours on end—*hey ya, hey ya, hey ya*—and read *Black Elk Speaks* and got yourself an "Indian name": these efforts have all been noted. But the role of "white pseudo–Native American girl" is not one we can recommend for you.

We appreciate the many times you took this man to the hospital or bailed him out of jail. You let him borrow your car, your truck, your money, your life. But we're sure that if you take a good hard look at your performance, you were using this man as a punishment for past sins. This kind of symbiosis is never good for anyone, so we bid you farewell and wish you the best of luck as you find spiritual salvation elsewhere.

Sincerely,
Yurok Elders

May 23, 1986
Dear Temporary Gatekeeper,

Thank you for your four years of service with Orr Hot Springs Resort, and in particular your role as the live-in girlfriend to one of our more depressed shareholders. We also appreciate your services as a godmother to our resident toddler and as a confidante to his parents (a relationship which did, ahem, *transgress* some boundaries, but you shaped up when this was pointed out).

So it is with great sadness that we inform you your services are no longer required. This dismissal in no way reflects on your job performance (well, you could have cleaned the lodge a little better and been a little more thorough when it was your turn to scrub the bathhouse—but no matter, it's all water under the bridge now, as they say). It's simply time for you to move on.

Please pack your two boxes of belongings into the car you bought for $200. Please do not dramatically extend the farewells—wandering the property "saying good-bye" to inanimate objects, to the gardens, to tub room #2, where you spent so many morning hours immersed in yourself. Please do not throw the I-Ching to determine your next steps, or read the Tarot, or take Ecstasy. Simply get in your car and chug up the mountain road at first light. You will feel a sensation of tearing—like ligament torn from a bone—but don't worry, this is normal. You will head north. You will be fine. You'll find the role that suits you.

Namasté,
Orr Hot Springs Resort, Ukiah, California

April 14, 1994
Dear Potential Wife,

Thank you for your application to get married. While I saw much to admire here, I regret to inform you that you do not meet my needs at this time.

I do want to commend you for your efforts over the past five years. You did your best, but your anxiety made it difficult to proceed on a clear path. Even so, we did love our coffee in the morning, the meals in the evening, the travels through the Middle East (let's just forget the argument we had while walking the walls in the Old City of Jerusalem. Water under the bridge . . .). You laughed at my jokes, thanks for that. And of course, being fledgling writers together, in the salad days of artistic expression, before the marketplace intervened.

Try to remember that we loved the way we could: not perfectly, not entirely well, but genuinely—one injury against another's. I loved your lisp. And the little mole above your lip. I touched your scars, and you touched mine. We tried. But at some point, a relationship shouldn't have to try so hard, right?

It may just be a timing thing. Best wishes in your future matrimonial endeavors; I'm sure your talents will be put to good use elsewhere. I hope we remain friends.

Your Grad School Boyfriend

June 30, 1999
Dear Applicant,

Thank you for your query about assuming the role of stepmother to two young girls. While we found much to admire in your résumé, we regret to inform you that we have decided not to fund the position this year. You did ask for feedback on your application, so we have the following to suggest:

1. You do not yet understand the delicate emotional dynamic that rules a divorced father's relationship with his children. The children will always, *always*, come first, trumping any needs you, yourself, may have at the time. You will understand this in a few years, but for now you still require some apprenticeship training.

2. Though you have sacrificed time and energy to support this family, it's become clear that your desire to stepmother stems from some deep-seated wound in yourself, a wound you are trying to heal by using these children. Children are intuitive, though they may not understand what they intuit. They have enough to deal with—an absent mother, a frazzled father—they don't need your traumas entering the mix.

3. Seeing the movie *Stepmom* is not an actual tutorial on step-parenting.

4. On Mother's Day, you should not expect flowers, gifts, or a thank you. You are not their mother.

5. You are still a little delusional about the true potential here for a long-term relationship. The father is not yet ready to commit so soon after the rather messy divorce. (This should have been obvious to you when he refused to hold your hand, citing that it made him "claustrophobic." Can you not take a hint?)

As we said, funding is the main criteria that led to our rejection of your offer. We hope this feedback is helpful, and we wish you the best in your future parenting endeavors.

XXX OOO

January 3, 2007

Dear New Dog Owner,

Congratulations on adopting your first dog! She will surely provide hours of love and enjoyment and be a great addition to your family.

Here are a few tips:

1. A dog is not a child, though do feel free to call yourself "Mom." Other people will now know you as "Abbe's mom," and you'll take a great deal of foolish pride every time you hear this moniker. But remember, a dog is not a child.
2. Though a dog is not a child, you will now need to plan your life around this creature: food, water, companionship, playdates, illness. And yes, there will be illness. You will need to make crucial decisions, while in tears at the vet's office. You will need to, perhaps, empty your savings to ensure your dog is no longer in pain.
3. You will, at some point, say to yourself, *I don't need to date; I have my dog.* Be very, very careful about repeating this statement in public.
4. You will grow very fond of this dog. You will overlook her shortcomings, her flaws (as they are, really, so few). Why can't you do this with a man?
5. A pet's love, contrary to popular belief, is not necessarily unconditional. There are many conditions: expensive food, regular walks, toys, and your undivided attention.
6. A dog such as Abbe makes a great, all-natural antidepressant! At some level, of course, you already know this; otherwise, why would you have spent so much time on Petfinder.com (other than that it was less stressful than Match.com)? When her little face appeared—all cowlicks and worry—you felt something in your body, something repaired, like a ligament reattached to the bone.
7. At times you'll feel rejected by your dog. Don't worry, this is normal. Since you have now invested all your emotional energy into this dog, your worry reflex might kick in if the dog appears uninterested in "snuggling." Though she is a very friendly dog, Abbe needs her space sometimes (as do we all!).
8. You will train to be a therapy dog team, though Abbe's better at it than you are. You like sharing your dog with those who need her. You like sitting by her side as she gets petted by a variety of hands, young and old. You'll

understand how this therapy is as much for you as it is for them. You'll stay quiet and simply observe, taking the background role, finding in this something to write home about.

Once again, congratulations on taking on this huge responsibility. It's an indication of maturity—growing up, finding your niche, and settling into life as it is.

Best wishes,

Furbaby Pet Rescue of Whatcom County

Here

In 1973 a volcano covered half of Heimaey with lava and ash.

No one died.

The lava moved so slowly that the people were ferried to Iceland's mainland before it threatened the harbor.

And when everything was over, most of them went back, rebuilding their homes in a valley between the mountains and the rock that buried the neighborhood they'd lived in before.

Back at college in Chicago, years before I took a boat from Reykjavik to Heimaey, my friends and I often snuck into classrooms in the middle of the night to watch movies on the projectors.

That was the first time I saw Chris Marker's travel documentary <u>Sans Soleil</u>, which begins on the same island.

"The first image he told me about was of three children on a road in Iceland in 1965."

"He said that for him it was the image of happiness."

"He wrote me, 'One day I'll have to put it all alone at the beginning of a film, with a long piece of black leader. If they don't see happiness in the picture, at least they'll see the black.'"

"So, it sufficed to wait, and the planet itself staged the working of time."

"I saw what had been my window again. I saw emerge familiar roofs and balconies, the landmarks of the walks I took through town every day, down to the cliff where I had met the children."

It was the "had been my window" that made me wonder.

"Had been" and the way he wandered, or the way I do, or how I looked across the island forty years later and thought:

Imagine wanting only this.

You and me, right here, watching the sheep grow ready to shear.

The summer light spreading low across the ocean at nine, eleven, midnight, dawn, then rising a few inches higher through the kitchen window to begin the day.

To see the lava coming, to lead your family to the boat, to watch the blackened sky of home across the water for years, until the volcano quieted and the ground had cooled enough, and say

"Children, we can finally go home."

THIHACOIAAGT

A mealworm farm is quiet as the fall of grain onto grain, like hair. Even mealtime potato noshing is hushed as a drinking peace lily. They undulate in their oat-bin barn like wind through alfalfa, curl in the corners like miniature golden pepperoni. I purchased my first clew of mealys to answer the increasing need for eco-efficient protein and to continue my family's seven-generation farming heritage. Cove Creek Farm has seen apple orchards rise and fall, clover fields churned to butter, turkey eggs laid and gathered. While I sleep, my great-great-great-great-great grandparents whisper in my ear ways to keep the farm going.

Initially, I offered my mini-livestock to a friend who raises chickens. The hens expressed their preference for this instinctual favorite protein by rushing in ecstatic stampede to pluck the ground clean. Their sunnier yolks made apparent the mineral boost mealworms provide of magnesium, zinc, iron, copper, and manganese, but their high proportion of omega-3 and omega-6 fatty acids inspired me to add them directly, sautéed, to my plate.

One of the ten marvels created on the twilight of the earth's first Sabbath, the shamir, a small barley-size worm, was used by Moses to engrave the twelve tribes of Israel on the High Priest's breastplate. Later, Solomon employed this supernatural creature to construct the First Temple by outlining every quarry stone needed and placing the worm on these lines. As the shamir crawled along, the stones split asunder without noise, "so that there was neither hammer nor ax nor any tool of iron heard in the house while it was building" (I Kings 6: 7).[1]

Though not Jewish, I appreciate the dream geneticist Paul Goldstein describes "of all Jews to assist in building the Third (and final) Temple" on a metaphorical level because, like the First Temple built by King Solomon at Jerusalem, it makes Earth a fit dwelling place for God.[2] The very name has been bloodied like the land under the Temple Mount, but the aspiration—to honor "The Highest Ideal Humans Are Capable of Imagining at Any Given Time"— remains worthwhile. Plus its acronym, THIHACOIAAGT, is as unpronounceable as the Old Testament YHWH.

"The Spirit That Moves through All Things," as one friend translates the Cherokee word *Unahlahnauhi*, might be a better term; or *prana*, as yogis refer to life force; or the Chinese *qi*, for the flow of energy that animates matter. All delineate more clearly an eternal constant than my THIHACOIAAGT, which evolves or devolves in relation to human consciousness. The limitation of this misnomer, though, has its advantage, since the transformation of human behavior can attest to evolutionary development subtler than skeletal structure or cranial mass.

In this era the highest ideal might be consideration for others—given that the planet supports billions of species and over seven billion humans—or gratitude for the many symbiotic relationships that make this planet habitable. Consider the 1018 (ten quintillion) insects that outnumber all other animals on this planet combined. Often unseen, they contribute to soil fertility, crop production, plant pollination, waste decomposition, pest control, and biodiversity. One could say in their multitudes insects comprise a scaffolding from the lower to higher realms, a pillar that supports earthly life, an invisible axis around which thirty-some phyla spiral in a millimeter-by-kilometer rise.

The original axis mundi in ancient cosmogonies was a tree, and various cultures and religions reflect that influence. In Scandinavian culture the universe flowered from the boughs of the Yggdrasil Ash, known as the Tree of Existence. The Bodhi tree Buddha meditated beneath illumined reality so purely he too came to mirror it. Hindus drink tea suffused with the divinity of Vishnu and his wife, Lakshmi, inherent in the leaves of the holy basil. The Cheremiss tribe that once existed in Russia protected at all costs their sacred groves from damage or interference. "A clump of trees made a great impression," John Stewart Collis reminds us. "Sometimes they were supposed to be the abode of gods, and sometimes they were regarded simply as natural temples in which gods might be approached."[3]

In *The Triumph of the Tree*, Collis muses that modern movement away from organized religion might indicate growing direct intimation of the divine. We may be ready to repair our state of being torn from a distant creator, nature, and one another, he says, through realization of "at-one-ment."[4] This underlying sense of unity could take precedence over varying theistic and nontheistic ideologies, he suggests. Beneath dogmas and dermis, blood and bone, nearer even than thought, we stem from the same substance. "We sprang from the oak," Czeslaw Milosz writes. We too send roots into "the dark womb of the earth."[5]

When I was growing up, our backyard hickory was tall enough that when the occasional nut dropped on our roof, it sounded with a sharp popgun blast. I imagined scenes unfolding in its wide-armed branches—a waifish grandmother braiding her granddaughter's hair, a straw-hatted farmer slicing cherry tomatoes—dreamscapes, since an adjacent ham hock would be wolfing mud pies, a tennis racket batting a giraffe's spine. The branches swayed and shuddered, contrasting each leaf with shadow's edge. When I lay daydreaming on my bed, "trees made conceptual thought possible," as Collis asserts.[6]

Thinking of that green imaginative stimulus, I can picture early humans leaping from their grasp of surrounding baobabs to comprehend the unseen support system bolstering such structures. But water's movement, bird's-eye views, and leafcutter ants' collaborative societies too have contributed to our brain's development. The key to appreciate is that we depend on the natural world directly and indirectly. How could we forget, when the arterial outspread feeding our gray matter resembles a *mopane* tree, named for the Shona word for butterfly?

"Until people start feeling a connection between their own body and mind and the rest of 'nature,'" David Hinton says, "until they come to understand this as a continuum—they're not going to care" about protecting nature or humanity as a whole.[7] A translator of ancient Chinese verse, Hinton has spent his life studying the deep ecology of poets in the rivers-and-mountains tradition. His work has led him to the same insights he finds in the poetry—that our thought-generated sense of separation is illusory.

The hickory was already mature when I began studying it, but history was writ large in its anatomy. I flashed my first poetic license noticing a fork spread from its base, like parents, from which emerged two limbs strong enough to support a swing apiece for my brother and me. Its canopy stretched as wide as the family history my Aunt Alpha was tracing. An early illustration of time's processes, decaying limbs had to be trimmed to protect our house, but green shoots flowered in their place. Under the crown, branches thickened and parted, but at the base a burl merged what never had been separate.

I live in one of the eight states whose percentage for food insecurity, ranging from 16 to 21 percent, is higher than the national 14 percent and global 12 percent averages.[8] How—I ask myself and neighbors—have we so poorly managed our needs? "It could only have happened," Wendell Berry says, "through our failure to care enough for the world to be humble enough before it, to think competently enough of its welfare."[9] The potential not only for a nation but also for this planet to provide enough for everyone without exhausting natural resources is achievable with conscientious cultivation. Is such an ideal not worth our highest regard? The word "worth" shares a root, *weorð*, with "worship," that intimidating noun that would exact excellence.

Solomon strove to build a permanent dwelling for God to reside among humankind, but in our century we have seen the conflict that arises when such an ideal is confined to a particular land or sect. Fixtures fall. Ownership is disputed. Our species might better attain its greatest heights the way forests do, by drawing on a more integrative foundation. One cannot point at, only toward, such undergirding. The temple lasts longest made not of marble or bone but of the most estimable action possible at any given moment.

Our national debt doesn't account for dung beetles, mayflies, honeybees, and thousands of other species that carry our food's chains. In exchange for their mutually beneficial services, we invent stronger pesticides, level forests, pollute waterways, and otherwise attempt to dominate our interdependent environment. But guilt will only daunt our power to act. Nor will we undertake responsibility we cannot manage, and nothing could bolster this charge but the kind of infrastructure that flexes in strong wind, draws on a fundamental substratum, and parses nothing unless it passes through the heartwood.

The past's failure to create a favorable present or to sustain a viable future prompted Berry to declare the need for a "new speech—a speech that will cause the world to live and thrive in men's minds."[10] It takes poetry as its inspiration, since metaphors connect humans to the world around them. Such dialogue would also reaffirm our participation in the ongoing process of creation, through which we might meet or remember spontaneous adoration and from that effusion of feeling make the kind of voluntary emendations that fulfill human promise.

Only a poet could conceive such possibility—perhaps a mad farmer, and the two billion entomophagists already eating insects worldwide.[11]

Subtitled *The Last Great Hope to Save the Planet*, Daniella Martin's *Edible* makes a case for entomophagy, or the human consumption of insects, to complement the livestock industries working to feed our densely populated planet. Though many contemporary westerners and Europeans startle at the suggestion, Martin appreciates the squeamishness that accompanies those knee-jerk reactions. Overcoming fear can maximize culinary adventure. In an age when familiar packaged and packaged-to-seem-new foods predominate, supplementing our daily rotations with edible insects might rouse the palate and awaken the tongue.

I have eaten mealworms baked on pizza, folded in tacos, mixed in cornbread, browned in oatmeal cookies, dropped in egg-drop soup, rolled into spaghetti meatballs, and stirred sautéed into tuna salad, which added crunch akin to when I layered my third-grade sandwiches with potato chips. As efficient as they are versatile, mealworms convert grain to protein at the rate of one gram per gram, minimizing agricultural land and water use.[12]

To silence the many arguments against lofty dreams with actionable means, one must rise high as a bird in flight. In European folklore several birds are granted the power to sever obstacles from some path. Such "opener" birds include the raven, the eagle, the bee-eater, the woodpecker, and the ostrich, among others, but by far the most important is the hoopoe, who holds the famous shamir.[13]

"*If we go down into ourselves, we find that we possess exactly what we desire*," Ewa Chrusciel writes (quoting Simone Weil) in her book of poems, *Contraband of Hoopoe*.[14] We carry our progeny on our cuffs, circulate inherited breath, and wear ancestral hopes in sheets of finest dust, shed cells skittering toward the earth when we drag our feet.

While it may seem contradictory to gratitude to cultivate another creature for protein, conscientious animal husbandry has deepened my admiration for other species and my awareness of reliance on them. My generation, though, has tipped the balance for raising enough traditional livestock in comfortable and growth-patient conditions.

This January I helped my father pull a larger-than-average calf from its first-time mother. After laboring for hours while Dad looked on with binoculars, the cow was exhausted before the head breached. "Once the nostrils make their appearance," he told me, "the calf has separated from the birth canal and relies on the oxygen it can get on its own." When the tired mother retracted the head into her womb, we drove toward them in the vehicle he uses to feed. The familiar engine didn't startle her, but cows separate themselves from the herd to give birth and Number 14 didn't want to be disturbed. Still, we were able to steer her toward a head gate to do what we could.

Dad slipped a finger-width chain around what would be the wrist joint on the calf's hoof to give us purchase to pull. Over the years he has experimented with other devices, but this technique for hand pulling has proven gentlest on the cow's hips. Like many jobs on the farm, it also requires strength. My boots threatened to slip on the manure-slick barn floor, but I dug in my heels and relied on friction from my gloves. "We'll need to protect the calf from falling on the concrete," Dad said, better assuming its odds for survival than I.

Before this calf, I had helped pull two, neither of which lived. Seeing the calf's tongue lolling from its mouth, I thought we were trying to save the young mother's life. Then the calf emerged, ribs expanding with ours while we rushed to prevent its spill.

In our exuberance, we named the calf Lucky. Lucky was lucky she made her appearance on a weekend. Dad has a full-time job to compensate for the vicissitudes of small-time farming. My grandfather could wait for late winter dawns, but Dad feeds before the sun comes up, and by the time he gets home from work, the fields are dark. Sun and stars both though shined on Lucky. Born a heifer on a small farm, assuming good health, she will live the full duration of her natural life, birthing calves in natural reproductive cycles, eating hay and grass from spacious pasture without ever seeing a feedlot, and dying of old age.

Michael Pollan, in *The Botany of Desire*, explains the compulsion of apples, potatoes, tulips, and marijuana to cast their seeds over the widest land possible. He elaborates how their needs drive human appetite as much as humans domesticate them. Applying the same concept to biology equally bends the mind. Like the kingdom *Plantae*, the kingdom *Animalia* strives to propagate foremost and diversely. Outside my parents' kitchen window, Lucky kicks up her hooves and dashes across the hillside, every cell bursting with Black Angus genetics.

Meanwhile, somewhere under a flour drift, the world's crispiest mealworm is strategizing ways to carry on.

After centuries of use and adoption by cultures around the world, a recent increase in insect diets by westerners and Europeans are prompting more research into mini-livestock's nutritional and ecological advantages. Scientists are learning which species provide the most health benefits, rear easily, best augment existing livestock industries as feed, and can thrive on food-industry byproducts like apple juice pulp, melon rinds, and carrot skins.

A Polish university study found the most nutritious way to serve meal-worms appears to be milling them into flour. As flour, mealworms yield twice the protein, fat, and mineral content as fresh. The high-quality meal this team studied was created by boiling larvae, as one might shrimp, for three minutes, then drying them at sixty degrees Celsius.[15] This form of processing has the added advantage of convenience. Enriching bread or protein bars with meal-worm flour takes less time than it takes to unwrap a package of ground beef.

Some have suggested, like beef and pork, mealworms need a name that distinguishes them as foodstuffs rather than creatures. Author Joanne Greenberg suggests the term "shamir," after the thought-to-be-vanished, heaven-sent creature.

Shamir tacos might stimulate more appetites on restaurant menus. Shamir burgers could pick up where ostrich burgers left off—their lean meat equally free of saturated fat but easier to tend. I particularly want to see shamir flour listed as an ingredient, because the English translation of mealworms' Latin name, *Tenebrio molitor*, stems from the root verb *molitus*, meaning to build or construct, to labor at, and to set in motion, with the suffix suggesting one who builds, constructs, mills.[16]

My uncle H.A. inherited Reed Creek Milling Company from his father after years hefting infant-size sacks of corn meal to stock local groceries. Until I visited when I was nine, I pictured a wooden wheel, as in our painting of Mabry Mill, churning the creek into frothy purls of mist. In reality, a sheath hides the wheel's action while grist stacks like snow clouds spilling powdery flakes. The heady smell of sweet grain fills the air, which one can just distinguish from grass cud, the sough of milled wheat from snuffling cattle.

It is not impossible to imagine a peanut-size creature carving its way onto the production line. Nor does it seem a reach to call such a solution miraculous, considering it could well-provision homes for the next highest human cause, befitting Solomon's goal, without the instruments of war.

NOTES

1. John Gotthold Kunstmann, *The Hoopoe: A Study in European Folklore*, repr. 1938 diss. (Charleston, S.C.: Nabu Press, 2014), 27

2. Paul Goldstein, "Modern Physics and the Shamir," *Kabbalah Online*, October 18, 2014, www .chabad.org/kabbalah/article_cdo/aid/380303/jewish/Modern-Physics-and-the-Shamir.htm.

3. John Stewart Collis, *The Triumph of the Tree* (New York: Sloane Press Archive, 1954), 73.

4. Collis, qtd. in Wendell Berry, "A Secular Pilgrimage," in *A Continuous Harmony: Essays Cultural and Agricultural* (New York: Harcourt Brace, 1970).

5. Czeslaw Milosz, "Into the Tree," *New and Collected Poems* (New York: Ecco, 2001), 416–17.

6. Collis, *Triumph of the Tree*, ix.

7. Leath Tonino, "The Egret Lifting from the River: David Hinton on the Wisdom of Ancient Chinese Poets," *Sun*, no. 469 (January 2015), 11.

8. U.S. Department of Agriculture Economic Research Service. "Household Food Security in the United States," 2013, www.ers.usda.gov/publications/err-economic-research-report/err173 .aspx.

9. Berry, *Continuous Harmony*, 7.

10. Ibid., 12.

11. Arnold van Huis, Joost Van Itterbeeck, Harmke Klunder, Esther Mertens, Afton Halloran, Giulia Muir, and Paul Vantomme, *Edible Insects: Future Prospects for Food and Feed Security* (Rome: Food and Agricultural Organization of the United Nations, March 18–22, 2013).

12. Marcel Dicke, "Why Not Eat Insects?," TedTalk, December 2010, www.ted.com/talks /marcel_dicke_why_not_eat_insects/transcript?language=en.

13. Kunstmann, *Hoopoe*.

14. Simone Weil, qtd. in Ewa Chrusciel, *Contraband of Hoopoe* (Richmond: Omnidawn, 2014), 27.

15. Ewa Siemianowska, Agnieszka Kosewska, Marek Aljewicz, Krystyna A. Skibniewska, Lucyna Polak-Juszczak, Adrian Jarocki, and Marta Jędras, "Larvae of Mealworm (*Tenebrio molitor* L.) as European Novel Food," *Agricultural Sciences* 4, no. 6 (2013): 287–91.

16. William Freund and Joseph Esmond Riddle, *A Copious and Critical Latin-English Dictionary* (Sheldon, 1866) 594.

The Girl, the Cop, and I

For nearly eighteen years, only three people knew that I'd been raped several months after I left police work in 1985. That number increased dramatically in 2003, when I told friends I'd been invited to give a talk at Vanderbilt University.

"About writing?" they asked.

"No," I replied, my tone matter of fact. "About my rape."

What followed were double or triple takes, stunned looks, breath sucked in sharply, averted eyes, speechlessness. My best friend said, "Oh my God." My therapist of six years closed his eyes briefly and said softly, "I'm so sorry," and then, "Would you like to talk about it?"

Not really.

It took me some time to figure out why I agreed to talk about my rape, beyond the wine-induced bravery after a conversation with a friend whom I trust deeply and who was arranging events for Sexual Assault Awareness Month at Vanderbilt University. The path to that understanding appeared only when I became conscious of word choice, when I thought about my response as a writer. Dialogue *is* character: the way a character says something—or what a character doesn't say—reveals perspective and experience; it reveals what's going on beneath the surface. Word choice is crucial.

"About my rape," I'd told friends. Why didn't I say, "About the time I was raped"? Or, "About rape"? Why the use of the possessive pronoun: *my*?

The answer, when it came, was disarmingly simple: I was ready to claim that it happened. It happened to me. It belongs to me—not that I want it—but it is mine. My rape.

This was no small feat, that claiming. Because it meant that all of me—all the parts of who I am—must now come to mutual acceptance and forgiveness. And that is much more difficult. Whenever I think about my rape, three distinct voices erupt in an often-convoluted dialogue: the twenty-nine-year-old girl who was raped, the woman I am today, and the police officer I once was.

The woman I am today has claimed the rape. She tells the girl that it wasn't her fault, that she didn't deserve it; she did nothing wrong. I know this. I believe this. And the girl nods, skittery-eyed, shame clogging her throat, wanting to believe, explaining again that she was just being nice, giving a man a ride home.

It's the cop who gets in the way every time. The cop is adept at pointing out how stupid the girl was, how the girl should have known better. Because the cop can't handle that she was raped. Cops aren't raped. Certainly not that way. Not without a fight that leaves either her or her attacker bloody and broken or dead. Not acquaintance rape. And so the cop stands in judgment of the girl, and the woman knows this is utterly wrong, utterly ridiculous, utterly cruel, and the girl is caught in the middle, looking at both of them, trying to figure out who's right.

He had dark curly hair, a Boston accent, Italian features, and a crooked nose. His hands were thick and muscular. He stood maybe four inches taller and had a good sixty pounds on me. He was an ice hockey coach for a Massachusetts high school. He reminded me of the boys I'd attended under-graduate school with in upstate New York—the accent, the features, the ges-tures, the East Coast attitude—little details I missed living in Louisiana. He was funny and witty. He wore a well-broken-in brown leather jacket, and he smelled like snow.

I'd quit my job with the Baton Rouge Police Department earlier that spring to return to college. Leaving police work had been hard, hard enough to send me into therapy for the first time. I was unsettled being a civilian again; I missed the work terribly, although I'd left in part because I simply couldn't handle any longer the misery I dealt with day in and day out.

That late fall evening I'd joined six off-duty female police officers at a bar. We lit up the room with our energy. Get us out of our uniforms and we were babes; men circled us like flies. Buying us drinks. Flirting. We were good flirters. You can't be a decent cop without knowing how to talk, how to handle people. And we worked in a primarily male environment. Many of the men we worked with had served in Vietnam; many were military reservists. So we knew men, we knew how to handle men, and we knew how to talk to them. Tell a civilian male you're a cop—or an ex-cop—and watch the wary fascina-tion skitter across his face.

So this man whose name I can't remember, the fellow with the Boston accent, was buying me drinks. His friends had left, but he stayed—leaning into me, putting his arm around my shoulder. We talked about New England winters and the pleasures of homemade pasta; we laughed about the incongruity of ice hockey in Baton Rouge.

When the bar shut down, he asked for a ride back to his hotel because he didn't have enough money for a taxi. My friend and long-time partner on the police department, Marian, stood behind him, her raised eyebrow unmistakable, shaking her head no. His hotel was four or five minutes past my apartment, but I said, "Sure."

Oh. The woman I am now sees this with a mixture of sadness and compassion. The cocky cop thinking, "Sure, I can handle anything." The girl who was in therapy, working hard to learn how to trust again, thinking, "Oh don't be so suspicious."

Before we left, Marian pulled me aside and made me promise to call when I got home. "So I don't worry," she said.

In my car, he kissed me. It was nice, although a little insistent. I pushed him away and said in my best southern, now-this-is-the-way-it's-going-to-be voice, "All right, enough of that. I'm taking you to the hotel, and you're going in there alone, understand?"

Sure, sure, sure. He understood.

Two minutes on the road and I knew I should not be driving. I'd had way too much alcohol. The man beside me chattered and laughed, while I marshaled every ounce of concentration to drive.

"Listen," I interrupted. "You'll need to get a cab. I'll give you the money. I'm too drunk to be driving."

That was fine by him.

"Nothing's going to happen," I said. "We're just going to my apartment to call you a cab. Understand?"

He said he understood.

The first rape I ever worked—that's how cops refer to it; we work a homicide or work a traffic accident or work a rape—was when I was a plainclothes police officer in the Crime Prevention Division with the LSU Police Department. I was twenty-one years old. The victim—that's how cops refer to rape survivors—was nineteen and did not know her attacker. She was raped in a narrow alley behind the electrical engineering building on campus. She sat in an overly bright interview room, minuscule tremors wracking her body, makeup smeared, clothing torn and dirty, with the faint, sweet scent of alcohol on her breath. I kept a hand light on her shoulder as she related her story to a male officer and me, as we waited for the detective and the rape crisis counselor to arrive. "I was just taking a shortcut," she said, "and there he was."

I murmured soothing words, kept my eyes trained on her face. She would not meet my gaze.

When we left to resume patrol, the other officer shook his head. "What was she thinking of, walking through that alley?"

"She didn't do anything wrong," I said.

"But she should have known better," he said. "Walking late at night by herself."

And then we parted: he in his police unit and me on foot, by myself, into the dark.

Six months later, for one long, hot summer week, I posed as bait for a rapist.

A man in his midtwenties had sexually assaulted four co-eds over several weeks. He held a knife to their throats and raped them. The assaults all happened in the same location after dark: the Greek Theater, located on the edge of campus under massive live oak trees. During the day it was a lovely place to hang out on the shaded, concrete seats that fanned up from the stage; in the early evening the sunken stage below frequently hosted plays or musical performances. At night it was spooky. Lighting was poor if you stepped off the paved path. Still, students often came here after dark to drink or smoke pot. It was also a convenient cut-through from the main campus to the commuter student parking lot and what was referred to as the Ghetto—cheap, off-campus student housing.

My supervisors decided we needed a stakeout with bait and that our three-person Crime Prevention Division should handle this task. Ron, Nancy, and I looked at one another. We were all close in age, early to midtwenties. We were a good team and had been working this division since it was formed a year ago.

Ron said, "Well, clearly I can't be the bait."

Nancy, a stocky, no-nonsense woman, looked at me and said, "I think you can do sexy and helpless better than me."

I wasn't sure whether this was a compliment or not, but that was it. I was the bait.

From nine at night until two in the morning, I sat midway down on those concrete seats, wearing shorts and a tank top and tried to look sexy and helpless and clueless and oblivious and, well, rape-able. This is difficult to do for five hours at a stretch. Especially when the mosquitoes are biting, which they were with a vengeance. It was sticky-hot and it was dark and my butt hurt after forty-five minutes. I had a few books—though it was too dark to read—and water and snacks. I chewed gum; I filed my nails; I sang to myself; I skipped along the edges of the seats; I inspected my split ends; I studied the stars; I smoked endless cigarettes. I did this for five nights with Nancy below, hidden behind a stage wing with binoculars, and Ron behind me, parked in a car with binoculars. They also had guns and portable radios. I didn't have a portable radio for obvious reasons. We had decided that I wouldn't carry a gun because it was hard to look sexy and helpless carrying one.

Five nights, tensing every time someone walked by or came into the theater to hang out. Five nights listening to rustling in the underbrush, trying to see in the dark, trying to stay alert and look oblivious. Several times young men approached me, and my heart tangled up in my throat. But they just wanted a light or to bum a cigarette. An older woman told me it was dangerous here, and I should go home. Mostly, though, I sat out there alone.

Then, the rapist attacked a co-ed during daylight, near the Greek Theater. Several bystanders tackled him, and that was that. End of stakeout.

I never told anyone that I was terrified every second I was out there. Utterly, completely, bone-exposed-to-air terrified. I imagined all the things that might go wrong: Nancy and Ron falling asleep, not seeing the rapist attack me; being stabbed, my throat slit. I imagined the rapist had graduated to guns and would put a gun to my head, would shoot me. I hated being that exposed and vulnerable. I hated not having my gun. I hated being that terrified. But I did it. I did my job. I sat out there night after night.

I was offered the opportunity to serve as bait again several years later when I worked for the Baton Rouge City Police Department. The guys in Narcotics thought I might be good. I turned them down without hesitation.

The first rape that I worked as a city police officer was at a hotel off Acadian Thruway—the same hotel that a man from Boston who smelled like snow would check into five years later.

I was dispatched to a Signal 51, an assault, and I entered a bedroom in disarray. One woman met me at the door. The other sat on the bed, mascara streaked. Fresh bruises clotted her cheek and arms. A man had raped her, she told me. She'd invited him into the room for a drink—she'd met him at the bar—and he'd raped her. She'd called her friend, and her friend had called the police.

When Detectives Heinrich and Howell arrived, I followed Heinrich out into the hallway, while Howell interviewed the woman.

"Jesus, Drummond," Heinrich said. "They're prostitutes."

Only a second of dismay at my naïveté, and then "so?"

"So they're fucking prostitutes. She wasn't raped."

"How do *you* know?"

"She's. A. Prostitute."

I stared at him open-mouthed before I found my voice. "Heinrich, if you think prostitutes can't be raped, you're dumber than me."

He laughed. It was a familiar response from some of the men I worked with, some of the women too—the good ole boy chuckle at that softy liberal northeasterner Drummond.

I shook my head, said, "It's not right."

I heard a variation on that same tune over the next five years as I worked other rapes. Why the fifty-four-year-old woman who lived in a high-crime neighborhood should have known better than to take her garbage cans out to the curb at night. Why the fourteen-year-old girl should have known that wearing clothing that displayed her knees, her collarbone, and her belly button was an invitation to the wrong sort of boy. Why the nurse, home to her apartment after a double shift, shouldn't have left her window unlocked. The message was always the same: somehow the woman had done something wrong; she'd brought this on herself. Only, mercifully, were children and the elderly exempt from this condemnation. Most of the time. Or, sometimes, if the woman had fought back and had serious injuries to prove it. Or, sometimes, if she'd died. But even then, not all the dead or injured were exempt. The same head shaking, the same, "She shouldn't have _____."

Hear that enough and eventually some part of you comes to believe it.

The man who smelled like snow followed me up the interior stairs of my garage apartment. I was wobbly and thick-tongued and tired of brushing off his hands, tired of playing the good ole gal, smiling through tight lips and pushing him away each time he tried to embrace me. "Enough," I said. I got him settled on the couch with the telephone book and phone, while I used the bathroom and put my purse in my bedroom before I returned.

He was fast. He had me up against a wall before I registered what was happening. His hands dug into my armpit and shoulder; his knee dug high into my thigh, trying to push it aside, his lips pressed against my teeth. I tried to knee him. I grabbed skin and twisted; I turned my head from side to side; I squirmed and fought with elbows and hands and feet. I said no. But I was drunk, and he was stronger. I got the palm of my hand up under his chin and pushed, forcing the heel in deep. He hit me once, with the back of his hand, hard across my cheek, and dragged me onto the carpet. He yanked my underpants below my knees. I kept fighting him, kept saying no until he entered me, and then all I wanted was it to be over and him gone.

When he was done, he rolled to his side, gave me a half smile, and said, "Damn, you're a fighter."

I stood, went into my bedroom, opened my purse, and returned holding my gun at arm's length.

His face changed expressions fast. Even before I spoke, he was scrambling backward, eyes on the gun, hands pulling up his pants.

"Leave," I said. "Now. Out of my house."

I followed him down the stairs, gun pointed at his back. I pointed south and said, "Start walking. I see you anywhere near here in one minute, I'm calling every cop I know."

I closed the door, double-locked it. Walked slowly back upstairs and turned off the lights. Looked out the window. He was walking south, rapidly.

When the phone rang, I knew it was Marian. I let it ring to silence. How could I explain what had just happened? I didn't understand what had just happened. But if I didn't call her back, she'd show up on my doorstep within the hour. Or worse, she'd have an on-duty officer swing by. That's what I would do if the roles were reversed.

So I picked up the receiver and prepared to tell her I'd made it home just fine.

I used to say that I'd kill anyone who broke into my house and tried to harm me. I'd seen firsthand the variety of things one human being could do to another, and that was not going to happen to me, not without a fight. I was a light sleeper; I had a .38 Smith & Wesson tucked under the second pillow on my bed, and a shotgun under the bed. I'd been trained in defensive tactics, street survival skills, and kung fu. And I was certified as an expert marksman.

I also used to say—and I still believe this—that you can never know how you'll react or handle a specific situation until you're in that situation. You can train for it by honing certain skills, you can plan out what you'll do, but you won't know until it happens. This was the advice I gave people, usually women, who were thinking about purchasing a gun for protection and visiting the pistol range a couple of times a year to qualify for their permit, a foolhardy move if I ever saw one. Having a gun doesn't mean you can protect yourself. It can easily be used against you if you don't handle one day in and day out. And target practice at the range doesn't mean you can hit anything when terror ricochets inside your body.

"There are certain measures you can take to make yourself safer," I would tell these women. "A gun is not necessarily one. But you need to understand and accept that you can never be totally safe. Thinking you're totally safe will get you hurt."

I applied this philosophy to my work as a police officer: I trained and I trained hard and I trained repetitively for a variety of situations, but I was never naive enough to think that I knew exactly how I would handle a situation until I was in the midst of it. I knew that nothing I did would keep me totally safe—at work or at home. I hoped, I prayed, I trained. I was relieved when I walked out of each new situation with my life and—let's be honest here—my pride intact.

I broke down on the phone with Marian, and she made the twenty-minute drive from her house in ten minutes. She was pissed; she wanted to call every cop we knew; she was ready to drive to the man's hotel and arrest him.

"No," I said.

She begged. I refused.

I knew that every cop who was my friend would be outraged, viciously outraged, just like her. My friends would see this as an attack on a cop, even though I was no longer one. But I also knew what would happen after the outrage dissipated, after the man was arrested, after my friends stepped back and looked at me.

I laid out every mistake I'd made, starting with giving the man a ride. "Look at me, Marian. I don't have a mark on me. I let him into my house. I've been drinking."

With two cool fingers she touched my cheek, red and slightly swollen, pointed to my torn underpants on a chair.

I shook my head again. "Think," I said. "Think how they are going to see this, the crime scene detectives, the sex crimes detectives, the assistant DA, how it will play in court. You know what they'll say: a police officer can't defend herself? She must have been willing at some level. She must have wanted it."

The girl I was—and every woman, no matter her age, becomes a girl again when sexually assaulted—was left little room in this debate. She was bewildered and traumatized. The cop refused to hear her or even let her speak. The cop refused to let her feel much at all. The truth was that the cop was deeply ashamed—*mortified*—that she hadn't been able to defend herself; the cop was deeply ashamed that she had *let* this happen. She knew better. He wasn't a stranger breaking into her house; he didn't have a weapon; he hadn't beaten her bloody. He was a man she'd met in a bar, a man she'd flirted with all evening.

I knew deep in my gut that the right thing to do was have this man arrested and prosecuted. As a police officer, I believed this; I'd encouraged countless civilians to file charges, to trust the process of the law. But I kept seeing my case from the point of view of everyone else. The cop saw all the weaknesses in my case. The cop saw each mistake the girl had made.

And so I would not budge. "No," I told Marian. "And you must promise me that you'll never tell anyone about this, not a word."

A promise that, as far as I know, she has kept to this day.

I was grateful for Marian's support, for her outrage, for her love. I was also grateful there had been only one comment, just after she arrived—"Why in fuck's name did you bring him back to your house?" Only a few small questions, all understandable, all a process of collecting information: where my gun had been, what I'd said to him as I tried to fight him off, whether I had injured him.

But of course I absorbed it, integrated it—what she did and didn't say. It simply confirmed what I already knew: the man who smelled like snow may have raped me, but I was guilty too.

I don't recall any training or seminars about date rape when I was a police officer; I don't think the term even existed then. We called it the "he said/she said" rape and considered this the worst kind of rape to work because you never could pinpoint the guilty party.

But as I moved into academia, as I became educated about women's and students' issues, I became increasingly aware of the prevalence of acquaintance rape. And then students started telling me about their rapes, confiding on the page or in my office. With each whispered, halting story, my own rape rushed to the surface: vivid and alive, rage and terror and shame intertwined. The girl and the cop listened carefully to each student's story too—the girl with empathy, the cop itching to administer equal parts revenge and justice.

In 1999 I was appointed to a judicial appeal board when a young man challenged his expulsion from our university for raping a student. Three of us were charged with reviewing the case file, reinterviewing all the witnesses and parties concerned, and either upholding or dismissing the young man's expulsion. It was a delicate and exhausting task. It was also a complex case.

The young woman, "Jill," attended a large off-campus party with some friends. Jill wasn't a drinker. But that night, for whatever reason, Jill drank heavily. The young man, "Sam," also drinking heavily, briefly talked to Jill several times. When a group of students decided to go to Denny's, they piled into a car so small that the girls had to sit on the boys' laps. Jill sat on Sam's. All the witnesses testified that Jill repeatedly said she didn't feel well and that Jill and Sam sat beside each other at Denny's but didn't converse.

Everyone returned to campus around three in the morning. Jill went to her dorm. Jill's roommate, who was asleep with her boyfriend, remembers Jill coming in and going straight to bed.

Sam, according to his testimony, returned to his on-campus apartment, took off his jacket, and stretched out on the bed. But he kept thinking about Jill; he wanted to talk with her some more. He rose, put on his jacket, and made the ten-minute trek to Jill's dorm. Because the dorm was locked, he waited until a female student passed, then he banged on the glass. The student let him in. He wasn't sure where Jill lived, so he wandered the halls until he ran into another student; she told him Jill's room number.

Jill's roommate answered the door. Sam said he wanted to talk to Jill. The roommate pointed to Jill's bed and returned to her own bed.

At this point, there was conflicting testimony, but what is clear is that Sam took off his clothes and crawled into bed with Jill.

Jill awoke to Sam lying beside her, under the covers. He was naked and his hand was on her thigh, pulling up her nightgown. She was still quite drunk, and she was very confused about why Sam was in her bed. Terrified, she couldn't speak. She pushed his hand away. He put it back. This happened several times. Jill lay there rigid; she couldn't even move. It was, she said, as though she was out of her body. "I wasn't sure it was happening," she said. Even when he was inside her, she said nothing, did nothing.

Afterward, Sam fell asleep.

Jill remained awake until daylight, when Sam woke, dressed, and left. Several hours later, after talking with her roommate, Jill called the university police.

This is a quick summary of what we discovered through our interviews. We were stunned at and saddened by the series of poor judgments by so many. One of my colleagues said that he understood that Jill was drunk; yes, he understood that she was confused and scared. But why not one single word, this colleague asked, one gesture that would have told Sam to stop? My other colleague and I pointed out that Jill had moved Sam's hand off her thigh several times.

"But then shouldn't she have been able to say something, done something else?" he asked.

And that's when I found myself arguing vehemently about how fear can make you immobile and silent, about disassociation—the body in one place while the mind is someplace else—about wanting to survive, about wanting it over and him gone. And how none of that, NONE of it, excuses rape. How poor judgment and mistakes do not excuse rape. How alcohol does not excuse rape.

Our appeal board ultimately, and unanimously, upheld Sam's expulsion.

I can be a slow learner sometimes. It took me a while to realize that the girl I was and the woman I am now had combined forces with all that was good and compassionate in the cop, and we were arguing about my rape too. We were starting to take on the judgmental cop, the ashamed cop, the cop who thought she should have been able to defend herself, the cop who did not want to admit that she had been raped. We were finding our voice, and we were getting louder.

One evening in 2002, on the way to dinner, my boyfriend mentioned that his former wife was a complainant in a lawsuit against an East Texas police officer who was accused of raping a number of women: some whom he'd worked with, some whom he'd arrested, some who'd called the police for help. Nearly ten women had come forward and testified that he'd raped them. My boyfriend's former wife was one of these women.

"But you know," he said, "I'm not so sure I believe her."

"Why?"

"She's a feisty thing, big mouth, big attitude. She doesn't take crap from anyone. And she always carries a gun, knows how to use it too. She used to say, anybody tried to rape or hurt her, she'd kill 'em. She'd die fighting."

"So you don't believe her because she wasn't hurt?"

He nodded.

"Yeah, I used to say that too." My tone was flat and hard. "Until I was raped."

He almost drove off the road.

I told him about my rape, every detail. When I was finished, he was very quiet and had a hard time meeting my gaze.

"Don't ever judge a woman for what she did or didn't do," I said. "Or for what you think she should have done. The instinct is to survive."

My boyfriend told me that if he'd known me back then, he would have killed the man who raped me. He'd kill anyone who hurt someone he cared about, especially a woman. His daddy had taught him that women were precious, that women were to be taken care of and defended and always treated with respect.

Really? the girl said.

Oh for fuck's sake, the cop said.

I shook my head wearily. "You still don't get it," I said.

In 1996 a woman whom I didn't know at the time was sleeping in her San Antonio bedroom when a man entered the unlocked front door and stabbed her so hard in the chest with a nine-inch kitchen knife that the tip embedded in her spine. Then he tried to rape her. When she asked if he had a condom, he fled.

The responding detectives were puzzled that there were no fingerprints, no blood anywhere except on her bed, no evidence of this intruder; that the woman was so coherent during her 911 call; that she'd remained conscious; that there was no bruising on her thighs or around her vagina consistent with an attempted rape. The intruder's MO didn't fit any previous MO. The detectives decided the woman was lying and that, in fact, she had stabbed herself. They changed the case file to Attempted Suicide and closed the investigation.

This woman, who has since become a close friend, fought ferociously to have her case reassigned to Attempted Homicide and Rape and reopened. She still talks about the trauma of the stabbing, the trauma of the attempted rape. But mostly she talks about the trauma of the police not believing her. She says she felt violated all over again, in a much more horrific way.

Several months before I agreed to talk at Vanderbilt, I read Alice Sebold's powerful and unsettling memoir, *Lucky*. Sebold explains the origin of her title in this way: "In the tunnel where I was raped, a tunnel that was once an underground entry to an amphitheater, a place where actors burst forth from underneath the seats of a crowd, a girl had been murdered and dismembered. The police told me this story. 'In comparison,' they said, 'I was lucky.'"

Sebold was eighteen and still a virgin. Weeks later she saw her rapist on the street, called the police, had him arrested, and testified at the grand jury hearing and at trial. He was convicted.

When she began research for her book fifteen years later, she obtained copies of the police reports and found a number of handwritten notes by the investigating detective, Lorenz. She discovered that he hadn't believed her, that he thought her account was "not completely factual." After several weeks of investigation, Lorenz recommended her case to the inactive file.

After the trial Lorenz acknowledged that he'd been wrong. He told Sebold, "I'm sorry if I didn't seem very nice [when you reported this crime]." He mumbled, "I get a lot of rape cases."

When I read that I paused, electrified and nearly breathless. I felt as though someone had grabbed me and the girl and the cop by the shoulders and shaken us hard. The apology. The admission. Yes, I wanted to shriek. Yes, that's it. There's the truth of it—the ugly, hard, undeniable truth, goddamn it.

Cops judge: we are trained to process dozens of different pieces of information to come to some sort of assessment about what happened. Part of that assessment comes from our prior experience and previous cases. And part of that assessment involves the victim: the choices he made, the things she did, how he appears, what she says or doesn't say. All in the attempt to get a clear picture about how the crime occurred and who is guilty. But with rape, we immediately look more closely at the victim's appearance and behavior than with any other crime. We almost always see the victims as guilty or complicit in some way.

Lorenz apologized. Sebold forgave him.

It's time for my cop to admit that our rape happened, to not silence the girl or the woman anymore. The girl and I, we don't need an apology; we forgave her long ago. It's time for the cop to forgive herself. She has not been happy with this disclosure, that part of me who is still a cop. She is terribly uncomfortable. She has fought every word you've read.

But that's okay. The girl and I understand. We sit on either side of her, pat her shoulder. "You were raped," we tell her. "You didn't do anything wrong. It's okay that you couldn't stop it."

We will tell her this as many times as it takes until she believes us.

Readings

Though I've obsessed over every bruise and scab of my childhood, my husband has resisted "all that bother" about growing up. And so I'm surprised one morning, two years into his recovery from cancer, when he says casually, "I might write to the Massachusetts Department of Children and Families and ask for my foster care files."

"You should," I reply, turning my attention to the faucet, where hot water cascades through my tea ball. I don't want to spook him. He was in foster care in the early 1950s—at least three years—before returning at age seven and a half to his mother when she married the man who would become his stepfather. Of course, I've heard the war stories of their lives together—the flailing fists, the weird "sick" punishments, the blame, the merciless scorn—but his first seven years are barely a Post-it note on the fridge.

I've often asked him about those early years, surprised at how little I know, how little he's revealed, how tense and secretive it feels. He's always noncommittal. "Can't really remember much," he'll say, yawning as if the thought of it makes him sleepy. "It was a long time ago." He was perhaps no more than three when placed in the system, and what do you remember at age three but delight—the prize of a big, yellow balloon; or fear—not knowing why the room's so eerily dark when you wake alone in the middle of the night?

The truth is, the only thing he's ever acknowledged is living in Sturbridge, Massachusetts, with Aunt Adeline and Uncle John (foster parents) and three foster girls in a blue clapboard house where, on Sundays, he stuffed himself with chicken and dumplings and rhubarb pie and played soldiers in the woods behind their garden. He doesn't know how long he lived with them, if he lived with other foster families, or even why he was put in foster care. He knows only that Aunt Adeline and Uncle John were decent, loving people who took him to Mass every Sunday at a French Catholic church, where the melodious cadences and the intricate formality of Latin and French entranced him. "But all I recall about that church is a space, about three feet between the pulpit and a woman's shoulder in the front row," he says, frowning as if puzzled, "and those chanted sounds. I just can't remember anything more."

But someone, the officials in Boston, might know where and with whom he lived.

Or, at least, know more than he did.

And yet he hesitates, a diver on the brink. He isn't, it turns out, that eager to get the files. Maybe it feels like asking for trouble. Maybe it's better to stay in the shadows, drowsing. In truth, he might have let the idea lapse, but there I was, finding the address for the Department of Children and Families on the Internet, printing out the application and putting it quietly on his desk. Still, for the next few days he doesn't bother to fill it out. I know. Like a spy, I creep up to his study and see it lying there, waiting.

And then, like magic, an addressed envelope appears on our dining room table waiting for a stamp, the words written in his clean, square script. Instinctively, I pick it up, then put a hand to my mouth to stifle a laugh: my God, he's transposed the first two numbers of the zip code and misspelled the abbreviation of his home state. Unconsciously, he's sabotaged the whole damn thing. If he mailed this letter, it would only circle back to us—*address unknown*—and who knows how many months or years might pass before he'd consider doing this again.

"Are you sure you want to request the files?" I insist the next morning after I've shown him the mistakes, but he's already addressing another envelope and attaching a stamp, the request ready to fly out into the world.

A few weeks later a caseworker calls to say that she's received and will be processing his request. "But the surprise of it," David tells me casually that night as we're fixing dinner, "is that she said I'd lived with *many* foster families. I couldn't get that phrase out of my head, like I had repetition compulsion, *many foster families, many foster families, many foster families.*"

I'm cutting up broccoli and peppers while he seasons the salmon, the rice already steaming in its cooker. I stop. "So, you didn't live only with Uncle John and Aunt Adeline like you remembered."

"Nope."

I look at him slyly. "Well, now you've got a right to be really fucked up!"

When he glances at me relief flickers across his face and he laughs such a big, happy laugh that I grin and do a little curtsy.

"Probably where I got my super powers," he retorts, an old joke between us.

"Fucked-up super powers."

"But super powers nonetheless."

I open up the rice cooker to a billow of steam. He'll be all right, I think. We'll be all right.

When the files arrive, David trundles them up to his study, then retrieves them after dinner, placing them on the dining room table like a gift or a penance, I don't know which, the manila envelope still sealed. "Let's read them together, okay," he says, pulling out a chair. "I mean, I don't want to pretend this will be easy. It's probably like chemotherapy . . . gotta hurt to make you better."

I nod at his little joke and tuck my hand into his. Then we sit side by side in the heat of the evening, reading the beginning dates and summaries until on the second page we both stop, jolted by the discovery that he was put into foster care before he was three months of age: *David received this date under Section 38.*

"You were just a baby," I whisper.

"It seems."

I squeeze his hand, but he only lets out a slow, thin breath, staring at the page. "Yeah, all these years I didn't want to know about my past because I thought if I found out more about my mother and why she let me go, I'd, well—" His face looks weighted, sad.

I've seen his sadness.

Months earlier we had visited Worcester, the city of his childhood, a place he hadn't returned to in over forty years, but where he insisted on showing me every flat he'd lived in with his mother and stepfather as if he needed to document their inevitable decline: Newberry Street, Congress Street, Cottage Street, West Street, Paine Street. That trek, a kind of nakedness, every nerve on fire. On Friday evening we drove down Lincoln Street, full of rush-hour traffic and a blur of lurid lights, trying to find the last place, a housing project where he'd lived when he was eleven. "The lowest of the low," he frowned, staring moodily out the window of our rental car, his face in shadow. I thought of cracked linoleum, skimpy curtains, torn shades, and dried ketchup on the floor. Did they have hamburgers? Meatloaf? Hamburger Helper? "Everyone knew when you got off the bus where you were headed. You were one of the untouchables."

But when we finally found the projects, David's face sharpened, surprised that the buildings, two- and three-story red brick apartments, looked as ordinary as married student housing in the university town where we lived, neat and orderly and plain. "They don't look so bad," I murmured, almost gaily, noticing a pink tricycle beneath a porch light and neatly shoveled walks.

"Yeah, they've added a few architectural flourishes"—he gestured to the arched, framed doorways and concrete steps—"but when we lived here, it was butt-ugly. And this is where my mother got so depressed she didn't get out of bed, so I had to stay in and take care of my half brothers." His voice took on a bitter edge. "Every few days I walked two or three miles to get milk for them. I hated those goddamn walks in winter."

I nodded, flexing my fingers. Even in the heated rental car, the air was chilled, the outside temps in the teens, the wind roaring.

"If she'd left that bastard, we'd never have ended up here." The stepfather, of course, a Stanley Kowalski type, thick-shouldered and rough in a wife-beater T-shirt.

As we turned back onto Lincoln Street, driving toward our hotel, the sky a deep smoky blue, the street lights blazing above layers of traffic noise, I imagined my husband as a boy, cooped up in an ugly room in that project or huddled in a cheap wool coat, walking listlessly down a highway scabbed with snow, cartons of milk in a paper bag clutched in one arm. To him, being back in Worcester meant a return to that trapped boy, one of the untouchables, his mother like a warden, oppressive and silent under a cloud of unhappiness.

But maybe it wasn't so simple. "Maybe your mother didn't know any way out either," I said tentatively, if only because it seemed too easy to blame her for everything. Her name was Ann. She was Italian. The stepfather beat her too. Those were the facts I knew. Maybe depression had yanked her into a savage sadness, an overwhelmed passivity, a not unfamiliar consequence of abuse and poverty. "Maybe she hated it as much as you, living with your alcoholic stepfather." I glanced at David, but he stared resolutely ahead, his jaw clenched. "I'm not excusing her," I said. "She let him hurt you and *she* hurt you, but maybe, I don't know, maybe we just don't know enough, maybe she wanted . . ." But, of course, I had no clue what she'd wanted, only fragments and snarls, her desires as blurred as our snow-smeared windshield. And yet some part of me wanted to find a reason, a kind of exoneration, a reprieve.

When we stopped at a red light, I saw tears in my husband's eyes. "I don't know why I'm doing this," he said, shaking his head. He looked away, opening a window, the cold air rushing in. "Just going back there . . ." He grew quiet for a moment, and I listened to the sharp sounds of the street trickling in, the screech of brakes, the hiss of tires, a bicyclist flashing past. "I used to think"—he whispered, his voice now low and muffled—"I thought she must have been a prostitute. I thought that's why I was in foster care, that I was *taken* from her."

But now . . . now, after reading the files, we know differently.

"*She was very attracted to the baby's father and appears sincere in her desire to do everything within her power for her child,*" the caseworker writes. "*In reference to the putative father, mother talked quite freely and with a great deal of feeling. She said she had known him for over two years . . . that a better job possibility had required him to leave this area shortly before she knew she was pregnant. It was apparent to worker that she is hopeful that marriage to David's father will ensue."*

Instead of a marriage, however, everything went sideways: she was alone, cast-off, an embarrassment, a problem, a woman bound to minimum-wage jobs with no help from anyone. Only the baby now claimed her urgent attention. *"Mother distressed that she will not be able to take him for day visits immediately,"* the caseworker writes, days after the mother had released him to foster care. Again and again she asks if she can visit; if she can take him to her brother's place; if she can have him overnight; if she can get his picture made; buy him new toys, new clothes; feed him; dress him; sing to him; soothe him, every sentence a hum of desire.

The next day at breakfast David pushes the stack of files toward me. "You can read the rest of them now, if you want." After page 15 we'd stopped reading last night and instead sat close together on the couch, my legs draped over his knees as we talked quietly about the revelation of the caseworkers' notes, of his mother's desires and constraints. Now he tells me he finished them alone, lying on the couch in his study, unfurling that chorus of notes about himself, his mother and his foster mothers.

Though anxious to read them all, I'm also tentative, uncertain how to interpret and understand them. After all, this isn't a childhood but a case study, my husband's early years documented by social workers and doctors, a clinical commentary with proscriptive expectations rather than an autobiography. *The 1950s.* Jesus, all that rigidity.

And yet that night, the house shuttered and still, when I slip the files from the envelope, I feel a moment of illicit fascination, a writer about to get the goods. I note where my husband's eyes clouded with tears (his mother's obvious pride and delight in him), where his interest sparked (the quickness with which he learned words, his *"diction and vocabulary are advanced,"* the caseworker wrote), where his face tightened (one doctor declared him *"mentally retarded"*). But it's different to read the files alone. The comments seem more personal—*"Foster mother said that David understands that his foster father is not his real father, but he is not quite sure why he does not have a father like other boys"*—and more bureaucratically distant—*"eczema has cleared up; fractured right clavicle; buttocks badly scarred with sores."*

After rereading the first few pages, I'm still troubled that he was "received" into foster care seven days shy of three months of age; that he was moved to at least six different placements before he was three and a half years old; that, as the caseworker drove him to his seventh placement—Aunt Adeline and

Uncle John's—a journey of thirty-five miles from his former foster home in Worcester, he was so distressed, they feared he was ill.

"*D. manifests great emotional disturbance because of being removed from one foster home to another. His hands are perspiring and he seems to have a slight temperature. Visitor (case worker) disturbed to learn that mother and foster mother (the one he is leaving, the one he calls Aunt Alma) prepared David for his leave taking by telling him that foster mother (Aunt Alma) is to be hospitalized and that he may hope to return there at some far distant time when she may have recovered. Visitor attempted to point out to foster mother that this deception is unwise and could have far reaching consequences for the child. However, the child is so confused that visitor does not attempt to give him any other explanation. On the journey to the new foster home David complains that he doesn't feel well and he is obviously extremely nervous.*"

Two days later when the caseworker returned to check on him, he was finishing his lunch in his new foster home. "*He immediately tells visitor that he does not want to go in her car and wants to stay where he is,*" the caseworker writes. On the next visit, he was playing happily outdoors "with his little cart and his tricycle." "*Again upon greeting visitor,*" she writes, "*he shakes his head very solemnly and says he doesn't intend to go anywhere else.*"

I put down the pages and a ragged piece of my husband's puzzle falls into place: he still *hates* to move, hates to disrupt one household and start another, hates packing and unpacking, hates not just the physical act of moving but the preparation, the concept: leaving the familiar for the unknown. Not only that. He resists all fantasies about the new place, never indulging in "imagining what it will be like" or "who we'll be when we're there" or "how this will change us" or "what we'll miss or forget."

Because he refuses to conceptualize moving, he never prepares until it's too late, making it a crisis, a disaster, every departure delayed, the two of us furious at each other because the movers are here and he's *still* not finished though he stayed up all night, sorting and discarding, half-empty coffee cups scattered around the room.

I see his face the day we packed for a temporary semester's move from our house in Iowa City to Auburn, Alabama, where I'd be a visiting writer at Auburn University from August to December. Though we took only clothes and books and laptops and art supplies, the move meant renting out our house and driving fifteen hours from Iowa City to the southeast corner of Alabama. That morning, when David finally arranged all of his photo equipment and suitcases in the car—two hours late—he was tense and distressed and complaining that he didn't feel well.

"It will be okay," I kept saying, wondering why I always had to coddle and soothe. And then my own irritation flared. "You're being ridiculous! Just stop!" All I wanted was for him to see this as an adventure, a pleasant little "getaway" from routine, but to him it was all rupture and trouble. *What's wrong with you?* I kept asking as we turned onto I-80 E, David slumped in the passenger seat, his face creased with worry, his shirt damp with sweat.

How little we know each other, I think now, as I sit writing at my desk on an ordinary summer day, the air thick and sultry, the sun hiding behind clouds, our laundry tumbling in the dryer downstairs. And yet it's all there. It's always been there, the past continuous, a momentum that pushes beneath the present, an undercoat wearing its way through the outer layer, exposing our beginnings, betraying our needs, telling on us.

Our traumas, it seems, will never abandon us.

To me, childhood meant a secure home and family in a small Alabama town with three meals a day, baths every night, and stories read to us under the oak tree in our backyard. At age five I could walk with my sister to the drugstore to get a Coke float or sit sucking my thumb in my mother's flower garden, squatting by the caladiums while she finished making the homemade ice cream, the clacking sound of the crank handle mingling with the shouts of the neighbor boys playing kickball. I knew that my mother would cook waffles and bacon every morning and that my father would return home from the clinic each night, fix himself a drink, and sometimes say, "Com'ere, Pooch," patting the sofa beside him. To my husband, childhood was a series of temporary exiles to unfamiliar places and new people, with no one at its center. True, his birth mother visited him at his first foster home four times a week, the files note, but after his third move, this was reduced to once a week, and with the last move, once every three weeks. Each time the caseworker took him in her car, did he worry about who would give him food and warmth and a cuddle?

Or did he get confused, uncertain how to act? The first foster mother, the file suggests, is befuddled and sweet and young, the next one middle-aged and strict, the next one soft-voiced but mentally limited. From my reading I know that children in foster care, especially when they're preverbal, sometimes have difficulty forming secure attachments to new foster parents if they've lived in compromised environments with frequent changes. When this happens, they often become confused about how to behave, having lost two of the things a child most needs: the familiarity of habit and the security of feeling safe. How can a two- or three-year-old know what to expect when he's presented so frequently with new and different mothers, new places to sleep—this bed too hard, this one too soft—new routines and rules, new foster siblings, new foods? Did David learn to fear a change in mothering, to associate dislocation with episodes of sickness and stress and anxiety about the unknown? *Where were they taking him? Why was Aunt Alma sick? Why was she abandoning him? Had he done something wrong?*

Though I know these questions are mere speculation, I am shocked to read days later that "foster care children are twice as likely to develop PTSD as war veterans."[1] I have to put the article down and stare out the window at the spill of impatiens hanging from my neighbor's back deck. *Breathe. Just breathe.* I learn that the HPA (hypothalamus-pituitary-adrenal) axis is "very reactive to adverse early experience" and that "foster children more frequently show 'atypical' patterns of cortisol production when compared with other children," which means the fight or flight response can go haywire, a twitch, a seam of fear, then panic swimming through the blood.[2] I think of the body fragile and clenched, the brain marbled with dread, a subtle but ghostly disruption of the neuroendocrine system, where nests of cells begin silently to rebel. I read these facts but I can't seem to take them in. I feel ambushed in this hot, silent room, flustered by how little I know, how powerless a child can be.

And yet in our life together my husband seems remarkably resilient: ambitious and friendly, a man comfortable with diverse groups of people, a man slow to take offense. How easily he meets new people, his energy kicking up at English Department parties or writers' receptions or community events, where he becomes instinctively charming, gregarious, often moving physically close to people as if establishing intimacy, though the talk might be about politics or art or music or a TV series, nothing personal or deeply revealing. "What did you talk about?" I often ask as we're driving home, jealous at how deeply engaged he was in conversation with my colleagues, people who seemed to laugh with him much easier than they did with me. "Oh, you know, we just played, batted the ball around," he'll say, never offering any concrete details. It's taken me years to recognize that he wasn't being intentionally evasive or simply bullshitting and that the right term for what he was doing is flirting. It doesn't matter the gender because flirting is about winning favor, making yourself charming; it's the ability to improvise, a natural instinct for many, but a heightened one, perhaps, for a man who seems to have learned so early in childhood that acceptance is conditional.

One Saturday afternoon we drive to the Hy-Vee grocery store in Iowa City to get broccoli and tomatoes and Skinny Cow ice cream sandwiches along with the usual household products. As we load our stuff onto the conveyer, the clerk says, "Well, hello there," to my husband as if they're old friends. She's a pleasant-looking older woman with graying hair, glasses and a flushed face, and my husband smiles and says something about our purchases or about the discounts, and then they talk for a few minutes about the repairs recently done to her car. I look on amazed. *He knows her.* They chat easily and he makes her laugh. "You must be David's wife," she says, smiling, offering her hand and including me in their conviviality.

Why, he's always creating potential family, I realize as we gather up our bags and head for the car. It's instinctive to him, a kind of security, a way of being, and, I admit, completely anathema to me. I glance out the window where our neighbors' gardens soften into evening, glad to have read these files, aware that I too needed to know something larger than the space between the pulpit and a woman's shoulder in the front row.

Near midnight I find the official petition for David's adoption by his stepfather, a report signed by the assistant supervisor of the Department of Public Welfare and distilled from summaries of the caseworkers' notes. On page 2 of this two-page document, the report reads,

"*During the period that he was under the care of the Department he needed many foster home replacements because of his asthmatic condition, eczema, temper tantrums and slowness of being toilet trained. Handling him was more difficult because of the frequent visits of his mother, who overly indulged him. Throughout his care, there has been a question of his general normalcy.*"

Incensed, I slam shut the document, frustrated at what is so conveniently left out: that he was removed from his first foster mother's house after four months (he was seven months of age) because the caseworker stated that this woman was "*too young and immature to care for the child,*" that "*the child got little fresh air and sunshine and was always sloppily dressed,*" and that the doctor didn't feel "*that she carried out his instructions (for medical treatment), but let the child 'do for itself.*'" There is no mention that at this house his carriage was placed on the back porch and toppled over and down the back stairs, and the child broke his collarbone. There is no mention that he had severe eczema and such a bad upper respiratory infection along with "*no training at all from the first home*" that the second foster mother felt she was "*not capable of keeping him.*" There is no mention that the first foster home was closed down as "*unsuitable for all children.*" Within a month he was shuttled off to a third foster home, in which the "*limited mental capacity of the foster mother*" and a four-year-old mentally retarded child gave the caseworker pause about David's adjustment, though he was kept there for several months—and labeled mentally retarded too—until another home could be found.

Though I can imagine my husband was a "handful" as a child, it might also be true that his stubbornness and tantrums allowed him to survive these places and become the man he became. If he'd been a docile child, he might have been left with the first foster mother who let a six-month-old "do for itself."

But why do I care about such vague diagnostic words as "general normalcy" when I know these terms are culturally imposed, defined by doctors who saw normalcy within the rather strict guidelines of postwar correctness: ease of toilet training, obedience to authority, participation with other children, cheerful affect, easily distracted from masturbation. I shouldn't care, but obviously, some part of me is outraged on his behalf. *Idiots!*

During the week that I'm reading the files, my husband and I go out to dinner with friends, people who will be sending their children, ages seven and ten, to a private school that costs $32,000 per student a year, people who are educated and decent, whose wonderful kids will have every opportunity in life: to learn languages, to travel, to focus on their unique talents with the best teachers, the most modern equipment, with familial support. The man, a friend and former colleague, talks about his work, a novel he's writing and the research he's doing for another book, and when he asks what I'm working on, I find myself tongue-tied. "Fucked-up super powers," I want to say, and for a moment I imagine blurting it to this man, so educated in entitlement and ambition. Instead, I ask him about his kids, about his wife's new job and his most recent travels.

Later, before I get ready for bed, I see my husband sitting at his desk, bent in a familiar posture toward the computer, studying a recent print he's made or perhaps just checking his e-mail. He glances up as if surprised to see me, and smiles. Sometimes now I see the boy in the man, the freckles scattered across his eyelids; the quickness with which he adapts to new people, easily befriending them; the entangled mess of his room as if each item tossed to the floor or the chair is a kind of claiming. *I live here.* Though it might be a romantic notion, I like to think that the man I fell in love with—witty, demanding, surprising, tender, moody, irritating, and sometimes infuriating—couldn't have emerged from any other world than the one he survived. There's no way to know. I know only that for most of our life together there's been a space between us, his past shielded, a kind of protective veil I couldn't push through until he reached out to tear it open. Perhaps he couldn't look at his past until he'd been thrust into the gray-dark world of cancer. Perhaps

I couldn't have shared it if I hadn't been there too, changing dressings, emptying drains, sitting those long hours in waiting rooms, watching the strained light fade to dusk.

I think now that cancer does this to some people, some marriages: once the illusion of normalcy is broken, what emerges is something sweeter, deeper, closer, as if the broken thing becomes, ironically, the healing thing.

Several weeks after my husband's surgery, when he could lie only on his right side in the hospital bed in our living room, his wound slowly healing, the sheet pulled up to his waist, his legs swollen with edema, the ankles as dark and spotted as bruised fruit, he called to me. I was making tea in the kitchen. "Come closer," he said, lifting his head, his eyes finding mine. He smiled. "I want to say something mushy."

I stood by the bed, the steam from my cup rising to my face. In one breath, he told me he loved me. "But that's not really what I wanted to say. Come closer," he insisted, as if he wanted to tell me a secret. In the waning light his blue eyes looked almost gray, his hair, once dark, was now threaded with silver. As I leaned nearer, he reached for my hand. "I just wanted to say"—his voice dropped low, edged with emotion—"I just wanted to say that this is the first time in my life I've ever felt safe."

I remember that I was stunned into silence, unnerved by the force of that word: safe. I nodded, but I didn't understand. I knew so little of his past.

But now, well, now I think I do.

On a late morning a few months after I've read the files, I come into my study—its French doors leading out to the deck—and see David standing outside in his black robe and bedroom slippers, cooking bratwursts on the grill. Overhead, the soft green of the Katsura leaves drift and blur. A garden hose spirals across our lawn. It's been a little over two years since his cancer surgery. His back is to me, his thick gray hair a whorl of cowlicks as if he's just gotten out of bed, his robe drooping slightly on one side. He's reading something, deeply absorbed, white pages fluttering in the light wind. I have that feeling of being a voyeur—he's completely unaware of my presence—as if I can secretly observe and study him, the bare, freckled skin of his neck, the flattened heel of his right slipper, the sag of his robe. . . . I can read him as I read the foster care files, but that's not what happens. Watching him, I feel such a surge of unexplained joy that he's *there* that I pause before opening the door, taking him, the whole of him, shadows and light, in.

NOTES

1. Cris Beam, *The End of June: The Intimate Life of American Foster Care* (Boston: Houghton Mifflin, 2013), xi.

2. Mary Dozier, Deane Dozier, and Melissa Manni, "Attachment and Biobehavioral Catch-Up: The ABC's of Helping Infants in Foster Care Cope with Early Adversity." *Zero to Three* 22, no. 5 (2002): 10.

There Are Distances between Us

The interstate highway system in the United States is the largest and most sophisticated in the world. It is named for President Dwight D. Eisenhower. There are two points and between them, a distance between you and me. These two points are connected in ways we will never fully understand but they *are* connected. You are there and I am here. We are red stars on maps protected beneath hard plastic in highway rest areas tired travelers touch to make sense of where they are. I have counted the miles, yards, feet, and inches between us. There are too many. When I was young, my father had an atlas I liked to study, bound in leather, worn. I traced tiny lines with my fingers and said the names of cities like Waukesha and Cody and Easton and Amarillo. I once came home to a canopy bed. That summer was long, hot, terrible. Before I left, there had been an incident involving some boys who broke me right down the middle and, after, I couldn't pull myself back together. I simply stopped talking. My hair started graying. I stayed in my room. My parents fretted. A change of scenery, they decided, would be good. I went to Port au Prince, the city of their birth, stayed with an aunt and uncle I hardly knew. Each time we needed to flush a toilet or take a bath or brush our teeth, we carried huge buckets to a well and carried those buckets back, warm water sloshing everywhere, all to wash ourselves clean in some small way. It was never enough. I never felt clean. I only felt those boys. When I returned home, I walked into a perfect bedroom. The wallpaper was covered in little corn-flowers. There was a canopy bed covered in gauzy material, draped perfectly. I loved to stare into the canopy and forget about all the ways I felt broken. Whenever we went on vacation, my father would study his atlas to find his way across America. My brothers and I sat in the back of our 1974 Grand Prix, bare legs sticking to the leather seat, hot and irritable, often bickering, forced to participate in my father's endless exploration of how far he could go. He often said the United States is a great country because with enough per-sistence, with enough patience, a man can travel from one end to the other. He said he never wanted to take for granted that he could not be kept from any place he wanted to be. Every morning, when I wake up, I think your name. I think, "Marry me," over and over and over. It shocks me, the clarity of those words, the intensity and depth, how the emotions behind those words defy logic, possibility. I do not say the words "I love you" often, not to anyone. Those words mean something. They shouldn't be used carelessly. In a photo album there is a faded Polaroid of my dad and my middle brother and me at the Grand Canyon before the third child came. We are painfully young, the four of us. I have no recollection of this trip. Behind us is our car and, on the roof, the atlas. My father stands with one leg on a rock. My brother and I hug his other leg, hold hands. My father smiles. He is not a man who smiles easily. There is a gravity to him. When he speaks or acts, he does so with purpose and sincerity. I have spent the past several years trying to become like him so when I say, "I love you," *you* can know I mean it. My father is a civil engineer. He is always concerned with infrastructure, the strength of holding the world together. He has always filled my head with information about highways and tunnels and concrete. I've retained little. The ingratitude of children is staggering. I do know this, however: if nothing else were in the way, we would always be able to reach each other. We could close the distance between our two points. We could point to a place on a map and say, we are here.

A Flexible Wolf

Of the "62 Interesting Facts . . . about Wolves," 23 are about how humans have nearly eradicated them: bounty, eradication programs, werewolf trials—you know, normal human reasons.[1] Another 24 are about how humans fear wolves (werewolves, cattle) or use them: wolf livers (to treat melancholy), wolf heads (to sleep on to treat insomnia), their teeth (to treat teething). Humans mimic wolves (their howls). They imagine wolves (John Milton's *Lycidas*, J. K. Rowling's Remus Lupin). They use them to explain autism (raised by wolves) and to stave off revenge (Cherokee). They use them to neologize (wolf whistle), to sex-up (see Red Riding Hood/hot chick/clitoris), to inspire (cave drawings), to treat infertility (Roman festival Lupercalia), to help man kill man (Charlemagne forced prisoners condemned to death to wear a wolf head as a mask before they were executed). Humans do not usually use them to protect their houses or their property: wolves aren't great guard dogs—they'd rather hide than be seen—but our guard dogs descend from wolves. Cleo, my dog, looks like a wolf. She is distinctly not (although also not a good guard dog—too nice). Humans do not go out of their way to protect wolves either.

Before North American colonization, there were two million wolves; now, maybe 65,000, most of them in Canada, about 3,500 in the United States. Another interesting fact about wolves is that they have in any number survived humans' attempt to eradicate them. Also interesting: "In order for a new wolf cub to urinate, its mother has to massage its belly with her warm tongue." Also, wolves run on their toes to prevent wear and tear of the pads on their feet. Also, "recent scientists suggest that labeling a wolf 'alpha' or 'omega' is misleading because 'alpha' wolves are simply parent wolves. Using 'alpha' terminology falsely suggests a rigidly forced permanent social structure," meaning we screwed over not only the wolves but ourselves, believing that social structures are based on something permanent and important and leader and male. Some wolves mate. They get named "alpha." When they mate, they mate for life. Their brothers and sisters join their pack to babysit. I used to babysit my nephew Cameron when he was newly born. I felt omega then but I was instead just a different kind of lucky.

Where there are wolves, there are often ravens (sometimes known as "wolf-birds"). Ravens often follow wolves to grab leftovers from the hunt—and to tease the wolves. They play with the wolves by diving at them and then speeding away or pecking their tails to try to get the wolves to chase them. If only the inverse were true and where one finds ravens one finds wolves.

Ravens live near (and possibly even in) my backyard in Flagstaff, Arizona. Wolves, as far as I know, did not live near or in my backyard, until recently, when a wolf was discovered on North Rim of the Grand Canyon. Separated from his pack in northern Utah, he has walked far and has only a hundred miles to go to reach my backyard, as the raven flies. My backyard hosts a play-set with two swings, a ladder, and a slide. The neighbor's house behind ours sits only forty feet away. It's a normal neighborhood, except fences are prohibited. Would, if the wolf wanted to visit my backyard, were he to walk another hundred miles of the more than five hundred he has already tread, appreciate the lack of barrier between houses? The lack of fences allows for the meanderings of deer. I can't tell if this is purely aesthetic or an actual deer management policy but rarely do I see deer run over by cars in the road by my house, possibly because they aren't stymied by a big wall of dead trees so they can leap faster and higher and more freely. Or maybe people drive more carefully, knowing that this is a "deer friendly" (as opposed to a "deer aggressive") neighborhood. Perhaps (the deer chomp the junipers that line my driveway, these fake arborvitae) the point of the deer is to keep invasive species to a minimum. That's what my Aunt Audie thinks when she calls to tell me that the deer, in her like-minded, unfenced neighborhood in Colorado Springs, have eaten her tulips once again. I would like a garden but we'd have to build a fence around it, which is allowed according to neighborhood policy but perhaps purely Sisyphean, as deer can jump fence and will, for the love of lettuce.

Would the wolf like my neighborhood? Would he find any use for the play-set? Could he climb up the ladder and use the slide-landing as a lookout tower? Could he pounce on deer, lured by the sweet tulip, or, in the winter, the sweet juniper, from above, taking down even a four-point buck? We still have a couple big bucks, wandering through the yards, nibbling on stubs of grass. The wolf more likely would not take down the buck—why risk getting stabbed by an antler? Why risk a hoof to the face? There's a deer that hangs back. He limps a little. Maybe he got his leg caught in one of the barbed wire fences that encircle the forest to remind us that even the forest isn't really ours, that the wild isn't really wild. The wolf is not like the hunter. He pulls the weak link out of the chain. He doesn't have any walls to hang the trophy rack anyway.

Which is not to say I'd want to see the wolf tear into the neck of the limping, lame, weak-link deer. I'm a big fan of the weak link. Underdog rooter. That's why I usually don't watch football. Somebody always has to lose. Of course, it depends on how you look at the underdog. I am flexible in my loyalties, which means people will not watch football with me. If the underdog is now winning, I switch teams. Maybe the team who is winning now has lost all season long. Maybe five interceptions do not an underdog make. Maybe this game will turn around and then I'll be on the losing side again. Maybe the wolf who walked six hundred miles to find this lame deer hasn't eaten for a week. Isn't he the underdog now? A hungry wolf can eat twenty pounds of meat in one sitting. That's a big chunk of deer. "62 Interesting Facts" compares twenty pounds of meat for a wolf to a hundred hamburgers for the human, but they don't say whether that number is with or without the bun.

Put a Go-Pro on the deer's head; you feel bad for him and his broken foot. Put the Go-Pro on the wolf's head and watch the cars he dodged, the streetlights he slunk from, the way he noted the smell of another animal, and thus the danger, from a mile away with his 200 million scent cells (compared to humans' 5 million), the millions of times he must have smelled the scent of humans and their delicious leftover meatloaf and their delicious backyard deer and had to ignore it to make his way south through Utah (to avoid getting shot) toward Arizona for some reason like territory or the seductive scent of the genetic material–deprived Mexican Wolf, whose range is confined by I-40 to the north, the Apache reservation to the east, and I-10 to the south—a big prison or a small territory. Maybe the Gray Wolf senses their need for new genetic material. He is willing and waiting—"an average size wolf produces roughly 1.2 cubic inches of sperm," which seems like a little but might be a lot. Enough, if he becomes an alpha male by impregnating a female wolf, who will gestate for sixty-five days or so. Her pups will be born deaf and blind. Who's the underdog now?

He'll travel where there's little water (Dugway Proving Grounds, the Navajo reservation) to where there's too much water (Lake Powell). He'll step on granite rocks, snow, and prickly-pear needles (which must be why he walks on his toes). He will step on hot asphalt and cold snow. He will take shelter under red rocks and tall ponderosas. He will see sheep and cattle and deer, and he will eat a squirrel.

He is a "he" for so many reasons, all human. He is what we think of as a long traveler. He is gutsy. He is horny. He is an explorer and a loner. He is everything we thought we saw in men but really read in books. He is a provider and a killer and will take over this country if we are not careful. He jumps out of the shadows at you. If only we had ever seen a real wolf before. Maybe we would see that its shape is not shadow. Maybe we would see its shape is not male. Or female. Just wolf. But, of course, we have never seen.

If you remove the forty-seven facts about wolves that are really facts about human impact on or human mythology about wolves, that leaves fifteen facts for the wolves alone. Their powerful jaws. Their sense of smell. Their tongue licking to teach their babies to pee. That they can run twenty miles an hour for distance and up to forty miles an hour for a sprint. Maybe wolves are boring without people. Imagine a world of wolves without humans. Walking on their toes through Montana without dogs chasing them. Walking on their toes in Alaska without hunters setting their scope sites on them from helicopters. Walking on their toes through the snow instead of the climate-change-makes-it-rain-in-the-mountains-now rain. Walking on their toes over forest humus instead of asphalt. Stretching out. Finding mates. Yawn.

You could maybe write a good story about them, one with a little drama. The way the smaller, nonalpha wolves suffer at the attitude of the powerful, swaggering alphas: "Lower-ranking males do not mate and often suffer from a condition of stress and inhibition that has been referred to as 'psychological castration.' Lower-ranking females are sometimes so afraid of the alpha female that they do not even go into heat." I think I saw this movie once. Was it called *Wolf of Wall Street*? Or was it called *Goodfellas*? Or *Mystic River*? Or was it that movie when the little kid did whatever his brother told him? His brother made him rob a bank. He got caught. Went to prison. Never said a word against his brother because that is man-code and they were brothers (neither of them had any kids so alpha was only as alpha claimed). Or was it that movie Thomas More made called *Utopia*, where everyone gets along, even though there is a bit of snipping about who the hell do they think they are, only two of every eight or so of them allowed to breed? The nonbreeders. They smoke a little too much weed. Population is kept naturally in check, no one runs out of food or forest or even out of pot. Hints of drama, but no real breakdowns. No one goes hungry. In Utopia there are no guns and so the only competition for the deer are the mountain lions and the tigers and the lions (wolves are everywhere) and the humans with their spears. If only the spears were as tidy and efficient as the wolves' powerful jaws—1,500 pounds of pressure. Twice as powerful as a dog's. Think of those teeth hooking you around the neck. The deer believes in the drama of the wolf. The deer doesn't care if it's a boy or a girl wolf. The deer doesn't care if you write a story about the wolf and his long trek from Utah to Arizona. Utopia is also a point of view.

Humans like a story. They like a story with a wolf. It gives them a good reason to get rid of the wolves, so the humans can be the center of the story. The Red Riding Hood story does a good job of making young girls look sexy and clitorises named red and hooded and the bad wolf, who is predating on the young girl, with his teasing pick-up line, "all the better to see you with," is turned cartoon when the savior lumberjack fills up the wolf's belly with stones. The woodsman is making the forest safe for little girls by getting rid of the wolves and the trees. Then he can have all the little girls and their clitorises to himself.

Once upon a time, there were over two million wolves in North America. Now, to repeat myself, there are sixty-five thousand. Considering, though, that humans tell stories about the abduction of babies by wolves, that the precious cattle are killed daily by wolves, that if you eat lamb that was killed by a wolf you will turn into a vampire, that wolves get in the way of your deer hunt, that wolves molest your daughters, that wolves are the reason you lost your job and the reason you need eighteen guns, considering all that, it is amazing there are any wolves left at all. Wolves are highly adaptable. Humans can make roads that bisect forests, pave the forest floor, make the backyards safe—so safe, no fence required. The world bends and breaks for the stiff humans. But the wolves are elastic, plastic, resilient, flexible, like yogis and rubber bands.

Even more flexible is the coyote, who is able, when populations are culled by coyote-killing population cullers (my euphemism, not theirs) to reproduce more kits. Their ovaries somehow sense their distant brothers' foot trapped in steel. He gnaws it off but bleeds out anyway. His death-by-stoning. His tongue as it licked poison. However many more coyotes, male or female killed, the females register and ratchet up their baby making. They can't quite keep up (it's like throwing a grain of sand into the Grand Canyon), but they slow the population decimation.

Their individual populations threatened, coyotes and wolves have begun to breed together, like polar bears and grizzlies will, because of proximity and because of innate recognition that they're going to have to adapt faster than regular evolution allows. Regular evolution has given the coyote ovaries that pulse six eggs instead of five, seven instead of six. Regular evolution has taught the wolf to walk on tiptoes. Regular evolution has taught coywolves to eat out of dumpsters and hide out in the trees of city parks. It's taught them to duck at the barrel of a gun. It's taught them to stay away from humans even as they live right in their backyards. In the night an invisible coywolf swings on my swing set. I don't see her. Unlike the wolf, I can't see anything in the dark, but she knows she's there.

If two distinct species can slide together, maybe so can two genders. The alpha female leads the pack. She's licking the pups so they can pee. The alpha male has a tongue too. He licks and licks. The pee trickles for the first time from the baby wolves. The woman wolf stands up on her toes. She peers over the edge of the Grand Canyon. She sees I-40 in the distance. She smells the Mexican Wolf. There are senses that outrank sex parts. A nose can smell humans before humans can know they're being smelled. A clitoris can become a penis. A girl can stuff a woodcutter full of stone. A wolf can walk on her toes all the way from Utah to Arizona and feel that, although she's never been anywhere near the Grand Canyon, she is coming home. She's impressed with the lack of fences—it's useful. In case a human does see her, she needs a way to run. Although humans can't see wolves, they can shoot them. Ending up as a news story is the last reason she walked this way.

There are sixty-two "Interesting Facts." I left some out. Maybe next time.

NOTE

All quotations and facts in this chapter have come from "62 Interesting Facts . . . about Wolves," *Random Facts*, November 15, 2009, http://facts.randomhistory.com/interesting-facts-about -wolves.html.

Difference Maker

The first child whose life I tried to make a difference in was Maricela. She was twelve years old and in the sixth grade at a middle school in the San Gabriel Valley, about a half hour's drive from my house near downtown Los Angeles. We'd been matched by the Big Brothers Big Sisters program. It had taken a while to get my assignment, as there were far more women volunteers than men and there often weren't enough girls to go around. But when the volunteer coordinator finally called, he told me I'd be great for Maricela and that she was well worth the wait. Though I'd wanted to be in the "community-based program," where kids went on excursions with volunteers and were allowed to visit their homes, there wasn't sufficient need so I was put in the "school-based program." This meant Maricela would be excused from class twice a month to meet with me in an empty classroom.

On our first visit I brought art supplies—glue and glitter and stencils you could use to draw different types of horses. I hadn't been told much about her, only that she had a lot of younger siblings and often got lost in the shuffle at home. Her family's apartment was close enough to the school that she could walk. She explained to me that her route took her past an ice cream truck every day but that she never had money to buy anything from it. She suggested we go to the ice cream truck together but I explained we weren't supposed to leave the school grounds. In fact, we were supposed to stay in the classroom. The classrooms were arranged around a courtyard, as is typical of California elementary and middle schools. Maricela spent most of our first meeting skulking around in the doorway, calling out to friends who were playing kickball in the courtyard. I sat at a desk tracing glittery horses, telling myself she'd come to me when she was ready.

The second child I tried to make a difference with was Nikki. I met her when I was transferred from the school-based program into the community-based program after it was determined that Maricela was merely using me to get out of class and therefore needed "different kinds of supports." Nikki was fifteen. She lived with her mother, brother, grandmother, and an inde-terminate number of other relatives in a crowded apartment in South L.A. Her mother worked as a home health care aide. Another brother had left the household before he turned eighteen, though she didn't go into much detail. Nikki had requested a Big Sister of her own volition, writing on her applica-tion that she needed "guidance in life." We met for the first time in an office at Big Brothers Big Sisters' Los Angeles headquarters. Her mother brought her to the meeting and they both sat quietly while an employee facilitated a rather halting conversation about what kinds of things Nikki liked to do and what particular strengths I might have as a mentor.

I can't remember exactly what I said, but I'm sure it was something about being available to help her with homework, especially English assignments. Though I would end up being Nikki's Big Sister for more than three years, I never once helped her with homework. I did take her to an experimental the-ater production of *Tosca* that my neighbor had directed and which Nikki, to her enormous credit, sat through without complaint. But mostly she wanted to go to the mall. These were outings on which she examined handbags at the Hello Kitty store while I feigned enthusiasm and scraped the reaches of my mind for conversation topics that might lead to some form of bonding or a teachable moment. With the exception of one occasion when I tried to explain that President Bush most likely did not, as she put it (actually as Kanye West had suggested on live television), "hate black people" but, rather, had policies that were unfavorable toward all but the wealthiest Americans, such moments never arose. When she came over to my house, she spent much of the time on my computer sending instant messages to friends and taking self-portraits (the term "selfies" had not yet been coined) with the Photo Booth application. A few times I ducked into the frame and the computer snapped the two of us together making silly faces. This was such an inaccurate representation of our actual rapport that I was embarrassed. It was as if we were imitating a Big and Little Sister. Or at least one of us was.

Later I found out Nikki actually had several different mentors from several different volunteer organizations. They came with different areas of expertise: help with college applications and financial aid, help finding a summer job, help with "girl empowerment," whatever that meant. This partly explained why nearly every time I asked her if she'd been to a particular place—to the science center or the art museum or the Staples Center to see an L.A. Sparks women's basketball game—she told me, yes, some other mentor had taken her.

I was thirty-five years old when I worked with Maricela and thirty-six when I met Nikki. These were years I would later come to see as the beginning of the second act of my adult life. If the first act, which is to say college through age thirty-two, had been mostly taken up by delirious career ambition and almost compulsive moving between houses and apartments and regions of the country, the second act seemed mostly to be about appreciating the value of staying put. I'd bought a house that I wasn't planning on moving out of anytime soon. I was in a city that was feeling more and more like home. And though I could well imagine being talked out of my single life and getting married if the right person and circumstances came along, one thing that seemed increasingly unlikely to budge was my lack of desire to have children. After more than a decade of being told that I'd wake up one morning at age thirty or thirty-three or, God forbid, forty, to the ear-splitting peals of my biological clock, I'd failed to capitulate in any significant way. I would still look at a woman pushing a baby stroller and feel more pity than envy. In fact, I felt no envy at all, only relief that I wasn't her. It was like looking at someone with an amputated limb or terrible scar. I almost had to look away.

I recognized that my reaction was extreme. I was also willing to concede that I was possibly in denial. All the things people say to people like me were things I'd said to myself countless times. If I met the right partner, maybe I'd want a child because I'd want it with him. If I went to therapy to deal with whatever neuroses could plausibly be blamed on my own childhood, maybe I'd get over myself and trust in my ability not to repeat its more negative aspects. If I only understood that you don't have to like other children in order to be hopelessly smitten with and devoted to your own (as it happens, this was my parents' stock phrase: "We don't like other children, we just like you"), I would stop taking my aversion to kids kicking airplane seats and shrieking in restaurants as a sign that I should never, ever have any myself. After all, it's such a tiny percentage of women—5 or 6 percent, according to the tiny handful of entities studying such things—that genuinely feel that motherhood isn't for them. This is the most minor of minorities. Was I really that exceptional? And if I was, why did I have names picked out for the children I didn't want?

For all of this I had reasons. I had reasons springing forth from reasons. They ran the gamut from "don't want to be pregnant" to "don't want to make someone deal with me when I'm dying." (And, for the record, I've never met a woman of any age and any level of inclination to have children who doesn't have names picked out.) Chief among them, though, was my belief that I'd be a bad mother. Not in the Joan Crawford mode but in the mode of parents you sometimes see who obviously love their kids but pretty clearly do not love their own lives. For every way I could imagine being a good mother, for all the upper-middle-class embellishments I'd offer in the form of artful children's books and educational toys and decent schools—magnet, private, or otherwise—I could imagine ten ways that I'd botch the job irredeemably.

More than that, though, I simply felt no calling to be a parent. As a role, as my role, it felt inauthentic and inorganic. It felt unnecessary. It felt like not what I was supposed to be doing with my life. What I was supposed to be doing was writing and reading and teaching and giving talks at colleges.

What I was supposed to be was a mentor, not a mom. My contribution to society was all about not contributing more people to it but, rather, doing something (and I felt this in a genuine way, not in an aphoristic or guilt-ridden one) for the ones that were already here. Ones like Maricela and Nikki.

Except Maricela and Nikki didn't really need me all that much. Or at least they didn't need me specifically. They each might have benefited from a real big sister, someone who shared their DNA and/or at least a common interest or two. But there wasn't anything about my particular skill set that was likely to improve their quality of life in any measurable way. After Nikki graduated from high school and aged out of Big Brothers Big Sisters (and went to college, I should add), I took a break from kid-related do-gooderism for a few years. During that time, I married my boyfriend, a man who seemed only slightly more interested in potential parenthood than I was, which is to say not enough to explore the issue in any depth. When I decided to return to volunteerism, I was determined to up the ante. So I became a court-appointed advocate for children in the foster care system.

Court-appointed advocacy is a national program designed to facilitate communication in foster care cases that are too complicated for any one social worker or lawyer or judge (all crushingly overworked) to keep track of. The advocate's job is to fit together the often disparate pieces of information about a child's situation and create a coherent narrative for the judge. This narrative takes the form of written reports submitted to the court several times a year and is supplemented with actual appearances in court, where the advocate can address the judge directly. Sometimes the information is simple: This child wants to play baseball but needs transportation to the practices and the games. Sometimes it's gothic: *This child is being locked in the basement by her foster mother because she's become violent and the state insurance plan won't cover her antipsychotic medication.* Advocates are required to see the children at least once a month, and are encouraged to take them places and help them with schoolwork. But they are not mentors as much as investigators—sometimes even de facto judges, since judges often rely heavily on advocates' recommendations when making their rulings.

Like my interest in being a Big Sister, the urge to be a child advocate was mostly an urge to inject something into my life that, for lack of a better way of putting it, had nothing to do with my life. As huge in many ways as that life was, it often gave the sensation of an isometric exercise requiring the foot to repeatedly draw very small, perfect circles in the air. I wanted some bigger, messier circles. Moreover, I didn't want these circles to intersect with anything related to my professional career. If I'd wanted to find volunteer opportunities that kept me in the orbit of my regular crowd, I could have taught creative writing to prisoners or joined the hipsters who worked at drop-in tutoring centers in gentrifying neighborhoods. But I didn't want to go that route. I wanted to be in a different neighborhood entirely.

Children who wind up in foster care aren't just in a different neighborhood. They inhabit a world so dark it may as well exist outside our solar system. This was certainly the case with Matthew, the boy I was assigned to shortly after I completed my advocacy training. Compared with him, Maricela and Nikki might as well have been upper-middle-class children of suburbia, complete with riding lessons and college funds.

Matthew was the child of no one. Of course, that's not literally true. He had parents. At least, he'd had them at one time. But they were permanently out of the picture, as were any number of others who'd endeavored at times to take their place. Matthew was a longtime foster child. He lived in a group home, one of a hundred or so children who had proven incapable of functioning in traditional family settings. He ate his meals when he was told to, watched whatever happened to be on television in the common room at any given time, and put himself to bed every night. When I met him he was about to turn twelve. He had been living this way on and off since the age of six.

There is very little I am permitted to reveal about Matthew, starting with his name, which is not Matthew (just as Maricela's is not Maricela and Nikki's is not Nikki). I cannot tell you about his parents or what they did to land their son in the child welfare system, but I can tell you that it's about as horrific as anything you can imagine. As with just about everyone else in this story, I cannot provide a physical description of Matthew, but for the sake of giving you something to hold on to I'm going to say he's African American, knobby-kneed, and slightly nearsighted. He's not necessarily any or all of those things but I'm going to plant that image in your mind and move on.

Was Matthew a cute kid? A charming kid? A kid with potential? People seemed to think so when they first met him, but then things had a way of going south. That was the pattern, anyway. His housing history covered the demographic spectrum. I can't give specifics, but let's say there'd been middle-class suburban couples, single moms, gay dads, and large evangelical Christian families. Some had wanted to adopt him but then changed their minds when he started feeling safe enough to test their loyalty by making their lives hell.

On my first meeting with Matthew, he wanted me to do what many advocates do for their assignees and take him to McDonald's for a Happy Meal (the meal of choice, it turns out, for the unhappiest kids in the world). But I wasn't allowed to take him off the grounds of the group home, so we sat in the dining hall and hobbled through a conversation about what my role as his advocate amounted to (he already knew; he'd had one before) and what I might do to help make his life a little better. In my training sessions, I'd learned that it was a good idea to bring a game or toy to break the ice. After much deliberation, I had settled on a pack of cards that asked hundreds of different "would you rather" questions: "Would you rather be invisible or able to read minds?" and "Would you rather be able to stop time or fly?" Matthew's enthusiasm for this activity was middling at best, and when I got to questions like "Would you rather go to an amusement park or a family reunion?" or "Would you rather be scolded by your teacher or by your parents?" I shivered at the stupidity of not having vetted them ahead of time. He had no parents to scold him or family reunions to attend. This was like asking someone with no legs if he'd rather walk or take the bus.

"We don't have to play with these," I said.

"Uh-huh," Matthew said. This would soon be revealed as his standard response to just about everything. It was delivered in the same tone regardless of the context, a tone of impatience mixed with indifference, the tone people use when they're waiting for the other person to stop talking.

The next time I saw him, I was allowed to take him out.

I suggested we go to the zoo or to the automotive museum, which had an interactive children's exhibit devoted to the inner workings of cars, but he said he wanted to go shopping at Target. He'd recently had a birthday and received gift cards he wanted to redeem. I would figure out soon enough that currency for most foster kids took the form of gift cards from places like Target or Walmart. The retailers allocated a certain amount for needy children, which meant that social workers and advocates would unceremoniously bestow them on their charges on holidays and birthdays. Matthew's moods, it often seemed, rose and fell with the cards' balances.

On this shopping trip, the first of many, he seemed upbeat, counting and recounting the cash in his pocket (he received a small weekly allowance from the group home) and adding it to the sum total of his gift cards, including a card worth twenty-five dollars that I'd picked up at the advocacy office and just given him. But, as with so many outings with Matthew, he had enough money to burn a hole in his pocket but not enough to get anything he actually wanted. He wanted something digital, preferably an MP3 player. The only thing in his price range was a Kindle reading device. I tried to explain the concept of saving up a little while longer, but he was determined to buy something right then and there and insisted that he wanted the Kindle. Even after I warned him that he was going to regret the purchase as soon as he got home, that he'd told me he didn't like to read and, besides, he would still have to pay for things to put on the Kindle, he remained adamant and took it to the checkout counter, where somehow it turned out he was twenty-five dollars short anyway. The cashier explained that there were taxes. Also, somehow it appeared that one of his gift cards had already been partially used. Matthew's face began turning red. I couldn't tell if he was going to cry or fly into a rage. There was a line of people behind us.

So I lent him the twenty-five dollars. I lent it on the condition that he'd pay me back in installments.

"Do you know what installments are?" I asked.

"No."

"It's when you give or pay something back in small increments."

I knew he didn't know what *increments* meant, but I couldn't think of an alternative word.

"So now you haven't just gone shopping, you've learned something, too!" I said.

I tried to sound light and jokey. I tried to sound like the opposite of how my mother would have sounded in such a situation. My mother would have pulled me aside and explained the conditions of the agreement in the most serious tones possible. My mother had been a very serious person. She would let you know your shirt was on backward using a voice most people keep in reserve for statements like "Grandpa's had a stroke." At some point in my early forties I realized that my primary goal in just about any verbal exchange is to lighten the mood. If a situation starts to feel too heavy, I will not hesitate to make a joke or say something sarcastic just to push away the feeling of my mother sitting me down and somberly telling me that black and navy don't go together. I do this to a fault. I do it especially with kids and I would do it with Matthew more times than I could count.

Once we were back in the car I found a piece of paper, tore it in half, and wrote out two copies of an IOU, which we both signed. Matthew seemed pleased by this and ran his index finger along the perimeter of the Kindle box as though he'd finally got his hands on a long-coveted item. I gave him command of the radio, and even as he flipped annoyingly between two awful pop stations I found myself basking in the ecstatic glow of altruism. I was a difference maker and a wish fulfiller. When I dropped him off at the group home, the promissory note tucked in his Target shopping bag along with the Kindle and the greasy cardboard plate that held the giant pretzel I'd also bought him, I felt useful. I felt proud. These were not feelings that rolled around all that often in my regular life.

It had been a long time between accomplishments. At least it had become hard to identify them, as most of my goals for any given day or week took the form of tasks, mundane and otherwise, to be dreaded and then either crossed off a list or postponed indefinitely (finish column, get shirts from dry-cleaner, start writing new book). Rarely did anything seem to warrant any special pride. And though I wanted to believe that I was just bored, the truth lay elsewhere. The truth was that the decision not to have children, which I'd made somewhat unilaterally around the time I signed up to be an advocate, was wrecking me day by day.

As much as I'd never wanted to be a mother, my relationship with my husband had turned me into a bit of a waffler. If I was going to have children with anyone, it was going to be him. He was patient and funny, not to mention tall and handsome and smart. In other words, outstanding dad material. So outstanding, in fact, that wasting such material seemed like an unpardonable crime. Besides, among my personal theories is the idea that it is not possible to fall in love with someone without picturing—whether for one second or one hour or fifty years—what it might be like to combine your genetic goods. It's almost an aspect of courtship, this vision of what your nose might look like smashed up against your loved one's eyes, this imaginary cubist rendering of the things you hate most about yourself offset by the things you adore most in the other person. And about a year earlier, this small curiosity, combined with the dumb luck of finding and purchasing an elegant, underpriced, much-too-large-for-us house in a foreclosure sale, had proved sufficient cause for switching to the leave-it-to-fate method of birth control. Soon enough, I'd found myself pregnant.

It was as if the house itself had impregnated me, as if it said, *I have three bedrooms and there are only two of you; what's wrong with this picture?* For eight weeks, I hung in a nervous limbo, thinking my life was about to become either unfathomably enriched or permanently ruined. Then I had a miscarriage. Given that I was forty-one, it was not exactly unexpected. And though there had been nothing enriching about my brief pregnancy, which continued to harass my hormones well after vacating the premises, I was left with something that in a certain way felt worse than permanent ruin. I was left with permanent ambivalence.

My husband was happy about the pregnancy and sad about the miscarriage. I was less sad about the miscarriage, though I undertook to convince myself otherwise by trying to get pregnant again (at least the kind of trying that comes before medically assisted trying, which for a forty-one-year-old may be tantamount to not trying). After three months of dizzying cognitive dissonance (This is me, using fertility-test sticks? This is me, seeing an acupuncturist?), I walked into the guest room that my husband also used as an office and allowed myself to say the thing I'd been thinking my whole life: I didn't want a baby. I'd never wanted a baby. I'd thought I could talk myself into it, but those talks had failed.

I remember that as we talked I was lying on the cheap platform bed we'd bought in anticipation of a steady flow of out-of-town company. I remember looking at the ceiling and admiring the lines of the window frame and the ceiling molding. I remember that the curtains, which were partly raw silk and looked expensive despite my having bought them for cheap on the JCPenney website, were lifting gently in the breeze. There was bougainvillea outside, along with bees and hummingbirds and mourning doves. There was a big grassy lawn where the dog rolled around blissfully scratching his back, and a big table on the deck where friends sat nearly every weekend eating grilled salmon and drinking wine and complaining about things they knew were a privilege to complain about (the cost of cable television, the noise of leaf blowers, the problem of not having enough time to pursue one's art). And as I lay on that bed it occurred to me, terrifyingly, that all of it might not be enough. It was possible that such pleasures, while pleasurable enough, were merely trimmings on a nonexistent tree. It was possible that nothing, not a baby or lack of a baby, not a beautiful house, not rewarding work, was ever going to make us anything other than the chronically dissatisfied, perpetual second-guessers we already were.

"I'm sorry," I said. I meant this a million times over. To this day, there is nothing I've ever been sorrier about than my inability to make my husband a father.

"It's okay," he said.

Except it wasn't, really. From there, a third party was introduced into our marriage. It was not a corporal party but an amorphous one, a ghoulish presence that functioned as both cause and effect of the presence that would have been our child. It had even, in the back of my mind, come to have a name. It was the Central Sadness; that was the only thing to call it. It collected around our marriage like soft, stinky moss. It rooted our arguments and dampened our good times. It taunted us from the sidelines of our social life (always the barbecues with toddlers underfoot; always a friend's child interrupting conversations midsentence; always the clubby comparing of notes about Ritalin and dance lessons and college tuition, which prompted us to feign great interest lest we come across like overgrown children ourselves). It haunted our sex life. Not since I was a (virginal) teenager had I been so afraid of getting pregnant. I wondered then, as I had a hundred times before when this subject arose, if our marriage was on life support, if at any moment one of us was going to realize that the humane thing to do would be to call it even and then call it a day. How hard, after all, would it be to go back to being the people we'd been before? How easy would it be to stop trying to become the people we apparently didn't have it in ourselves to be?

Compared with this existential torment, foster care advocacy was a cakewalk. Though it was certainly more demanding than Big Brothers Big Sisters, I found it considerably easier—or at least more straightforward—than traditional mentoring. For one thing, advocating for foster kids mostly required dealing with adults. It meant talking to lawyers and meeting with school administrators and sitting around the courthouse all day when there was a hearing. It meant spending a lot of time on the phone with another, much more seasoned advocate, who was supervising me. As onerous as all of this might have been for most people, I found that I loved it. I loved talking to my supervisor. I loved hanging out in the tiny attorneys' lounge outside the courtroom, where there was always a plate of stale supermarket pastries next to the coffeemaker and the lawyers stood around in clusters complaining about the judge, their clients, the whole hopeless gestalt. I was fascinated and moved by the family dramas playing out in the courthouse waiting areas. There, teenage mothers wept into their cell phones and men with shaved heads and tattoos sat glumly next to women who were presumably the mothers of their children but might also have been their own mothers—or their sisters or cousins or aunts. Everywhere there were children with women who were not their mothers but who had taken custody of them when those mothers got arrested or became otherwise indisposed. Occasionally there would be a physical altercation and an officer would have to intervene. There was a sheriff's station in the basement next to the cafeteria. There was paternity testing on the second floor. The courthouse was its own little planet of grimness and dysfunction. By contrast, I felt bright and competent.

And I took genuine pleasure in helping Matthew. He may have seen me largely as a chauffeur, but the truth was I actually had pushed for some changes on his behalf and thus solved a few problems for him. I can't disclose what they were, but suffice it to say they were the kinds of problems that a kid with a family would simply never run up against, problems stemming mostly from the fact that he lived in an institutional setting and was essentially being raised by committee. It was the kind of help I think I'd subconsciously wanted to provide for Nikki. I wanted to contribute to her life without intruding upon it. And deep down maybe that's what she'd wanted, too, when she signed up for all those mentors.

As it was, I always had the sense with Nikki that she'd rather be just about anywhere else than with me, even when she'd been the one to initiate an outing. One year, near her birthday, we'd been at the mall and she'd expressed a desire to celebrate with her friends by going to a certain movie on opening day. Unfortunately it was one of those movies that sell out before their titles even go up on the marquee, even if they're playing on multiple screens, and Nikki didn't have a credit card or any way of purchasing tickets ahead of time. And though she didn't ask me to buy her anything, I considered her plight and offered to buy six advance tickets for her and her friends. This would be her birthday present, I told her. As long as she was sure she'd be able to secure a ride to the theater and assemble the whole group with no one dropping out at the last minute. She said she was sure. She seemed happy as she tucked the tickets into her purse, taking care to put them where she wouldn't lose them. I was happy, too, though somewhat surprised at myself for impulsively forking over more than $100.

When I saw her a few weeks later, I asked how the movie was. She told me they ended up not going, that she and a smaller group of friends went out to dinner instead.

I didn't say anything to her. By that I mean I didn't say anything beyond "What? Really? After all that?" I didn't say the thing that even then I knew I should have, which is that $100 was not a small amount to me and that not using the tickets was disrespectful and inconsiderate. I didn't say it because I didn't feel like our relationship was such that I could scold her. I also didn't say it because she hadn't asked me to buy the tickets in the first place. Looking back on it now, I see that they were more of a burden than a gift. As much as she'd insisted that going to the movies with her friends was exactly what she'd wanted to do on her birthday, I now know that you cannot expect a teenager to plan more than one day into the future. It's hard enough to get adults to commit to a social activity until they're sure they're not getting a better offer elsewhere. But I suspect that ultimately what I wanted most from Nikki was for her not to act like a teenager. I didn't like teenagers. I hadn't even liked them when I was one myself. I wanted her to act like an adult, which as it happens was what my parents had wanted from me when I was a teenager and even a young child. So I didn't say anything to her about wasting the movie tickets. I merely reminded myself that this was yet another example of why I should never have children. Childhood itself was anathema to me. The very condition gave me the shivers.

I think in part that's why I was interested in foster children. In some cases, childhood had literally been beaten out of them. And though I had grown up a million miles from anything resembling physical abuse or neglect—if anything I'd been overparented, oversupervised, vested with far too many unmeetable expectations—the foster kids I met seemed alienated from their own childhoods in a way that felt familiar to me. Whereas with Maricela and Nikki the idea in some ways had been to keep them from growing up too fast, foster kids were essentially victims of their own youth. And they knew it as well as anyone. As much as they wanted to be normal kids, there was almost always a sense in them of wanting to get on with things. This phase of being a minor, of having no control over your fate and no say over what you eat or where you sleep or who's acting as your guardian and for how long, was a phase to be endured. No one ever said to a foster child, "Enjoy being a kid now, because one day you'll have to be a grown-up." It was no accident that when they aged out of the system it was called "emancipating." It seemed to me like the perfect word. What was adulthood, after all, but a permanent release from the chamber of childhood? Why would they have referred to these children as "minors" (in court documents, Matthew was never referred to as Matthew but as "the minor") if there wasn't at least some hope of major improvement down the road?

But that was my particular view, which was colored by my own particular experience as a young person who couldn't stand being young—in other words, a twisted view. It also doesn't really hold up when it comes to kids in the child welfare system, since the data on what happens to kids after they age out of the system without a permanent family is dismal. Statistics from the Department of Health and Human Services consistently show that more than half end up either homeless or in jail. Within two years of aging out of the system, as many as half of the young women will be pregnant. Besides, time moves at an excruciating pace for all kids. A month might as well be a year. On the days I went to court with Matthew, I watched child after child, some of them infants in plastic bucket carriers, appear before judges whose jobs essentially boiled down to issuing timelines. Parents were given six or twelve or eighteen months to get their acts together. They were told to go to rehab, to anger-management therapy, and to parenting classes. And when they failed to do so, the clock would start all over again. The children would hear this news and sometimes their faces would go jagged with despair. How was it that they'd been taken away in fourth grade and now they were in sixth? Sometimes they were afraid of the parents and secretly didn't want to go back, though they told the judge otherwise.

Matthew, for his part, was an old hand at court. He looked forward to it because it meant missing school and watching movies in the day-care area, where kids of all ages were kept behind locked doors as protection from abusive parents who might also be in court that day. Though he wanted to be adopted, he no longer expected anything to happen at his hearings. There were no major decisions to be made or battles to be fought. Usually the judge would just remark on how tall he'd gotten or how nice his hair looked.

Initially, I'd thought Matthew would grow on me. But though I learned to identify some of his charms—his facility with technological gadgets, his GPS-like knowledge of the location of every video arcade and big-box store within a twenty-mile radius—I can't say we were great friends. Not that we needed to be. I was never going to be his role model. I certainly wasn't a mother figure. I was more like a random port in the unrelenting storm that was his life. And that was enough. Matthew's lot was so bad that it could be improved, albeit triflingly, with one minipizza at a food court. A kid with higher expectations would have been more than I could handle.

I was comfortable with that admission. I was happy to state my limits. I was proud, in fact, to stand up and be counted among those who knew themselves well enough to know that they wouldn't do right by a child and that therefore the only ethical and, for that matter, remotely sensible choice was to bow out of the whole enterprise. But a member of a childless couple can only be as strident as the other half of the couple. And in the aftermath of my miscarriage, during those confused, angry months when I was struggling to understand how it was possible to feel so sad about not having something that held so little appeal in the first place, my husband began to say out loud that he wanted to be someone's father—or at least that he might not be okay with never being someone's father. He wanted to use what he knew about the world to help someone find his or her own way through it. He wanted "someone to hang out with" when he got older. That said, he didn't necessarily need the baby- or toddler-rearing experience. He didn't particularly want to give up his weekends for kids' birthday parties or spend half our income on child care. He didn't need the kid to look like him or even be the same race. When I asked if these needs could be met through teaching or mentoring or even being an advocate, he said he wasn't sure.

And so were planted the seeds of a potential compromise. Maybe we could take in, or possibly even adopt, a foster child. This would be a child old enough to go to birthday parties on his own, a child old enough that we might actually qualify as young or average-age parents rather than ones of "advanced age" (if I adopted a ten-year-old at forty-three it would be the equivalent of having had him at the eminently reasonable age of thirty-three).

Of course, the experience would be nothing like the typical child-rearing experience, but neither of us was after that, especially not me. Having never craved a child, I didn't crave the intimacy that came from raising someone from birth. This child could be more like a mentee, an exchange student, a distant relative who visited for the summer and decided to stay on because we could afford him opportunities unavailable back home. Of course, any child we took in would surely need intense therapy for years or even forever. He would have demons and soul-breaking baggage. But they wouldn't be Matthew-level demons. We would find the needle in the haystack that had Ivy League potential. We would find the kid who dreamed of being an only child in a quiet, book-filled house with parents who read the *Times Literary Supplement* over dinner. Sure, I would probably still be a bad mother, but I would be one according to such wildly different standards than those set by the child welfare system that it wouldn't matter if I dreaded birthday parties or resorted to store-bought Halloween costumes. All that would matter was that I was more fit than the teenagers weeping in the courthouse.

I knew this was 90 percent bullshit. I knew that it wasn't okay to be a lackluster parent just because you'd adopted the child out of foster care. A few times, my husband and I scrolled through online photo listings of available children in California, but we might as well have been looking at personal ads from a sad, faraway land that no one ever traveled to. There were cerebral-palsied three-year-olds on respirators, huge sibling groups that spoke no English, girls who had "trust issues with men." Occasionally there would be some bright-eyed six- or seven-year-old who you could tell was going to be okay, who had the great fortune of being able to turn the world on with his smile. So as the Central Sadness throbbed around our marriage, threatening to turn even the most quotidian moments, like the sight of a neighbor tossing a ball around with his kid in the yard, into an occasion for bickering or sulking or both, the foster child option functioned as a pacifier. It placated us with the illusion that all doors were not yet closed, that we still had the option of taking roads less traveled, and, best of all, that we could wait ten years to decide if we wanted to.

Or we could look into it sooner. One day, while my nerves swung on a longer-than-usual pendulum between pity for Matthew and despondency over my marriage, I decided to call a foster and adoption agency. Actually, I told my husband to call. Advocates aren't supposed to get involved with fostering and I didn't want to do anything that might give the appearance of a conflict of interest. He signed us up for an orientation and I told him he had to do all the talking. He agreed to this plan in much the same way he agreed to certain home-improvement projects when I suggested them, which is to say mostly accommodatingly though without tremendous relish. When we arrived at the meeting, I signed in using his last name, something I'd never done even once before.

"I've got to be incognito," I said. "Let's not call attention to ourselves."

There were about thirty people at the orientation. It was the most racially and socioeconomically diverse crowd I'd seen since I last appeared for jury duty. This agency was known for its outreach to the LGBT community and there were several gay couples in attendance. There were also a lot of singles, including a man wearing a dress, jewelry, and full makeup, though he'd made no attempt to hide his five o'clock shadow. We were each asked to introduce ourselves and say what had brought us. One male couple said they were deciding between adopting out of foster care and working with an egg donor and a surrogate. They both wore hipster glasses, and one had on what appeared to be a very expensive suit. They sounded like they had big careers. A young woman explained that she'd spent time in foster care herself as a youth and was now ready to give back by adopting a baby. She couldn't have been older than twenty-one and was wearing a hat and a puffy coat, even though it was probably seventy degrees outside. If I'd seen her in another setting, for instance the public library, I might have thought she was homeless.

"I'm interested in an infant only," she said. "But also LGBT. Those are my main two things."

She wanted a gay baby. Or a transgender baby. No one in the room seemed to find this unusual.

When our turn came, my husband spoke briefly about how we were just exploring things in a very preliminary way. Then I spoke about how I was ambivalent about children but that this potentially seemed like a good thing to do. I then proceeded to completely dominate the rest of the three-hour meeting. Instead of being incognito, I acted like I was back in advocacy training. I raised my hand constantly, asking overly technical questions about things like the Indian Child Welfare Act and the American Safe Families Act and throwing around their acronyms (ICWA and ASFA) as if everyone knew what they meant. I asked what the chances of getting adopted were for a twelve-year-old who had flunked out of several placements.

"Maybe this isn't the right setting for these questions," my husband whispered.

"But I genuinely want to know the answers," I said.

As the meeting wrapped up, the woman from the agency announced that the next step was to fill out an application and then attend a series of training sessions. After that, she said, prospective parents who passed their home-studies could be matched with a child at any time and theoretically be on their way to adoption.

Her words were like ice against my spine.

"We're not at that point!" I said to my husband. "Not even close. Not remotely close."

I suggested he apply to be a mentor for "transitional-age youth," which are kids who've emancipated but still need help figuring out the basics of life. He filled out a form, again with the slightly bewildered resignation of someone agreeing to repair something he hadn't noticed was broken in the first place. The agency woman said she'd call him about volunteer opportunities. She never did. We both figured it was because I had acted like a complete lunatic. If the agency had any sense, they'd give the homeless-looking woman a gay baby before letting us near any kids for any reason.

After the meeting, I was mortified for weeks. I felt like I'd gotten drunk at a party, like I'd launched into some blowhardy rant before throwing up into a ficus tree. Slowly, though, I began to understand why I acted the way I did. The notion of adopting one of these kids was so discomfiting that I'd unconsciously tried to soothe myself by turning the meeting into something I could handle, which was being an advocate. It was one thing to look at the children in the photo listings and imagine which one might be bookish and self-possessed enough to live comfortably under our roof. It was another to sit in a room with people who were really serious about it, people who were going to work fewer hours or go out to dinner less often or travel less freely in order to have the family they had always wanted. And I knew we were not those people. We did not match the profile of foster parents—the good ones or the bad ones. We were not known for our patience. We were not ones to suspend judgment or lower the bar. We'd once entered our dog in a charity "mutt show" (ironically, of course) and seethed for days when he didn't even make the finals in his category, which was "best coat." I told my husband that if he was really interested in mentoring he should call the agency and tell them so. He said he'd try, but he never got around to it.

When I was Nikki's Big Sister, one thing I'd always noticed was that people smiled at us a lot when we went out. At least they did when we were in the various necks of my woods, like the Farmers Market or the independent movie house or my local Trader Joe's. I guess it made sense. She was a black teenager and I was a white woman. Moreover, I was a relatively young woman. Both of us looked like we quite possibly had better things to do than hang out with the other. But there we were nonetheless, and baristas and ticket takers would subtly nod their heads in approval. The few times I actually ran into acquaintances when I was with Nikki, I'd introduce her as "my friend" and then watch their faces leapfrog from confusion to curiosity to surprise before landing on (at least what I assumed to be) blazing admiration.

"It's so amazing that you do that," friends would say when the subject of my mentorship arose in conversation, which rarely happened unless I brought it up, which I almost never did. Though I put in the requisite time with Nikki, even taking her to a Big Brothers Big Sisters holiday bowling party, which I think she might have enjoyed even less than I did, there always seemed something counterfeit about our dynamic. Very few people knew I was doing this volunteer work, mostly because in mentioning it, I felt like I was eliciting praise for something that didn't actually warrant any. Back when I'd been attempting to mentor Maricela, I'd actually gone out and bought a Polaroid camera so that we could take photos and incorporate them into a scrapbook made from construction paper and what was left of the glitter I'd brought in the first time. This activity hadn't been my idea. It had been among the suggestions listed in the Big Brothers Big Sisters orientation pamphlet. Maricela had been less than keen on the project, wanting to talk instead about how she needed a new soccer uniform but her mother wouldn't pay for it.

Around that time, I visited a friend who had just had twins. I picked up each of her babies, patted their bottoms, and then put them back down. They were warm and soft, yet still at that scary tiny stage. Truth be told, I love babies when they're between about five and eight months old, and I told my friend she'd be seeing a lot of me when they reached that age. She laughed and asked what I'd been doing lately. I had a Polaroid photo of Maricela in my purse and I took it out.

"She's pretty, isn't she?" I said.

"She's gorgeous," said my friend.

It was true that Maricela was a very pretty girl. But I'd spent a total of about three hours with her at that point. The ownership implied by that statement felt almost obscene. On our second session, she'd turned to me and asked, "What's your name again?"

"You're going to be an amazing influence on her," my friend said. "She is so lucky to have you."

A few months after that, I met my husband. I was attracted to him immediately. As I've done with just about every man I've dated, I thought about what it would be like for us to be parents together. I pictured us coaxing our child to take at least one bite of peas. I pictured us shaking our heads in bemusement at her precocious vocabulary. But you're never the real you in the beginning of a relationship. Eventually things get serious and you return to yourself. And from there the relationship either ends or makes a commitment to its imperfections. Either way there is loss. That's not the same as saying either way you lose. It's more like either way you have to accept that you didn't go the other way. But that acceptance is itself a loss, the kind that if you think about it too much might cause you to go a little crazy.

A phrase you hear a lot in the foster care world is that a child has "experienced a lot of loss." It will often come up in the blurbs accompanying the photo listings. *Jamal has experienced a lot of loss but knows the right family is out there. Clarissa is working through her losses and learning to have a more positive attitude.* At first glance, you might think these are references to the original loss, the dismantling of the biological family. But most often they mean the child has gotten close to being adopted but that things haven't worked out. With Matthew I often got the feeling that the trauma of being removed from his biological parents had been dwarfed by the cumulative implosions of the placements that followed. He seemed to know that he'd had a hand in at least some of these disruptions, that he'd lost his temper too many times or let himself lapse into behavior that frightened people. But when I asked about this, which I did only once or twice, he tended to offer some standard-issue excuse on behalf of the estranged parents, which he'd surely heard from his social workers. He'd say they lacked the resources to sufficiently meet his needs. He'd say they didn't have the skills to handle a kid like him.

Matthew had been taken to a number of adoption fairs over the years, a concept that floored me when I first heard about it. These were organized events such as picnics or carnivals where adoptable kids and prospective parents were supposed to mingle and see if they liked one another. It struck me as a barbaric form of speed dating. But caseworkers insisted that the events were benign, that the point was for kids to have fun regardless of the outcome. The same went for a local television news station with a regular segment that practically advertised kids who were up for adoption. *Clarissa is a wonderful young lady who likes to play dress-up and needs a forever family,* the anchor would say. *Jamal has a mean jump shot.* Then there would be a field report showing the child "having a special day" riding trail horses or getting "ace tips" from a professional athlete who'd been enlisted to show up for half an hour and interact with him on behalf of some charity. This same news station also had a weekly segment featuring shelter animals that needed homes.

About a year into my work with Matthew, he experienced yet another adoption-related loss. A couple that had been visiting him at the group home and later hosting him for weekend visits had decided he wasn't the right fit for them after all. He'd been hopeful about this placement, and when I visited him a few days after things fell through I found him pacing around his cinder-block dormitory like a nervous animal. The prospective mom had given him a used MP3 player, perhaps as an unspoken parting gift, but the group home staff had locked it up for some kind of disciplinary reason. He had his Kindle, however, which he'd never used, and now he sat on a bench outside the dormitory, bending the plastic until pieces of the device began falling off.

"I know what a huge bummer this is," I said. "I'm really sorry."

"I don't care," he said.

I wasn't sure how to respond. Every possible option seemed inadequate, maybe even capable of doing long-term damage.

"I know you probably do care," I said finally. "But sometimes we care so much about stuff that it's easier to pretend for a while that we don't care at all."

The temperature was in the high nineties; the choke of autumn in Southern California was in full, scorching force. The Kindle was practically melting into soft, curling shards as Matthew tore it apart. I thought about the twenty-three dollars he still owed me for it and wondered which was worse, enabling his mostly consequence-free existence by letting him destroy it or lecturing him about how money and the stuff it buys aren't disposable. Both tactics seemed fairly useless, but the latter seemed almost like a joke. The kid's whole life was disposable. Like most foster kids, he kept many of his things in a plastic garbage bag so he could grab and go as needed.

Through angry tears Matthew was now declaring that he was never going back inside the dormitory and would sleep on the lawn until he could live in a real home. He said he'd gotten mad at the prospective mom for not buying him something he wanted but that he hadn't done anything too bad. He said he'd kicked some chairs over but they weren't broken or anything. He said he just wanted another chance, but they wouldn't give him one and it wasn't fair. After a while, I suggested he put his feelings in writing. Admittedly, this suggestion was based on what I would do in his situation, not what he was necessarily inclined to do, but it was all I could think of.

"Let's go inside and get a piece of paper," I said. "And you write down what you want and how you feel. I'll walk away so you can do it in private."

He agreed, which surprised me. We went inside the building and into his room, where blue industrial carpet covered the floor and a low-slung twin bed was covered with a thin blue blanket. He got out a spiral-bound notebook and lay on the floor on his stomach, legs spread slightly and elbows propped up as he began to write. He looked more like a normal kid than I'd ever seen him. I left him and headed down to the common room, where about six boys, some of them as tall and muscled as men, were sprawled out in front of a too-loud television. A staff member sat on a stool in the kitchen examining her long, freshly lacquered nails. I asked where the bathroom was, and, without looking up, she directed me down a corridor that ran through an adjacent dormitory.

In that dormitory I passed another common room, this one filled with younger children. They were seated at a long table set for dinner, and they squirmed in their chairs and fiddled with their utensils, and of course there was one kid shouting above the others and holding a basket of bread sticks over his head where no one could reach them. Unlike the boys in Matthew's unit, these were actual children, little tykes who looked in some cases as young as four and five. Gathered there at the table, they could have been tiny summer campers in the mess hall. They could have been Cub Scouts gearing up for their nightly eating contest, after which they'd go off to the evening sing-along and then their cabin bunk beds and, eventually, home to their parents, who would take both pride and sorrow in the knowledge that their children could cope so well with being away from home at such a young age.

But these children were already home, of course. There was no going anywhere from here, except maybe to foster families or, if they smiled big enough, adoptive families that may or may not have the resources to sufficiently meet their needs. I slowed my pace slightly as I passed the entryway. It had been a while since I'd looked through the state photo listings (the more time that went on, the more my online self-soothing practices leaned toward looking at photos of puppies), but seeing the small, open faces, the feet that barely touched the floor, the institutional food heaped onto institutional plates, I was reminded of the tiny spark of hope those listings once gave me. I was reminded of the small handful of kids whose profiles I'd looked at more than once. I was reminded of the few occasions in which the conversation with my husband about adopting from foster care didn't necessarily feel like bullshit or a pacifier but, rather, a viable antidote to the Central Sadness.

I returned to Matthew's room. He was sitting on the bed, reading over his statement. He handed me the notebook.

I want to live with —— and ——. I'm sorry I got mad. If you give me another chance I promise I'll never get mad again.

"Will you give that to them?" Matthew asked me.

"If I can," I said. There was no way I could give them anything. The decision had been made. Later I would look back on this moment and realize that telling Matthew to write that note was the cruelest thing I could have done to him.

Sometimes I think perhaps my greatest wish is that one day my husband will get a call from a person claiming to be his son or daughter. Ideally, this person will be in his or her late teens or early twenties, the product of some brief fling or one-night stand during the Clinton administration. My husband will be shocked, of course, and probably in denial. He'll say, "I'm sure you're mistaken" and "I don't recall the woman you're talking ab—" and then suddenly his face will blanch and his jaw will grow slack. It will be like that absolutely tour de force moment in the Mike Leigh film *Secrets and Lies*, in which Brenda Blethyn, playing a mother who gave her daughter up for adoption decades earlier, meets the young woman for the first time and sees that she is black. With great kindness (with a maternal sort of kindness, actually), Blethyn's character explains that she cannot possibly be the girl's mother. But then she gets a faraway look in her eyes and is jolted by a long-suppressed memory, her face scrolling through several lifetimes' worth of emotion in just a few seconds.

My husband will have that kind of moment. And then he will tell me the news and I, too, will be shocked. Eventually, though, we'll both be thrilled. This new relation will breeze in and out of our lives like a sort of extreme niece or nephew. We'll dispense advice and keep photos on the fridge but, having never gotten into the dirty details of actual child rearing, take neither credit nor blame for the final results. My husband would experience the satisfaction of having a grown child to hang out with and be proud of when the occasion called for it. I would experience the satisfaction of not having to be anyone's mother.

Barring that scenario, I've sometimes thought my husband should donate sperm to a lesbian couple. They would live far away and send us photos every now and then. We'd visit sometimes and attend graduations and maybe by the time the child reached college age we'd have saved so much money not raising kids ourselves that we could kick in for the tuition. Once the kid was at college, my husband could get on the phone with him and help with assignments, lecturing him on comparative politics and trying to explain organic chemistry. I'd overhear snippets of the conversation as I puttered around our pristine, art-filled, and distinctly child-unfriendly home (perhaps there's a steep spiral staircase or a large malamute) and smile at the it-takes-a-villageness of it all.

If I learned anything from working with Matthew—and with Nikki and Maricela—it's that no such town exists. I thought I'd undertaken this volunteer work because I was, above all, a realist. I thought it showed the depth of my understanding of my own psyche. I thought it was a way of turning my limitations, specifically my unwillingness to have children, into new and useful possibilities. I thought the thing I felt most guilty about could be turned into a force for good. But now I know that in some ways I was under the sway of my own complicated form of baby craziness. As wary as I've always been of our culture's rote idealization—even obsessive sanctification—of the bond between parent and child, it seems that I fell for a whole other kind of myth. I fell for the myth of the village. I fell for the idea that nurture from a loving adoptive community could triumph over the abuses of horrible natural parents.

I'd also tricked myself into believing that trying to help these kids would somehow put the Central Sadness on permanent hiatus, that my husband and I could find peace (not just peace, but real satisfaction) with our life of dog hikes and quiet dinners and friends coming over on the weekends. Instead, we continued to puzzle over the same unanswerable questions. Were we sad because we lacked some essential element of lifetime partnership, such as a child or agreement about wanting or not wanting one? Or were we sad because life is just sad sometimes—maybe even a lot of the time? Or perhaps it wasn't even sadness we were feeling but, simply, the dull ache of aging? Maybe children don't save their parents from this ache as much as distract from it. And maybe creating a diversion from aging turns out to be the whole point of parenting. Maybe, since the beginning of time, it's never really been about anything more than that.

Matthew got transferred to a new group home shortly after he turned thirteen. It was practically indistinguishable from the old one, right down to its proximity to the local Target. I took him there to spend the $25 gift card I'd mailed him, but when we reached the front of the checkout line the cashier said there was only $3.29 left on the card. Matthew claimed it was defective. He said he hadn't used it. On the conveyor belt sat several bags of chips, a package of cookies, and multiple boxes of macaroni and cheese that he wanted to keep in the kitchen at the group home. He hadn't even bothered to try to stretch his budget to buy electronics. There were several people behind us. I was afraid he'd have an outburst either right there or in the car, so I pulled out my credit card and paid. I knew he was lying and I told him so. He said he wasn't. He said no one ever believed him. He said he had nothing, that no one cared about him or ever did anything for him. He said no one ever gave him a chance or cut him a break. He said everyone in his life was useless.

We got in the car, and he ate his chips as we drove in silence. When I pulled up to the entrance of the group home, he gathered up his loot without looking at me.

"Happy birthday," I said.

"Uh-huh," he said.

He slammed the door behind him and walked quickly toward his dormitory, as though late for something. Dinner would be served at five. At the old place dinner had been at five thirty and Matthew was peeved at the change in schedule.

Back at home, my husband and I sat down around our usual time of eight thirty. We ate some grilled fish. I drank a glass of wine. We looked through the magazines that had come in the mail, pointing out articles to each other while intermittently talking about our day. It was a good meal. The evening air was still cool but the daylight was beginning to linger. Soon it would be summer. Friends would start coming over to eat on the deck. After that it would be fall and what passes for winter. Then the spring would roll around again, and we would still be right there, eating our fish and reading our magazines. Our conversations and our sleep would remain uninterrupted. Our lives would remain our own. Whether that was fundamentally sad or fundamentally exquisite we'd probably never be sure. But who can be sure of such things? And what's so great about being sure, anyway?

The Truth

You make me feel (mighty real).—Sylvester James Jr., the Queen of Disco

I begin with an obvious lie: nonfiction writers tell the truth, fiction writers don't, and poets don't have a place in this conversation.

No wait. Better to start with a joke.

A poet, a novelist, and an essayist walk into a bar.

Oh but why is it always a bar? Right away, an unchallenged tradition—tradition of the joke, tradition of the writer—is substitute for the peculiar and thus more interesting truth. Might we see something truer if we move to another angle?

So let's make it a coffee shop, one of those crowded pretentious places, a silver sea of laptops, smart phones (the eyes of the table) fluttering on and off.

This type of joint has a turntable and vintage vinyl on the back counter and a myriad of brewing devices that look like exhibits from a medical apparatus museum.

The menu at the coffeehouse around the corner from where I live in Chicago describes their coffee selections as glossy or supple, loamy or buttery, velvet or ripe or bright, and the baristas—I've found this out the hard way—will only answer questions that adhere to the vocabulary they've established. You MAY ask, which is the ripest brew. You may NOT ask, which is the darkest brew, or rather you can, but the response will be "well, we don't really use that language to describe the coffee."

So these three writers, they say to this barista with her deep terminology knowledge and limited parameters of description: *All of us, see, the poet here, that novelist there, or the obvious choice, this here nonfictioneer, which one of us do you think can handle your most velvet, most robust, most truthy brew?*

There's a scratch in today's vinyl platter, a Sylvester single from the late 1970s, *You Make Me Feel (Mighty Real).*[1] The record is skipping, and the barista is also stuck. She stares back at the three writers as Sylvester's falsetto repeats, "*tyreal, tyreal, tyreal.*"

Which genre can best handle the truth? I repeat the word "handle" intentionally here. If literary artists had job descriptions, Language Handling would have to be one of the first required skills, as would Story Archiving and Deep Subject Excavation. Genre Policing will probably not be high on the list. Which genre can best handle the truth? This is the wrong question.

Dear Truth-Seeker,

If you come to me worried about the consequences of writing the "truth" about your subject—worried over your husband, your wife, your lover, your children, your neighbors and friends, I will try to convince you to just keep writing. If you write forward you will stop worrying, or at least stop worrying in the way you are worrying now, which is the type of worrying that works against the discovery of writing because your husbands, wives, lovers, children, friends have all crowded into the room of your own that is your process, squeezing out your writing. But if you write past your gripping fears and just keep writing you will stop overthinking what you are or are not revealing on the page and will instead flow with language, sound, voice, and moment, and the subject will organically open before you. You will become so selflessly and even ecstatically caught up in word-that-follows-word-that-follows-word, the brick-after-brick of your subject, what will come to your page will be truths, untruths, and the passageways between, not the truth you were afraid to write but other, realer, and more interior truths, the truths you were afraid to think. You will find truth is not what you thought truth to be. Only then will you really be writing.

We are not yet finished with these three writers in the coffee shop, but allow me to interrupt with another joke, this one popular in Alcoholics Anonymous circles.

QUESTION: How can you tell an alcoholic is lying?
ANSWER: Check to see if her lips are moving.
MY QUESTION: Does this joke still work if we replace alcoholic with writer?

When we talk about literary truth we so often act as if we really believe fiction is the drunken liar, nonfiction the breast-beating missionary, poetry the laughing spirit speeding past in a convertible, her scarf, sheer and malleable as language, as the poetic line, streaming behind.

You see here the reductions and logic flaws that come of defining genre through a righteous lens.

Fiction, nonfiction, and poetry differ not, as we so often seem to think, because of their relationship to truth. The genres differ simply because they are different, each their own distinct brew. SUPPLE. Fiction is the unreeling of action, obstacle, and change.

LOAMY. Poetry is internal awareness opening through language.
BRIGHT. Nonfiction is the attention that illuminates actuality.

But here's where it gets tricky, where I'm tempted to say, "Well we can't really use that language to describe the truth," because all the genres contain one another.

Truth is a jolt, an awakening, a coming to new consciousness. When the blurbs on the back covers read, "this book will change your life," they don't mean the physical trappings—your address, your clothes, your diet—so much as they mean this book will change the direction from which you listen, observe, think. "This book in your hand"—those blurbs should say—"will change the direction of your truth."

Truth is not a genre.

Sylvester rewrote the genre of bodies in the 1970s dance clubs.

Sylvester
performing onstage
in a nightclub, 1970.
Echoes/Redferns/
Getty Images.

One story of the body is the Sylvester's truthy falsetto wail to the mighty real. Today, assuming she/he approved, we might describe Sylvester as transgender, or perhaps just an out and proud gay femme, but the queen died before we got to that conversation. In the 1970s she was the Queen of Disco, a beautiful African American boy-girl with huge gloss-and-kohl-lined-give-good-face eyes, well known for a few hit club tunes still playing in the Chicago Boystown bars near where I live today. But she was also a gospel singer with a wide range and repertoire and described as the most diligent and talented member of the legendary, hippy, gay performance artist troupe the Cockettes (according to filmmaker John Waters, who with his collaborator, the drag performer Divine, hung out in the San Francisco gay performance scene in the 1970s).

There's a story about Sylvester, from before he succumbed to complications of AIDS but after she hit it big and signed with a corporate record company. Sylvester was known for big hair, armfuls of boho bracelets, shimmery flowing hippie-girl gowns and even, sometimes, bejeweled Mata Hari headpieces. Watching Sylvester on YouTube today, we see these intersections of gender-meets-Motown-meets-Diana-Ross-meets-Mama-Cass-meets-Labelle, as she moves through the spangly and platform-shoed multiculti of the dance bars, the singer in alternating male and female-ish drag, though never a drag queen, Sylvester was quick to repeat. John Waters backs him up on this point: "He did it seamlessly. He was never a drag queen. He was a great beauty who came out and I'm sure many straight boys liked him too."[2]

So Sylvester flutters a paper fan while barefoot white girls and black girls perform a choreography in matching satin track jackets and shorts, while a ring of boys of all races in the same shorty shorts but in gym socks and shoes cavort in the background, the world over which the Queen rules. The mighty real here is more and more clear; the formerly hard lines between things are harder and harder to see in the spastic light of the strobes and disco balls.

But the president of the record company wanted Sylvester to tone it down, more in line with Teddy Pendergrass, they instructed. The singer tried; there is film footage of an elegant black man in a finely cut suit, smoking and singing over cocktails, but the new image wasn't the truth. Sylvester, the story goes, marched up to the president's office in full makeup and high chiffon, announcing THIS is my image. THIS is my voice.[3] Long live the mighty real voice of the Queen.

Dear *Flamethrowers*, by Rachel Kushner,

I started out loving you. Oh dear novel, I loved you a lot. So much that I texted some of you to my friends, to tell them how crazy happy I was to be reading you. This passage, for instance, spoken by your protagonist, Reno, a young woman artist in the USA, riding west on an Italian motorcycle, watching a bird, and the road, and her life: "*I thought of Pat Nixon, her gleaming dark eyes and ceremonial outfits stiff with laundry starch and beading. Hair dyed the color of whiskey and whipped into an unmoving wave.*"[4]

This bit of you, oh dear summer novel, published in 2013 but about art and insurrection in 1970s America and Italy, reads to me as the truth because of the way we engage, together, so intimately with America, observing and entering time through the howling images of the day, carrying us into aliveness, saturated with poppy moments of now or then, bringing me into your you-ness dear book, but also into memories of living within the American hall of mirrors.

Another body's view from the American hall of mirrors, one of my own pop culture beloveds, is Sally Bowles, as remade by Bob Fosse, an American choreographer and director of a film based on a play, based on an autobiographical novel by Christopher Isherwood, set in a musical theater rendering of Weimar-era Berlin, as portrayed (inaccurately, according to Isherwood) by gay icon Judy Garland's daughter Liza (with a *z*) Minnelli.

Liza Minnelli in Cabaret, 1972. Bettmann/Corbis/AP Images.

(Because whom might I write of as my inherited American body? TV's Sock-It-to-Me Judy Carne in a yellow bikini and flower power body art, the one pummeled with a comedy water bomb at the end of her weekly "Laugh-In" sketch or, yes, Liza Minnelli's damp bangs, full thighs, and tender exposed flesh where the breast meets the underarm, as she dances in *Cabaret* with that banister back chair or, later still, the shorn and unprotected scalp, squinched face, fret of dyed red hair and heart-shaped open mouth of Cyndi Lauper's *Girls Just Want to Have Fun* days—because the pulsing of change across decades speaks to me of how any woman's passage will be of the body.)

Cyndi Lauper rewrote the genre of bodies on 1980s MTV.

Cyndi Lauper accepting her award for Best Female Video at the MTV Music Awards, 1984. AP Photo/G. Paul Burnett/AP Images.

Dear *Flamethrowers,*

You had me on page 4 but lost me by page 104, when your pictures became brittle. You show us the artists at the parties—the man who won't stop pitching his films made of white light, the woman whose waitress job is an Edward Hopper painting, the woman who puts her live naked genitals in a frame, the lover who makes boxes, the man who carries a pole, each one of them ridiculous, none of them represented as the makers of something real. But in caricature, dear *Flamethrowers,* the people lose breath. You get me back again on page 294, when the middle-aged artist, Sandro, Reno's now-former lover, the one who makes boxes, returns to his body, inviting history, his story of self, back into the rendering, which becomes then supple again with time and body and breath. Dear book, your middle plot, stacked with voices and art, revolutions and countries and cruel Italian mothers, allows dramatic happenstance to get in the way of narrative interior, and this, dear *Flamethrowers*, is when you cease, to me, to be true.

And why is it so hard to write the truth about conceptual artists? They are easy to make fun of, to be sure—with their time-bound walkings and unhangable hangings out; concept is always more ephemeral than object, and yet the conceptual, the happening, the art of being, that new way of seeing, of knowing, is a direct pathway into the truth. Or perhaps not? Perhaps the conceptual is just another surface performance, an empty box posing as the packaging of a new way to know as worthy of mockery as my neighborhood hipster coffee shop? Perhaps *Flamethrowers* isn't about art but fakery? Perhaps young Reno just doesn't know yet that she's the only artist in the mix? But aren't even fakes and posers motivated by some form of wanting?

Christopher Isherwood, one of the first novelists and memoirists to bring not just Sally Bowles but also the bodies we now understand to be homosexual to the literary page, says this about what he calls the "nerve" of the novel, which seems to me the same as what I mean by the truth. "*The most dreadful descriptions of agonizing death are, artistically speaking, just as enjoyable as great love. . . . [The subject] is quite, quite immaterial. The sense of joy, of contact with life, of the vitality of life, can be related to any set of circumstances you choose to name.*"[5]

I venture that this is one of the reasons we read, and write, to gain new and still moving access to the vitality of all forms of life.

Dear *Flamethrowers*,

Your protagonist, that young Reno, named after her neon-desert America hometown, is silent, but not brittle. Her interior frustrates me, but we do see she has one. This young woman entering the minimalist and conceptual art world of the 1970s starts out by making art but also loving that much older Sandro, figure of the New York scene, and is this merely a loving of all that he gives her access to? Though she is the speaker through so many of these pages, we are never entirely sure. Yet we do see her well near the start, leaning forward on this boyfriend's Italian motorcycle, a gift of his aristocratic family business, the business he vacates to make art, all those minimalist boxes, vacant packages we are perhaps meant to understand, while his much younger lover accelerates into the bend of desert time. Body and time, this much reads through.

One early poem by Greek American poet Olga Broumas is one of my own most true, keeping in mind, of course, the slippery aspects of truth, trueness differing in degree and impact, depending on culture, identity, experience, the body of the reader. "Sometimes, as a child" is true, *to me*, because it speaks in some but not all ways (I've never been to Greece and never made love in rain-green Oregon) to my culture, identity, experience, body. She reimagines a lover's childhood dive into a calm Greek sea with the words "*through water so startled / it held the shape of your plunge.*"[6] To me—once an avid swimmer—that elongated moment where the startled water holds the shape of the body having just moved through is the perfect lyric. The image cracks open time, enters the shock of aliveness, and the speaker leaps from ecstatic childhood moment to the resonant adult experience of not just lovemaking but woman-to-woman lovemaking, thus carrying the body across decades of living and immersing adult lesbian experience with childhood awareness, a body continuous rather than a body exiled. This poem tells the truth by giving us back the body as one story, a whole, a completion.

Which returns us to the coffee shop, where the coffee is fine, if a bit sharp, an acquired taste not everyone hangs around to acquire, though to be sure the pricey baked goods are exquisite here. Meanwhile the poet, the novelist, and the essayist still cannot agree. The novelist says truth needs better scenes, the poet wants the language to bring us to see anew, and the essayist wants a more explicit subtext. Sweeter. Sharper. Deeper. But that's too easy. Perhaps this novelist wants a new turn on the old arc, and perhaps this poet wants more of the language of speech, and this essayist might just want movement more like the tension and release of the most urgent story ever told. Buttery. Velvety. Vibrant. True. But they all agree, truth is not a genre, and the best flavor, in any form, comes of a measured manipulation of time. They are certain what we need here is not yet on the menu.

Truth will always be bound to time.

Natasha Trethewey's poem "Theories of Time and Space" appears in *Native Guard*, her collection about history, place, racism, and her mixed-race family, but is reprinted in her book-length cross-genre essay about going home. *Beyond Katrina*, about the posthurricane fates of her people on the Mississippi Coast, west of New Orleans, living in the devastation that followed the storm, includes most poignantly the story of her brother who lost the meager economic gains he'd achieved before the disaster and ended up serving time in jail. The prose in *Beyond Katrina* is wavelike and repetitive, exploring remnants and recoveries, witness and erasure. What is the story we tell about a story? Whom do we remember and what is forgotten? Trethewey describes the essay as "a love letter, a praise song, a dirge." The truth is time changes everything, but we might not remember what the chroniclers of time leave out. "*You can get there from here, though / there's no going home.*"[7]

The book tells the story of Katrina as a metanarrative, just as this poem speaks truth through doublings, through the impossibility of returning home, paired with the inescapabilty of home, this tension shored against the documents and erasures of time. The speaker is both witness and elegy-maker, charged with the complexity of returning to where and what time has made certain she has never been. We have no truth without space and time.

Dear *Flamethrowers*,

Your Reno is fully and truly present on page 29, on that fast Italian motorcycle, as she accidentally breaks a speed record, making her, for a moment, the fastest woman alive. "*I moved through the gears and into fifth. The wind pushed against me, threatening to rip my helmet off, as though I were tilting my face into a waterfall.*"[8]

I love how she remakes herself against moment here, her evocation of speed and time making this passage true, if even just through her submission to the agency of the engine, that power of the futurist perceivers of movement and machine as beauty, *vanitas* plus velocity adding up to narrative change.

Truth. Time. Space. Voice. Truth.

But, again, what of the conceptual center of the artist? What troubles me in *The Flamethrowers* is how Reno begins with an interior artistic voice but then moves into the voice of what some reviewers have described as the novel's many mansplaining men (the condition described so well by Rebecca Solnit in her essay "Men Explain Things to Me"[9]), whose presence or absence, devotion or betrayal, define her through Reno's flat reportage in much of the 190 middle pages, those rooms full of artists who chatter but do not make, the empty conception of their conceptual art, the space where what Isherwood called the joy and terror of aliveness is absent.

I can't help but compare Kushner's artists with the protagonist in Don DeLillo's *The Body Artist*—his curious allegorical ghost story about a woman's relationship with the strange and not fully existing man that enters her summer home and becomes her charge, her lover, and finally her art. The reader does not become aware until late in the novella that her strange and hidden relationship has become her art making, when finally we read a review of a body-art performance we never see but have lived through in the pages that precede: "*The power of the piece is Hartke's body. . . . What begins in solitary otherness becomes familiar and even personal. It is about how we are when we are not rehearsing who we are.*"[10]

The Body Artist is not realism, but as a book it's true because the conceptual foundation of the performance is bound to conceptual interrogation and so becomes an opening, a reclaiming, a reseeing realer than the seeing that came before.

In his book-length series of essays, *White Girls*—part criticism, part essay, part veiled-yet-intimate memoir, part biofiction—Hilton Als redefines the meaning of whiteness, girlness, white girlness, and any other category having to do with the culture-made colors and culture-hushed proclivities of the human body.

On the subject of truth—most particularly the truth of voice, intersections, contradictions, and fluid meanings—Hilton Als is everything. In his recalibration of the term "white girl," his subjects may be actual white girls, might be dead screen divas, might be straight black men who identify with white lesbians and sleep with straight white women, might be Michael Jackson in all his pop genius and misbegotten body erasure, and most certainly might be early Truman Capote, as captured by the languorous, come-hither author photo on the dust jacket of his first book, *Other Voices, Other Rooms*. Als writes, "*the watered or greased hair flattening the top of his head with the light hitting it just so, his eyebrows plucked or raised in mild astonishment, something to be fucked somehow—was too much for a number of his peers who did not possess the kind of will it took to deconstruct their bodies.*"[11]

I'm not concerned here with whether or not Als is correct in his interpretation of Capote or any visual version Capote offered of himself over the time of his career, from his nubile beginnings to the booze-spotted cartoon of himself gesticulating from one of the comfy chairs, stage right of the old *Johnny Carson Show*—the first image in my life, along with that of Liberace, I saw of obvious homosexuality anywhere, and no wonder so many of us who were young in that time had to overcome a stumbling and unintentionally comic inner script before we were able to come out to ourselves.

The inner truth of Truman Capote, if such could be determined, even by Truman himself, will forever elude us. The actor Philip Seymour Hoffman, who portrayed him on film, might be the only one who could come close, and he's lost to us now as well, his end quicker, but of similar means, as Capote's.

But Als is not trying to psychoanalyze the author so much as he means to interrogate the meaning of the author's performance as author, as well as all the raced and gendered influences that create the meaning of images, as viewed by all of us on this faraway side of the liberation movements yet to happen when Capote's author photo was first taken. Truth is time plus place plus change plus body plus voice.

Dear *Flamethrowers*,

Yes, I DO see the parody and humor of the excesses of your Warholian figures whose ideas have more texture than their works. And I do see a woman entering a male realm in the time and space that didn't invite her, these being the sock-it-to-me-girl days, flower power still wriggling her painted belly. And I DO see Reno's identity absorbed rather than taken. Through the power of passivity, of nonaction, does Reno gain access to life through the actions of others? Does Reno gain place or lose her own internal space? I see this young American Reno, on the clock of the decades, caught between "Sock It to Me, Baby" and "Girls Just Want to Have Fun." Her speed is internal, her engagement a silent sponge. I've gone back and back over what to make of her. I want her to throw a leg over a chair, have her show us that soft sexy spot on the top of the thigh, flip off her hard-to-love mansplainers, dance any dance of her own making, and yet I see historical truth in her waiting, her internal record taking, witness on delay. Reno does, after all, near the finish of your pages, dear book, end up back on a motorcycle, traversing Manhattan with an engine between her legs, as the rest of New York City is lost in blackout. Is her bike light the only illumination the broken city allows? Is Reno a winner, the only artist after all? Is it my own former self I really want to slap for all the unchoosing of my worst choices? Dear *Flamethrowers*, is this how you mean to make me feel?

I don't believe inaction is agency. I do believe performance is more than posture. I take my coffee strong and roasted so dark it stripes my lips with grounds, which I understand is not everyone's cup of tea.

QUESTION: How do you know a book is lying?

ANSWER: Well books might not lie exactly, at least no more than people commonly do, but sometimes authors do omit, or hold back, or simply fail to embody all there is in any life. Sometimes, most times, I fail on all these counts. So how do we know when our writing is not true? When the lips are moving but the desire is stuck in place?

The artifice of 1970s queer glam art world is surely some of what rewrote the genre of Sylvester.

Sylvester James with a blond woman and man, Los Angeles, 1972. Richard Creamer/ Michael Ochs Archives/Getty Images.

Dear Sylvester,

You always stop me cold, whenever I hear your voice, whenever I hear those mighty real words, still cutting through queer urban time and space, reminding us of all our departures and arrivals, your performance still a literature of the body, not just a dance anthem, not just a love song, but a clarion call for visibility. "I'm NOT a drag queen. I'm Sylvester," you told Joan Rivers in 1987 on her short-lived late night talk show, just a year before the end of your life.[12] Your saying so is the realness, and the realness of many others who come into focus again here, for a moment. Some of what I love in you, if I may love you, is so personal, as my own story will always be that of coming to queerness before there was the Internet, before your explicit queerness or anyone else's explicit queerness was regularly on TV.

Still I resist appropriating your body for my own purposes. My own womanhood grew so slowly through these years, through the sock-it-to-me girls and fleshy cinema cabaret singers made by gay men (from Capote and Isherwood, Holly Golightly and Sally Bowles), then remade again for audiences who don't see what's queer here. My own liberation is carried best, and still, by Cyndi Lauper's lower middle-class 1980s happy girl urban parade. So I'm good—but Sylvester, so many bodies are still too unseen, still balancing in gold platform sandals on the precipice of their self-made lives, the edges of those stairs that lit up in the wake of your tread. Too many more, like you, have been dead now for over twenty-five years. Hilton Als describes how you continue: *"In New Orleans, the late Sylvester glowed like an angel as one of his old videos played in a dark, wooden, bar, the rain falling out of a sun-bright sky."*[13]

As Cyndi Lauper still rewrites herself.

Cyndi Lauper at age fifty, on tour in Mansfield, Massachusetts, 2004. AP Photo/Robert E. Klein/AP Images.

Dear Sylvester,

You stop me cold every time as well, because you showed us the best performance is not merely a gesticulation, is more revelation than mask—*I'm NOT a drag queen; I'm Sylvester*—because you are body plus intersection plus language plus fabulous plus the unrelenting hereness of voice; because you are an angel, the angel of mighty real. Why is that so hard to write about?

Dear *Flamethrowers*,

I love you enough to have given you my summer, yet you break my heart when you stop throwing the flame. Where is the artistic logic, the artist realness, of these artists in Reno's new world, whether misguided or genius? What is the texture of the world inside them, their intersections of voice, not just their pomposity, their guns and their affairs, not just their Italian aristocrat parents and their place in the intrigue of European class wars? What of the truth seeking of actual conceptual artists, especially the women, such as the way Yoko Ono, in 1964, performed resistance through intentional vulnerability in *Cut Piece*, when she asked strangers to come up to the stage to cut off hunks of her clothing; the way Marina Abramović performed love through fleeting intimacy with strangers in *The Artist Is Present*, when she sat in a MoMA gallery and stared in patrons' eyes until some actually broke into tears. *Flamethrowers*, I love you finally more than I don't, but not because of your unlikely plot and unlikeable artists. I love for your attempt, for your horizons, for the truth of that young absorbent woman who does notice that performance is not always an empty box, but can be too an interpretation of breath, the unrehearsed act, the femme tough whiskey of Pat Nixon's hair.

As Yoko Ono still remakes herself.

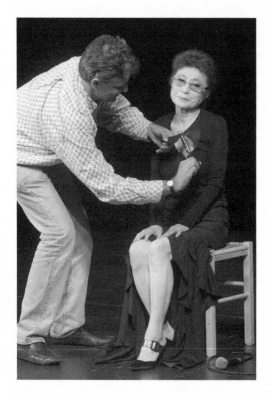

Yoko Ono repeating *Cut Piece* at age seventy. Paris, 2003. AP Photo/ Michel Euler/AP Images.

Truth is not factual. Truth is not static, or singular, or located on the surface. The best truths might be lies, as long as they are not the lies authors tell to themselves.

A poet, and a novelist, and an essayist walk into a coffee shop. By the time they walk out the record has stopped skipping, and they are wearing one another's clothes. They've agreed to overlook a few hipster pretentions and try harder to notice the actual subtleties between all those fancy beans, and they've agreed to use a new language to describe the work. The loamy is supple, the velvety now bright, but their tongues have failed them, as Rebecca Solnit has written in *The Faraway Nearby*, her book about stories that nest in stories, that nest in stories: "*Is it that the tongue fails where the fingers succeed, in telling truths so lengthy and nuanced?*"[14]

Not news that writers are not at their best when they are talking, and in fact these three have stopped talking altogether. *You make me feel* is what each of them is thinking, about one another, about their hard-won nuances—but realness, that gender bender, that pulsing shifting reversing current running under genre, that's only the horizon. We'll never get there, but we write because we live to try, and until we try we won't really be writing.

NOTES

1. Sylvester, *You Make Me Feel (Mighty Real)*, vinyl recording (San Francisco: Fantasy Records, 1978).

2. Sylvester, *Mighty Real*, directed by Tim Smyth, 2008, YouTube video, 11:21, accessed February 2, 2015, www.youtube.com/watch?v=r3lww-USS7Y&feature=youtu.be.

3. Ibid.

4. Rachel Kushner, *The Flamethrowers: A Novel* (New York: Scribner, 2013), 4.

5. Christopher Isherwood, *Isherwood on Writing*, ed. James J. Berg (Minneapolis: University of Minnesota, 2007), 66.

6. Olga Broumas, *Beginning with O* (New Haven: Yale University Press, 1977), 1–2.

7. Natasha D. Trethewey, "Theories of Time and Space," in *Beyond Katrina: A Meditation on the Mississippi Gulf Coast* (Athens: University of Georgia Press, 2010), 66, 5–6.

8. Kushner, *Flamethrowers*, 29.

9. Rebecca Solnit, "Men Explain Things to Me," in *Men Explain Things to Me* (Chicago: Haymarket, 2014).

10. Don DeLillo, *The Body Artist: A Novel* (New York: Scribner, 2001, 111–12.

11. Hilton Als, *White Girls* (San Francisco: McSweeney's, 2013), 95–97.

12. Sylvester, *Mighty Real*.

13. Hilton Als, "Versions of Masculinity," *Et Als: My Life in Culture*, June 27, 2011, www.hiltonals.com/tag/sylvester/.

14. Rebecca Solnit, *The Faraway Nearby* (New York: Penquin, 2013), 64.

Transgender Day of Remembrance   *A Found Essay*

Compiled and arranged from the "Remarks" sections of "List of 226 Reported Murdered Trans Persons from October 1st 2013 to September 30th 2014" (2014), a report by Transrespect versus Transphobia Worldwide, http://www .transrespect-transphobia.org/uploads/downloads/2014/TDOR2014/TDOR -14-Namelist-EN.pdf.

Brunete was beaten to death with a stick. The victim was shot by two men on a motorcycle in front of a motel. The victim was shot in the head. The suspected murderer is a former military police man. A neighbor heard the victim scream at night and saw two men walking out of the victim's room but could not remember their faces. The case is under investigation. The victim was found tied to a chair with multiple stab wounds in her abdomen. Police reported that the trans person was well known and admired and murdered by her lover with 7 stabs. A 14 year-old trans person was found strangled. The victim was stabbed 8 times. The victim was shot by a man on a motorbike. The victim was shot two times by two men on a motorbike. The victim was found in a lake. She was a Romani person. The body of the victim was found handcuffed. The body of the victim was found dismembered. The body of the victim was found handcuffed. The victim was a person of color. The undignified way her burned body was dumped in a trash bin indicates transgender hostility. Rosa was a person of color and of Indonesian descent. Police is investigating a possible hate crime. Police is investigating the crime as a possible homophobic hate crime. Alondra was a person of color. Police suspects that more than one person was involved in what they describe as a barbaric murder. The victim was slaughtered, beaten and stoned; the corps was found half naked in a wasteland. The face of the victim was smashed by the client with a stone after having sexual intercourse. The victim's body was found with tied hands in plastic bag on the road. Investigations revealed that several cars had run over the corpse. Noe Lopez was attacked at a sex worker's place, forced into a vehicle by a group of armed men wearing bulletproof vests and balaclavas. Amnesty International see this murder in connection with a series of murders of sex workers in San Pedro Sula. The note in the newspaper reports that the homicide is the product of insecurity and violence lived in the city. Sanchez was on her way to a party dressed in a skirt, when she was attacked by two men who stabbed her to death. Belizean LGBT NGO UNIBAM called the murder a hate-crime. Sanchez had been harassed and received death threats before in the days leading to her murder. The victim was killed with an axe after having a dispute with a young man in a bar. Witnesses reported that the victim was verbally assaulted and later shot. The victim was set on fire by four persons, and died from burn injuries in a hospital. Buxexa was a person of color. The body of the victim showed signs of torture. The police believe that the murder took place because the victim was a trans person. Strangers shot towards the victim's house, causing her death. According to a newspaper report the victim was tortured and beaten to death by a lawmaker and four of his assistants accusing the victim of theft of a mobile phone. The murder is described as a barbaric crime. The victim was dismembered and her face totally destroyed with a knife. The victim was killed by a 14 year-old minor. The police is investigating the crime as a possible hate crime as this is the second stabbing of a trans person within one month and under similar circumstances. The victim was beaten to death by a group of people and found hanged. The victim was a person of color. Raissa was shot six times on the head and thorax. The victim was using a public phone when she was shot to death with 10 shots by two men on a motorbike. Denise was tortured with the peak of a bottle. The victim was stabbed 11 times. She was attacked by a man in a group of 5 men. The murderer claimed that the victim criticized on his unimpressive sex they just had. He was angry and then beat her with a hardwood and stole her valuables. The victim was found wrapped in a black plastic bag. The NGO Red Umbrella reports that Sevda's murderer was her boyfriend, who fled to Serbia from where he called the police and confessed the murder. Police reports that the murder was the result of fights between trans people. "Alex", an 8 year-old child moved six months ago to Rio de Janeiro to live with the father. The father has beaten the child to death to "teach him to behave like a man", as the child did belly-dancing, wore female clothing, and loved dish-washing. Camila was executed with 15 shots. CCTV footage shows how a trans sex worker is approached by a man sitting in a car and then shot from the inside of the car. The victim was stabbed to death and her personal belongings were stolen such as her laptop computer. The murderer is still unknown and the case is under investigation. The victim's body showed signs of torture. Andressa was attacked by several persons at a cemetery and stabbed 15 times. Rose Maria was stabbed 12 times. The murder happened several weeks after the implementation of the so-called Anti-Gay-Bill in Uganda. Queen, a trans sex worker, has been attacked by a guy, whom her friends believe she met at a bar. During the attack she called her friends by phone saying "the guy is beating me, the guy is killing me." She was found later by her friends with severe wounds and signs of torture (cuts from a bottle on her body and in her anus). Queen was hospitalized and died several days later. Coco was a well-known drag queen. The victim's body was thrown to the street, allegedly the police saw the event and did not intervene. Vanessa received death threats before she was murdered. Paulete was executed with 15 shots, when she approached a client in a car at night. The murder was reported as homophobic hate murder. Dani was beaten in the face, before she was shot to death. Parts of the body of the victim have been found in different garbage bags at a cemetery. The skin of the torso was torn off. The suspect is a special force police officer, who wanted to pay less for a service and killed Jade Esmeralda inside his car, when she didn't agree. Giovana was a person of color. The victim was found stabbed to death in her condominium unit. The victim was beaten to death by a group of people in the middle of a street at night. The victim was hit in the head. Giovanna was stabbed 11 times. The victim presented stabs all around the body. She was murdered by two clients in her own apartment due to an argument over the price for the sexual service. The victims body showed signs of physical violence and was hit on the head. The victims body showed multiple wounds on its body. The victim was stoned. Nicole was shot five times in the head. The victim was found stabbed four times and her body was burned. The victim was a person of color. The arrested suspect offended Jenifer and two other trans women who were sex workers. Later he returned with another man in a car and stabbed Jenifer to death. The victim was a person of color. She was shot by two men. The victim was found tied up and showed signs of torture, with her face burnt on purpose. Marcia was executed with a shot in the head. The victim's body was found in a pit and showed signs of torture, plus a shot to the head. Other bodies were found in the pit. The victim was a person of color. The victim was found tied with multiple stab wounds and with her genitals exposed. The victim was a person of color. Shayara was found beaten to death with a stick on a hill in Rio de Janeiro in the morning. A news magazine reported that she provided sexual services to a policeman the night before. The victim was a person of color. She was found burned behind a garbage bin. The victim was a person of color. The victim was raped before she was beaten to death with a stick. The victim's body was beaten multiples time on the face. The suspected murderer strangled Kellen and threw her body into the swimming pool of the hotel. Makelly was found naked and with signs of hanging. Police is searching for a man who is chasing and killing trans persons. Two men in a car approached Dennysi and shot four times at her. Dafine was walking in the street with another trans person, when two men on a motorbike approached them and shot Dafine to death. They also tried to shoot the other trans person, but failed. The victim was having a drink in a bar, when two men on motorcycles passed by and shot her in the head. The victim was suffocated with a plastic bag. The victim's body was found with both hands and feet tied-up. The victim was stabbed 15 times. The victim's body was found in female underwear and as a newspaper reports "without eyes." Two other trans women in Detroit were shot within days of the murder inside Palmer Park. Geovana was stabbed 6 times. The victim was found inside of her own apartment. The suspected murderer had an argument with Alexandra in the street and shot her in the back only steps away from her home. Karen was seriously injured and thrown out of a moving car by a client. Cris was shot 4 times by a man passing by in a car. The Police affirm that the victim was raped before being killed. The victim was walking with another person and was stoned, causing her to die. The victim's body was found in her apartment. Her body presented 18 stab wounds. Mahadevi was impaired and pushed out of a moving train by two adolescents. It seems to be that the aggressors harassed the victim, who tried to hide, but they killed her with a shotgun. Bili was standing with two other trans people near a bus stand, when a man namely Raja started misbehaving with Bili and got annoyed and stabbed and injured her. Bili died in the hospital. The body of the victim was found floating in a creek. Bruna was shot by a man on a motorbike, when talking with a client in front of a motel. A local LGBT NGO speculates that the motive could have been "transmisogyny."

Light, from Faraway Places

And now a thing that can't be told. Not because I won't tell, but because the thing that wants telling is only partly revealed, a girl in a small room, flickering while she waits—for, clearly, she's waiting—but for what? It's impossible to know because the girl comes undone when I look too long in her direction. Like a ghost sign, she is. An old sign painted on the side of buildings, advertising turn-of-the-century hotels and dry-goods stores and Sweet Caporal cigarettes, the letters gauzy and half-gone, the images occasionally layer on one another so that signs for flour and aluminum castings blur together. But they persist, ghost signs, so that with patience and adequate desire, the wash of white on brick can still be read sometimes.

Step back and the room blooms into a bathroom. Turn your head to the left and it's clear the child sits on the toilet—lid closed, she makes it into a perch. There's comfort in her sitting, the sense that this is a girl who spends great portions of time in the bathroom, the only private room in the house, a respite from a pack of sisters and brothers, refuge from the slant and motion of the house. But no. This is something else. Someone else's bathroom, a quiet house, dark except for the trickle of light filtered through muted glass. She sits on the lid, legs pulled up at times or dangling against the cool porcelain bowl, as she makes a study of the floor, the countertop, the ceiling tiles. She looks into the surface of things, stunned, as if she already understands that the world she inhabits is not her own. The vanity's counter is constructed of cream-colored plastic, hard as ivory, with gold flecks floating throughout. The window glass is etched and frosted so that the view from outside is mottled, making the room a place in which to hide. Shapes like stars hang in the glass, the girl on the toilet notices. She seems not to have to pee and does not know much about prayer but clearly the room with a sun-starved plant on the windowsill is a sanctuary. From her family or something else?

Such girls know to beware of boys, to steer clear of men, but people being people and girls being the least among them, they are occasionally snared.

This is not high drama. It is only a rule of the forest—those outside the forest are naturally more surprised than those who must learn to live within in the heart of woods. The girl is snared, of course, which is to say that there will come a day when she's made to understand that she is more hard plastic than gold fleck—but will it be this day—her legs still too short to reach the floor from her toilet lid perch?

The moment matters. Why else would it rise and flare? For all its sloshy flailing, memory is not accidental. Memory is not the drunk girl at the party. Or, if she is, she's of the perceptive variety, the sort of drunk who spills soft secrets into the air. Memory does, in fact, know what she's about, even as she issues her unmoored invitations, returning us to the salt of early oceans, the lull of nursery rhymes, paths once traveled through green fields, the feel of August surging, insects and corn tassels brushing against bare legs as we return to a house lit against the coming night.

What does she wear, our girl? The colors shimmer and fade, everything yellowing under the filter of long-gone days. It must be summer, for how saturated the air. Perhaps she's outfitted in a pair of shorts, a blouse with a missing button. It's possible the day has found her in a ruffled dress or a new denim skirt—there are such days in nearly every life, even if they are rare. It's more likely, though, that the cloth covering her body is broken with wear. Only the strawberry hair seems certain. Fine and slippery, it falls into her eyes as she bends to make a fuller examination of the floor.

Later, this same girl will thumb through catalogs to choose the most glorious of tulip bulbs to set in the ground. Later, she will find a man who carries with him oil paints with which to fashion for them both a new sky. Later, there will be crisp dresses, if she wants, and buttons made of shell, more fine things than she could ever hope to count. There's goodness to come, yes, and maybe her looking so deeply into the grain of things allows her to see it mapped out in the ceiling tiles, the room lying like an open palm waiting to be read.

But what is she waiting for? This child staring now at the plant on the sill, its leaves faded for lack of pure light. It's possible she waits for the sound of his voice, for there's the slightest suggestion of a boy in the next room, older and growing restless, as the girl traces the movement of stars in the glass and contemplates the mystery of glitter trapped inside the laminate countertop—how can something so brilliant be bound? How can stars be caught in panels of frosted glass? Will it always be like this, the wondering and the waiting? She's delaying perhaps, or dallying—does he call out to her finally, say to her *enough already, come here*—or is this a different place, a different day and year altogether? Her sister might wait downstairs while the girl attempts to master the only universe they know. It's possible, of course, that the girl, with her limited understanding of botany and plant cycles, waits for a flower to bloom from the ragged plant while savoring the moment before the boy in the next room says her name—not quite like a command, but neither like a song. Or else she's waiting for the world to tilt on its axis. For the days to flutter forward and reveal themselves. For something to loosen with a sudden lack of gravitational pull, allowing her to free-float to other planets or to visit the other side of this one, which can look so different when the angle changes—the gold flecks beginning to spin and lift themselves from the hard plastic in which they once seemed so firmly contained.

Good-bye to All That

For me, New York ended as soon as it began. The day I moved into my first apartment, I discovered that the reason the kitchen had looked so big was that there was no refrigerator. I also discovered that water didn't flow out of any of the taps. Sal, the plumber who scolded me for letting him in before I asked if he was the plumber, stood in the doorway to my bedroom after he fixed the sinks. I was staring at a wall, holding a paintbrush and a can of paint. He asked, "Did they teach you to paint like that in college?"

So Sal painted my room while I listened to the story of his life and the story of my neighborhood. It had been Finnish when Sal moved there from Sicily as a young boy, and then it was Italian, and then Jewish, and now it was Puerto Rican. After he finished painting my room, Sal drove around looking for used refrigerators, found one, fixed it, put it on my front stoop, rang the bell, and drove away. By the time I got downstairs, the refrigerator had already been stolen.

But that is not the way it really happened. That is how I learned to tell the story of my life in New York. I learned to make my experience of being young and new to the city sound effortless and zany. It was not.

I didn't mention that I couldn't go down to get the refrigerator Sal found because it was impossible for me to carry it up four flights of stairs alone. It was taken only after I left it on the stoop for an entire day while I tried to think of someone I could ask for help. I didn't mention the animal-piss stink of my room or the extreme aching sense of helplessness that overcame me when I realized that I would have to buy a refrigerator. I didn't mention that I couldn't hear out of my right ear because it became clogged from crying. I didn't mention all the time I wasted in bed, staring at the ceiling, debilitated with dread. Or the time I wasted trying to find out if landlords were required to provide refrigerators in units over a certain size. Or the call to my landlord, when he laughed at me, saying, "Look, either you take the place as it is, or you find somewhere else to live." I didn't mention hurting my hand when I punched the door frame in frustration. Or my sickening realization that Sal was helping me because I was white. He made me aware of this fact with a barrage of racial slurs that I failed to respond to with anything but silence. Silence because I needed his help and I suddenly understood the contract.

"You gotta get a better lock on that door," Sal advised. I pointed out that I didn't own anything except a bed. "Yeah, well these Puerto Ricans will steal that bed right out from under you," he said. Silence.

I ran into Sal once more before I left the city. He was getting into a car in Brooklyn's Chinatown with his daughter, who was not white at all. Sal, like everyone else in New York, was not exactly who the story might lead you to believe he was.

I hardly even knew the story back then—I had only a vague sense that the heroine was young and that the moral had something to do with being in the right place at the right time. I was ready for anything. I moved to the city during a record heat wave and calmly braced myself for an entire summer of filling the bathtub with ice cubes to cool my body at night. But it was never again that hot in New York. And I learned every detail of the story just as fast as I discovered its falsehood.

I remember a moment from my first days in the city when I was lost in Brooklyn somewhere around Avenue J. Sweat was trickling over my breastbone and the sun was burning my scalp. I couldn't identify the exact nature of any of the businesses I was walking past, but they seemed to deal in car parts. Dozens of taillights in all different sizes and shades of red hung, sparkling, from chain-link fences. Suddenly, I felt a desperate need to call my mother. I tried three pay phones and lost five quarters before I found one that worked. When I got her on the line, all I could do was lean against the searing metal phone booth and sob.

Not that I wasn't dazzled by the city. Every nerve in my body was electrified by New York. I was on an endless sidewalk surrounded by bare bulbs and whistles and sudden flocks of pigeons and huge fading stretches of concrete. I believe that I will never feel like that again—so raw and so moved.

I was always lost in New York, even after I stopped walking east when I intended to walk west. There were just ways in which I fundamentally did not know where I was. I grew up north of the city, in the Hudson River valley. But the water that flowed through upstate New York might as well have been a different substance from the water that flowed into New York Harbor. Where I came from, the river smelled distinctly of crayfish and grew a leafy skin in the summer. In the winter the ice groaned and cracked under the weight of all the surrounding silence. I would not have had any trouble believing, when

I arrived in New York, that the water in the harbor had all been brought in on barges. Everything about the city seemed at least that absurd.

I was naive enough then to imagine that living a few blocks from the harbor would be pleasant. And I was innocent enough not to know that I should not walk down the street carrying two melons in my arms at about the level of my chest—even if melons were two for a dollar. From the roof of my building in Brooklyn I could see giant barges silhouetted against the hazy pink horizon at dusk. I tried to walk down to the water and promptly dead-ended at a huge, windowless building labeled Terminal Warehouse. On my way back, a bus driver at a red light yelled to me that I shouldn't be walking around down there. I got on the bus just to humor him and rode past train yards bordered with barbed wire. Then I took a train to Coney Island.

The station at Coney Island was half-charred from a fire decades ago and packed with giant inflatable pink seals for sale. An abandoned wooden box read, "The world's tiniest horse!" Caramel apples were seventy-five cents and the din of the fair games was intolerable. One freak-show announcer screamed, "If you love your family, you will take them to see the two-headed baby!" It was gross and crazy and base—it was everything I would ever love about the city. The beach was packed with naked flesh and smelled like beer and mango. And the Wonder Wheel inspired real wonder as I rose up over Brooklyn in a swinging metal cage.

Did I know it would all cost something sooner or later? All the bewilderment and disorientation? I'm not sure. But I remember the moment when I realized exactly what it had already cost me. A friend and I thought it would be fun to go ice-skating in Prospect Park, but, like most things in New York that are supposed to be fun, it was miserable. The rented skates were as dull as spoons, the ice was slush, and it was so crowded that all we could do was keep ourselves standing and try to avoid being burned by cigarettes while we were pushed and shoved in a slow circle. We had both been very good ice-skaters as children.

I arrived in New York at twenty-one, with a poor sense of direction and a worse sense of time. I set my watch first five minutes fast, then ten, then fifteen. I was only going to stay six months. I stayed three years, and I never stopped thinking about leaving. But when I left, I left my entire life behind. I have to explain to you why I no longer live in New York, but first I have to explain to myself why I stayed so long. Because what I want to say about living there is that it is not, as the mythology goes, more real than anyplace else. In some ways, it is less.

I noticed during my time in New York that many of the people I met there had a habit of describing how miserable they were, then arguing that they couldn't leave the city because it was so wonderful. When someone who spends the better part of every day in a cubicle and only occasionally makes it out to sit in a loud, dull bar tells me that she is living in the city for "the pace, the excitement, the culture, the—you know—stimulation," I have trouble fully believing her.

The myth of New York seems to be sustained by the fact that so many people who live there are from somewhere else. They come to the city and immediately dedicate themselves to making it the city of their imagination. The—you know—glittering city of endless opportunity that oozes riches and delights for the young and talented. I also came from somewhere else. Somewhere not far away but so clearly foreign that people often asked what country I was from. I always felt like an expatriate in the city, and I came knowing just a few of the stories that everyone has been told.

By now I consider almost everything that is often said about New York to be false. To begin with, the city is not that big or that worldly. An astonishing number of people who live there rarely leave their borough, let alone the country. And if you are part of the elite, as Joan Didion found, New York is like a small town. A tiny population of New York is rich or famous, and much of the rest of the city is in service to that population. For most people, even the elite, it is a city of drudgery. You sweat in the hot station, then you shiver in the crowded train, then you walk for ten blocks without an umbrella through a pounding summer thunderstorm . . . and you do this with desperation, because you have no other obvious choice. You do it every day. There is a series of statements on the supporting beams of one of the tunnels under Forty-Second Street that reads,

> Overslept,
> so tired.
> If late,
> get fired.
> Why bother?
> Why the pain?
> Just go home
> do it again.

Those words always affected me, although I never worked long enough at any one job to fully understand that particular brand of drudgery. I read them as words of caution. My work in New York was, like the work of everyone else I knew, whatever I could find. I watered plants in the offices of TV *Guide* at one point, I cleaned a bookstore twice a week for a while, I was a waitress for a few days, I did inspections of community gardens under the parks department for quite some time, I proofread just long enough to learn proofreaders' marks, I did transcriptions now and then, I opened mail, I taught writing for a couple of years, I temped, and I was briefly an editorial assistant at a major publishing house. My job as an editorial assistant was by far the most menial work I ever did in the city. I remember it mostly as a series of pointless trips in elevators. And I remember the way my friend described a similar job: "I professionally destroy paper clips."

But I still believed in the mystical power of the city to transform me into a writer—a real writer. I wasn't sure exactly how this alchemy would happen, which is one reason I kept changing jobs, but I was convinced that just living in the city could make my writing more legitimate. By the time I left New York, I had learned that the distinction between a writer and a real writer is superficial. And I suddenly understood the advice that more established writers had been giving me all along. "Move somewhere else—anywhere else," one journalist had recommended soon after I moved to New York. "Pick any other city."

There is a popular legend of New York as the gritty city of hard knocks and rough neighborhoods and real danger and police chases and wild nights. I suppose that watching a bum with no legs being dragged out of his stinking pile of blankets by four policemen is gritty, but it lacks any of the dirty romance implied by the word. Standing for an entire day in a clinic crowded with sick babies and pregnant women because you don't have health insurance and you've been ill for several months also lacks romance. So does spending hours on the telephone, waiting for the chance to explain that you were billed twice for the month of June. One of my most vivid memories from that first year in New York is the smell of the oil soap I always used to clean my floors. While I was on hold with the telephone company or the gas company or the credit-card company, I would sit on the floor, examining the splinters in the wood and inhaling the strange scent of oil soap.

Not even the dangers of New York are what the story dictates. I was harassed by children nearly as often as I was harassed by men in the city. I remember smiling at an eight-year-old boy on the train who stared at me stonily before he half closed his eyes and slowly ran his tongue across his upper lip as he fingered his crotch. While I was working for the parks department, I spent most of my time in neighborhoods imagined as "rough," where one or two people might ask me if I was lost. Often I *was* lost, and I got directions that were usually wrong from people who were always nice. The worst thing I was ever threatened with in New York was a lighter. And it was terrifying. But the man standing in the middle of the sidewalk in front of me, flicking his lighter, didn't hurt me. He stared at me and said softly, "How ya doing, princess?" I told him that I had been working all day and that I was very tired, and he said he knew how I felt and walked away.

I often woke before dawn and could not fall back to sleep. I lay there listening to the car alarms cycle through all their different sounds while my heart raced for no reason. It is hard for me to separate my experience of living in New York from the sensation of reaching the limits of my own independence. I was excruciatingly lonely, and everything was unfamiliar and difficult. But, in a way, I was living my dream. Long after I discarded every illusion I ever had about New York, I still treasured the empty fantasy of complete autonomy.

If I had entertained more illusions, I might have been able to stay in New York longer. I might have even considered myself happier. But I was not tickled by the daily opportunity to change trains in Rockefeller Center, I did not feel lucky to be surrounded by merchandise I couldn't afford, and I had absolutely no interest in the nightlife, whatever that is.

I didn't participate in the New York of the collective imagination, which may be one reason that I don't believe in it. My interactions with people I didn't know were always brief and often painful. One afternoon I crashed my bike into a man just as he stepped off the curb in Chinatown. Our heads slammed together, and I fell onto the sidewalk. For an instant I lay there, looking up at an advertisement for Asian escorts on the side of a building, smelling the reek of the fish market and listening to the humming motor of a tiny scuba diver who swam in a washtub next to me. The man I had hit was holding his forehead and seemed to be getting more and more agitated as people with orange bags of bok choy crowded around me to make sure I was all right while they left him standing alone. Scared and still seeing a few swimming lights from the impact, I got onto my bike quickly and rode away. I stopped after a few blocks and cried hysterically in dismay. No one looked at me. In ways I find hard to explain, most of the interactions I had in New York were like this one. Which may be why I always felt more comfortable simply observing other people's lives.

I watched everything carefully and never quite lost the conviction that I was missing something. *So, what's so good about all this?* I kept thinking. I suspected that there was a secret I hadn't been told. I was convinced that I had only one chance to do the right things and meet the right people and that I would surely fail. Everything was irrevocable, and nothing was within reach. The peculiar paralysis I felt when I first came to the city was mostly from the sense that every decision I made would last the rest of my life. I know now that I was right and I was wrong. Success and failure were the terms in which young people who had just moved to the city spoke. It was not a place to live as much as it was a test or a game. I despise both. "Why don't you leave?" I asked people endlessly, even though I could not yet explain why I didn't leave. "Because I don't want to admit that I failed," one friend said. "Because I have to prove to myself that I can do this." By the time I left New York, I knew that success and failure are silly terms in which to speak of living a life.

I read Joan Didion's essay "Good-bye to All That" before I ever saw the trenches of New York. All I remember of that first reading is that I didn't like the title. I knew nothing at all back then. I did not know that I would return to that essay again and again, and that I would eventually feel compelled to rewrite it.

But I remember, distinctly, walking down Fourth Avenue in Brooklyn for the first time, past the car wash and the huge windowless warehouses and the brick buildings bristling with TV antennas and the billboard that read, "Se Hacen." I looked around and thought, with wonder, *I'm going to love all this someday.* And I did.

Still, I feel jarred by "I♥NY" bumper stickers and repulsed by "I♥NY" T-shirts. Especially now that the slogan has become so grossly fetishized, like the flag. I don't want the New York I loved to be confused with the New York the T-shirts love. That isn't the same city. I didn't love the *New Yorker*'s New York or the New York of the *New York Times*. I didn't love Joan Didion's New York, or anyone else's fantasy of the place. I loved my own experience of the city, which was rarely what I expected it to be. I loved the people I knew there, who were unlike any character in any TV show or movie set in New York that I have ever seen. I was most comfortable with people for whom New York was not a mirage, and I most trusted people who hated it there.

New York took everything I had. I moved four times, and each time I owned less. I left New York without even a bed. I no longer had potted plants, or framed pieces of art, or a snapshot of my father. I remember the moment when I threw that snapshot out. I was sifting through my things before another hurried move with a borrowed car, and I looked at the photo, thinking, *I don't really need this—he still looks almost the same.* That was just before I noticed that my father had gone gray.

In New York, even one snapshot became too much of a burden to carry from one place to another. The mementos of my childhood began to weigh like lead. And so did my adolescent preoccupation with the real. Like many young people who go to college immediately after high school, I had learned to talk about the real world as if it were in an entirely different universe from the one I lived in. With the blind enthusiasm and embarrassing ignorance of a colonial explorer, I left college determined to discover the real world. I didn't just want to live there—I wanted to be made real myself. This might be the saddest part of my story, because New York did not make me feel more legitimate or real. Actually, it made me feel as if l barely existed. As I wandered through the surprisingly solid streets of that mostly fictitious city, people often bumped into me very hard, as if I were invisible. Now I agree with my grandmother, who recently said, "The real question is—what is authenticity, anyway?"

For most of my time in New York, I lived in Brooklyn and worked in Harlem. I considered this a clever evasion of The City. Where I lived was just a place to live, not The Place. And where I worked was just a place to work, not The Place. I rode my bike to work early in the morning, when even the streets of Midtown were still empty. I rattled over the Brooklyn Bridge, looking down through the wooden slats at the water below. I swerved through Chinatown. And then I rode up Mulberry Street, through Little Italy, where the street carnival had been the night before. The strings of lights were still hanging, but not illuminated. The cobblestones were covered with trash. And the sausage vendor was asleep at the wooden counter with his head resting on his folded arms.

The New York I knew was always the city of the morning after the carnival. I rode all the way uptown on First Avenue, from Little Italy to Harlem. I walked from 110th to 140th, from Frederick Douglass to Martin Luther King Jr. Boulevard. I passed murals painted on the boards that covered the broken windows of the old brownstones—the Virgin Mary on one window, Saint Lazarus, with his crutches and his dog, on the other. I read the messages chalked onto the sidewalk by De La Vega every morning: "You are more desirable as a servant of the machine than as a free thinker." I saw the glorious graffiti on the basketball courts. I stepped over dog shit. I watched the eastern European woman who worked in the pizza shop grow thin and develop a sore on her face while the boys from the school came in and yelled at her to hurry up with that slice, bitch. I glared at the boys and they didn't meet my eyes. Almost no one did. I listened to the guys in the bodega betting on the Mets and laughing. I smiled at babies in strollers. I watched kids on bikes ride through traffic and pop up onto their back wheels. Sometimes I ate in the hospital café, because it was the only place I knew I could get spinach for lunch. I watched women in hot, hot dresses, and I watched the men watching them. I listened to Rosie, the police officer, singing Aretha Franklin in the bathroom of the school where I worked. I knew, intimately, the empty lots where grandmas from Alabama grew okra and collard greens. I found a cat that had drowned in a rain barrel and was gathering mold. At the bodega on First Avenue I saw the old man who was always trying to remember my name. "Ida!" he would jump up and yell, "Ursula, Ursula, Ursula!"

This was the New York I loved, with the imperfect, ambiguous, hesitant love that I have come to recognize as my own. It was the city that existed on the margins of the story. It was the New York of Harlem and Inwood and Washington Heights. The New York of the outer boroughs. The New York of Brooklyn and Queens and Staten Island and the Bronx.

But see, the name of every place in New York serves as a code word or a racial cue. The code shifts slightly, depending on whom you are talking to, so at times the word "Harlem" will mean "dangerous" and "tough" and at other times will mean "vibrant" and "real." But it is always a setting for our same old stories. What an injustice to a place. A place that is, incidentally, real. When I moved to New York, I had the luxury at first of living in a neighborhood that most of the people I met had never heard of. Sunset Park meant nothing. But Fort Greene did, and so did Astoria, and the East Village meant so much that I tried to avoid admitting I lived there. "It's temporary," I would say. But so was everything.

My friends often say, "When you come back to New York . . . ," assuming, of course, that I will come back. And maybe I will, despite it all. Joan Didion did. But for now I prefer to think that I will go somewhere that is not so overimagined.

I lived in the city just long enough to see Coney Island begin to be destroyed. The spring I left New York was the same spring I discovered that the old vine-covered roller coaster had finally been torn down. So had the ancient candy shop with the homemade caramel apples. And the burned train station was being renovated.

It has been said that New York is a city for only the very rich and the very poor. Joan Didion suggested that it is a city for only the very young. In my worst moments, especially when standing on Madison Avenue, I have suspected that it is a city for only the very desperate or the very deluded.

I have at times been mystified by Joan Didion's ability to tolerate certain myths while she so fiercely and effectively destroys the foundations of many others. But I know now that it is very difficult to dismantle one story without replacing it with another. The romance of narrative is so hard to resist. Like Joan Didion, I made a yellow curtain for my first bedroom in the city because I had a romantic notion of light and color. My curtain also became grimy in the rain.

It is not that the heroine is no longer as optimistic as she once was. It is that the heroine is not convinced she is the heroine or that the story is true. The heroine knows that New York is just a city—just a place to live. And, like any other place, it demands that you make your own story.

I came to New York very young, and I left still young but not the same. The Wonder Wheel is still there, true, but everything else is gone.

The Art of Being Born

In what I hope will be our final appointment with the midwife, she guessed you weigh eight pounds and four ounces and that you will come soon.

I woke up late, having spent the night beached on the couch in the living room, memorizing the distinguishing signs of every rash chronicled in Dr. Spock's baby book, until nodding off around six. The book lay open to cradle cap, flaking patches of skin on the tops of newborn heads, which might be "cracked, greasy, or even weeping."

I'm ten days past the date you are supposed to arrive and too uncomfortable, too wrung out with anxiety to sleep. In the last weeks, after an hour or so of tossing in bed each night, I've been shuffling to the couch so that your father might sleep undisturbed. In the mornings I lumber into the shower, stand under the spray, and cry. I brace my arms against the shower walls and let the water rain down my face and stream over my breasts and enormous stomach.

This morning, I waddled to the bedroom and sagged in the doorway. Your father took one look at my forlorn figure and said, "Come on, let's get out of here."

We wound our way slowly down Twenty-Second Street to the entrance of Ravenna Park, and inside the park to the old-growth ravine with freshwater springs welling from the tall walls and flowing into Ravenna Creek.

As we entered the muddy trail down to the creek, Richard took my hand in his to brace me for our descent. We walked at a glacial pace, mimicking the first untroubled humans, on the path that looped through the waterlogged ravine, Richard consciously slowing his pace, me trying to move myself forward. At the end of the mile loop, we huffed up from the ravine and emerged by the tennis courts, where we rested a bit, sitting on a bench beneath a bracelet of blooming cherry trees, the branches dipping down around us. Though it was only noon, I lay on my side on the bench and put my head in Richard's lap. Sitting on the bench, we spoke of our anticipation and wondered how much longer we had to wait until you, our first child, would be born. At that moment we weren't anxious. How could we be anxious, sitting on the warm bench, the world alive and green, and the branches of the cherry framing our hopes?

I'm telling you this because few events are more momentous than birth. Every child wants to know about their birth and asks, *where did I come from?* Many are answered with a birth story that speaks to the child of who she is and will be, and that sets her life in motion in a particular way. Mothers know the story and tell it like a favorite fairy tale to the child, who rests her head on her pillow, on her way to sleep.

But sometimes the stories of origin are troubled, riven with complexity and unanswered questions and bespeak a cloudy future.

My parents never spoke of the circumstances surrounding my birth, and I am in possession of only a few meager facts.

I was born on February 26 in the dead of winter.
No baby pictures were taken.
No baby book, where the important milestones are recorded, exists.
I was installed in a wood-paneled room down a long corridor at the back of the house.

My mother's defensiveness on the subject of my birth led me to believe that the day, the event, my first entrance onto the stage and into my mother's life was complicated by emotions I didn't understand and would never understand. I came to think, perhaps irrationally, that from my mother's point of view my birth was a mistake and that was why all the memorializing forms were blank. Instead of caressing the event in memory, she entered a state of amnesia from which she never awoke.

In high school, on the bus ride, while some of my girlfriends were making up the names for their future children, I'd make up stories of my birth, as if I were a character in search of a play. The births I imagined all took place out-of-doors as if I was a wild animal—

In fields
In meadows
In mountains
In a valley
In the woods
In a ravine
By a stream

And my mother and I were always alone, mother and daughter, the essential couple.

Here is one story I made up:

On a Sunday morning in September, my mother drove out of town, by herself, deep into the country of farms and pastures and ponds until she reached an orchard. The orchard was on a rough incline, under an open sky. She was in the midst of pulling apples down from the branches and putting them in her bag, when she sunk down among the dropped apples and I was born.

This story is preposterous on many levels. I wasn't born in September. I never knew my mother to pick any fruit by hand, and certainly the apples we ate were all store bought. You can tell I don't know the first thing about birthing. Imagining my mother making a bed below the boughs and giving birth to me as if she were a doe and I her fawn is a fairy tale. I don't ever remember my mother lying in the grass or on the ground of any sort. We never even had a picnic at a table. Yet, despite its utter lack of veracity, this was one of my birth stories.

After my mother's death, my father discovered a cache of photographs she had stashed away. All the photos were a revelation; just their existence required me to rethink my portrait of my mother. But one photo stood out: it was a baby picture of me. No one is holding me, neither my mother nor my father. I'm lying awake on my mother's bed, the one place where I most longed to be as a child. In this photograph I seem to be looking up at the person taking the photo. It must have been my mother's shadow pointing the camera. The bedspread is white, and the blankets I'm swaddled in are white. I look small and dwarfed among the snowy folds. I'm holding my hands up in a defensive position, and even then my hands were clenched. I can hardly say what I felt looking at this picture after having spent the bulk of my life believing no pictures of me as a baby existed. And here I am, at long last, on my mother's bed. It's just a little square photo, so small, it could easily have disappeared and never been recovered. But it has; it is a fact, and, like other facts, it complicates everything.

I thought I was the wounded party. It never occurred to me that perhaps I wasn't the only one who had been deprived of a birth story, or a story one would want to share. It never occurred to me that there were no baby pictures because my mother was denied access to me in the first weeks. In my mother's proper middle-class circle, birth wasn't talked about. Women didn't share the gritty details of birth, the bloody show. A doctor and medical staff kept women medicated and deadened to the actuality of birth. Perhaps my mother never spoke of my birth because she didn't know the details. In some ways she wasn't present for my birth—she was the vessel that carried me. She was knocked out; there's no other way of putting it. She saw me only through the nursery window, too heavily sedated to hold me. My mother went home without me. In the case of my birth, my mother had little say in her experience and little to say about her experience. And she never talked about what had been denied her.

After our afternoon appointment with Patricia, our midwife, when she announced your weight, we returned home, ate dinner and watched the Sonics playoff game on our tiny black-and-white TV, which Richard set up on a bench in front of the couch. Around halftime I started having contractions. Just in case this was the real thing, I packed my bag, a suede blue overnight bag, and put it by the door. In the bag was my hospital reading, Nietzsche and Schopenhauer, which I needed to get a grasp on for my upcoming comprehensive exams. I can imagine you shaking your head and laughing—I obviously knew nothing about labor or hospital stays.

Unlike my mother who took no class and had no birth partner, we had prepared for your birth by taking a class offered through the midwife's clinic that included drafting a birth plan. Yes, we had a plan. We paid scant attention to the physical exercises but spent an inordinate amount of time figuring out what music we wanted to hear during labor, as if it were a dance party requiring a playlist. The birth plan called for a teddy bear as a focal point for me to concentrate on, a tape player and tapes, a mat to lie on, and a baby bag full of clothes and blankets for you. When it started looking bad for the Sonics, Richard hauled all the birthing assemblage to our car, filled with boxes of books we had neglected to clear out.

The time between contractions was shortening, and they were intensifying, rapidly and uncomfortably so. It seemed like real labor, what we had been waiting for, not a false alarm, not the practice Braxton Hicks contractions. We called Patricia and were told to come on in. Back into our little Civic we went, packed now as if we were heading on safari.

The ride, our second in not many hours, was excruciating. The rhythmic bounce of the car as it passed over each seam of the bridge shot pains through my body. Richard tried to listen to the basketball game through my groans. Back to the parking lot that five hours ago seemed like heaven—only now I could barely lift myself out of the car or walk across the lot. If I didn't move, the contractions might not be so bad or might not come at all.

When Patricia measured my cervix, it was as it had been at my office visit earlier in the day. She wasn't certain I was in real labor. Without declaring labor, I couldn't be admitted to the hospital, couldn't be assigned my own room. I was instructed to walk up and down the back stairwells to stimulate labor. The optimism of the morning and afternoon had vanished.

At eleven o'clock I was measured once again. Slight progress, but not enough to declare active labor. Patricia sent us off wandering once again.

Midnight came, and still I hadn't been formally admitted. We climbed a few stairs, only to have me fall against the cement wall and slump to the steps when a contraction seized me.

You should know that contractions operate in stages like a thunderstorm. You feel them rumbling toward you from far off, tremors building incrementally until they arrive dead center.

At full strength, you feel as if every inch of your brainbodysoul has been taken captive by the seizure, and there's nothing you can do but give in to its superior power.

And then, when you feel you have been wrung out, it lets you go and rumbles off until the next tremor begins.

When this contraction lifted, Richard hauled me to my feet, and we once again climbed the stairs. Up and down we went, stopping and starting until we exited the stairwell and staggered by the nurse's station like beggars searching for a handout.

"Couldn't someone do something? Give me something to move the labor along or ease the pain?"

"No," replied the nurse manning the station, referring me brusquely to my birth plan, which was pinned on her clipboard. The plan firmly stated my opposition to drugs. I had wanted a natural birth, to be awake and alert, to feel everything. "What you are going through is perfectly normal," the nurse said. "Not an emergency."

I screamed—I'm sure I screamed—"But I didn't know what labor was when I wrote the plan. Give me something, *please.*" She offered me ice chips. Richard rubbed my back. I cried.

I thought I was going to die and that you would never live through this. How could something so painful result in you? How could babies survive the turmoil of birth, the violence of it? Because make no mistake, labor is violent: it squeezes the air out of you. In the moments between contractions, when pain waited in the wings, I thought about women who had given birth before me, women who were at this very instant giving birth alongside me, in fields, in hospitals, in apartments, in elevators and makeshift infirmaries, women of all colors, sizes, shapes, who spoke languages I couldn't understand and ate food I had never tasted. We were united by this scorching labor.

At twelve thirty Patricia rechecked me. I had progressed and was officially declared in labor and admitted to the hospital. I was going to have you after all. Finally, we moved to the birthing room we had toured nearly nine months ago, decorated like a bedroom at home, with pictures on the walls, rocking chairs, and a flower-patterned quilt. The walls were mauve with a burgundy border—rich and warm.

Unfortunately, by this time labor was so advanced that I was barely conscious of the décor that had been so important to me in the planning stages. I lay down in the quilt-covered bed, but had even more difficulty getting through the pain. I tensed up, gripped Richard. I forgot about the quick shallow puffs of breath I had practiced in birthing class. I cried and looked to Richard, who was the only person in the room. I refused to let him go, even to bring our birthing accoutrements in from the car. I was long past teddy bear focal points or playlists. I looked into his face during the contractions as he dutifully chanted, "Breathe, breathe, breathe." When the contraction was over, I drifted out of consciousness. Far away.

Spent, and traveling out of the body, I returned to the apple trees of my earlier birth fantasy. This time the trees were in blossom, in sunlight, under a pale blue sky, and my friend Elizabeth, who had her daughter Emma a year before, stood beneath them. In between contractions I went to this place with Elizabeth and Emma. They seemed to be welcoming me. Emma was perched at her waist, stiff legs supported by Elizabeth's cradled arm, while the apple tree's canopy of branches crowned Emma's head. Elizabeth grasped a branch, pulling it down as Emma pushed on her stomach to reach the blossoms waiting above them both. Early in pregnancy women can forget they are pregnant for an hour or two, a day perhaps. They can walk the fields at their usual pace, bend down and lift laundry baskets easily. They can hop, skip, jump, and run after a bus pulling away from the curb. In the last trimester every second is colored with the knowledge that you have something living inside you and it's growing—it's pushing against your being. When you turn on your side, you are turning for two. Nothing about me remained as it was.

Our midwife suddenly noticed Richard—how shaken and pale he was. He looked like he was going to faint. He alone had been my companion in labor; it was his face I looked at when trying to focus through the contractions, his hands I gripped, his voice trying to talk me through the pain, and it was his frame upon which I collapsed. There was no one else in the hours between arrival and admittance.

"Go down to the cafeteria," Patricia said. "Get some coffee, something to eat. It's going to be some hours before the next stage." I let go of his hands that I had been holding onto like a life raft in a storm.

When Richard came back I was in transition, that period between the first stage of labor and the last when you push the baby out. I had been drifting in and out of consciousness, when suddenly I got up, went to the bathroom and threw up. Then the mucus plug that blocks the opening of the cervix was expelled and my water broke. It was as if a small balloon had burst, and out came the water in one big gush. And then, I had to push. There was no stopping, no slowing the need to push, a push that originated somewhere else, far behind me, a great epic push, and I was the instrument of it.

I had been steadfastly uninterested in having children. Nothing moved me from my refusal, not holding a newborn in my arms or the transformative tales of motherhood. I was too wrapped up in the trouble of being a daughter forever waiting for her mother's love that would never come. I was surprised when I was seized by a great longing for a child.

Husband, midwife, and nurse huddled about the fetal monitor in the birthing room because it had started to register distress. Something was wrong—I could hear it in their voices, in the low tones, though I couldn't hear what they said. I was concentrating on pushing. I had to get out of my bed and lie on a gurney being rolled in. Then away I went, wheeling toward an operating room. Patricia was trying to slow down my pushing—there was talk of a C-section, getting you out quickly, calling a surgeon. But I couldn't stop pushing, and you crowned. Richard said he could see your head. I had never heard such excitement in his voice. Out you rushed with your umbilical cord lassoed around your neck. That's what was causing the distress. Each time I pushed, the cord tightened around your neck, cutting off oxygen and blood. Later I wondered if this was the origin of the term *mother knot*. But what could have been dire was not. As you crowned, Patricia was able to unloop the cord from around your neck, and all was well. It was 4:19 a.m. on April 18, and you weighed eight pounds, four ounces.

Richard wiped you off, wrapped you in a blanket, and put you in my arms. And a new story was born, a story I am passing onto you. And while I hope you live in the here and now, in a present so full that you have no reason to look back in puzzlement about how you came into the world, remember I know the story of your birth by heart.

PERMISSIONS

The following previously published essays are reprinted here with permission.

"The Art of Being Born" by Marcia Aldrich. First published in *Hotel Amerika* (Spring 2012). Reprinted by permission of the author.

"Difference Maker" by Meghan Daum. Reprinted from *The Unspeakable* (New York: Farrar, Straus and Giroux, 2015) by permission of the author.

"Dumb Show" by Neela Vaswani. First published by *Manhattanville Review*, May 23, 2013, http://mvillemfa.com/journal/dumb-show/. Reprinted by permission of *Manhattanville Review* and the author.

"Girl Hood: On (Not) Finding Yourself in Books" by Jaquira Díaz. Reprinted by permission of the author.

"Good-bye to All That" by Eula Biss, from *Notes from No Man's Land: American Essays*. Copyright © 2009 by Eula Biss. Reprinted with the permission of The Permissions Company, Inc., on behalf of Graywolf Press, www.graywolfpress.org.

"Grand Unified Theory of Female Pain" by Leslie Jamison, from *The Empathy Exams: Essays*. Copyright © 2014 by Leslie Jamison. Reprinted with the permission of The Permissions Company, Inc., on behalf of Graywolf Press, www.graywolfpress.org.

"Grip" by Joy Castro. First published in *Fourth Genre: Explorations in Nonfiction* 11, no. 2 (2009). Reprinted by permission of the author.

"Here" by Kristen Radtke. First published in *Essay Daily* (essaydaily.org). Reprinted by permission of *Essay Daily* and the author.

"Portrait of a Family, Crooked and Straight" by Wendy Rawlings. First published in *Colorado Review*. Reprinted by permission of the author.

"There Are Distances between Us" by Roxane Gay. First published in *Brevity*, May 15, 2011. Reprinted by permission of the author.

CONTRIBUTORS

MARCIA ALDRICH is the author of the free memoir *Girl Rearing*, published by W. W. Norton and part of the Barnes and Noble Discover New Writers Series. She has been the editor of *Fourth Genre: Explorations in Nonfiction*. Her *Companion to an Untold Story* won the AWP Award in Creative Nonfiction. Her essays have appeared in *The Best American Essays*.

JOCELYN BARTKEVICIUS has received the Missouri Review Essay Award, the Annie Dillard Award in Creative Nonfiction, the Iowa Woman Essay Prize, the Vogel Scholarship in Nonfiction at Bread Loaf, and the 2016 John Guyon Literary Nonfiction Prize. Her work has appeared in anthologies and in such journals as the *Hudson Review*, the *Missouri Review*, the *Bellingham Review*, and the *Iowa Review* and has been selected for the notables list in *The Best American Essays*.

CHELSEA BIONDOLILLO is a prose writer from Portland, Oregon, and the author of the chapbook *Ologies*. Her essays have appeared in *Orion, Passages North, River Teeth, Brevity, Diagram*, and others, and they have been listed as notable in *The Best American Essays 2014* and *2015*. Her journalism has appeared on state and national public radio and in *Nautilus, Discover Magazine*, and *Science*. In 2014 she received the Carter Prize for the Essay from *Shenandoah*.

EULA BISS is the author of three books: *On Immunity: An Inoculation, Notes from No Man's Land: American Essays*, and *The Balloonists*. She is the recipient of a Guggenheim Fellowship, a Howard Foundation Fellowship, an NEA Literature Fellowship, and a National Book Critics Circle Award.

BARRIE JEAN BORICH is the author of *Body Geographic*, winner of a Lambda Literary Award and an IPPY (Independent Publisher Book Award) Gold Medal in Essay/Creative Nonfiction. Her previous book, *My Lesbian Husband*, won the ALA Stonewall Book Award in nonfiction. Borich is an associate professor at DePaul University in Chicago, where she edits *Slag Glass City*, a digital journal of the urban essay arts.

JOY CASTRO is the author of *The Truth Book: A Memoir,* the post-Katrina New Orleans literary thrillers *Hell or High Water* and *Nearer Home,* the essay collection *Island of Bones,* and the short story collection *How Winter Began.* Winner of a Nebraska Book Award and an International Latino Book Award, she edited the collection *Family Trouble: Memoirists on the Hazards and Rewards of Revealing Family.*

MEGHAN DAUM is the author of four books, most recently the essay collection *The Unspeakable: And Other Subjects of Discussion,* which won the 2015 Pen Center USA Literary Award for Creative Nonfiction and was featured in *The Best American Essays 2015.* She is also the editor of the *New York Times* bestseller *Selfish, Shallow, and Self-Absorbed: Sixteen Writers on the Decision Not to Have Kids.* Her work has appeared in the *Los Angeles Times,* the *New Yorker,* the *Atlantic,* and *Vogue,* among other publications.

JAQUIRA DÍAZ has work noted in *Best American Essays* and *Best American Nonrequired Reading* and anthologized in *Pushcart Prize 37: Best of the Small Presses.* Her stories and essays appear in *Ploughshares,* the *Kenyon Review,* the *Sun,* the *Southern Review, Salon,* the *Guardian, TriQuarterly, Ninth Letter, Brevity,* and the *Los Angeles Review of Books.* She is the recipient of fellowships from the Wisconsin Institute for Creative Writing, the MacDowell Colony, and the *Kenyon Review.*

LAURIE LYNN DRUMMOND is the author of a collection of linked stories, *Anything You Say Can and Will Be Used against You,* which was a finalist for the PEN/Hemingway Award and won the Best Book Award from the Texas Institute of Letters and the Violet Crown Award from the Writers' League of Texas. She has also published in journals such as *Creative Nonfiction, Fourth Genre, River Teeth, Brevity, Southern Review, New Delta Review, Story, New Virginia Review, Black Warrior Review,* and *Fiction.*

PATRICIA FOSTER is the author of a memoir, *All the Lost Girls,* which won the PEN/Jerard Fund Award for Women's Nonfiction; a book of essays, *Just Beneath My Skin;* and a novel, *Girl from Soldier Creek.* She is also the editor of the anthologies *Minding the Body: Women Writers on Body and Soul* and *Sister to Sister,* as well as the coeditor with Jeff Porter of *Understanding the Essay* and with Mary Swander of *The Healing Circle.* Her essays have appeared in numerous journals.

ROXANE GAY is the author of *Ayiti, An Untamed State, Bad Feminist,* and *Hunger.* She is also a contributing opinion writer for the *New York Times.*

LESLIE JAMISON is the author of *The Empathy Exams,* a *New York Times* bestselling essay collection; and a novel, *The Gin Closet,* a finalist for the Los Angeles Times First Fiction Award. Her work has appeared in *Harper's, Oxford American, A Public Space, Boston Review, Virginia Quarterly Review,* the *Believer,* and the *New York Times,* where she is a regular columnist for the *Sunday Book Review.*

MARGO JEFFERSON is the author of *On Michael Jackson* and *Negroland: A Memoir*. She received a Pulitzer Prize for criticism in 1995 and teaches in the Writing Program at Columbia University.

SONJA LIVINGSTON's essay collection, *Ladies Night at the Dreamland*, provides lyrical profiles of little-known historical women. Other books include *Queen of the Fall: A Memoir of Girls and Goddesses* and *Ghostbread*, which won an AWP Book Prize for Nonfiction. Her essays have been listed as notable in the *Best American Essays* series and anthologized in many texts on writing. Sonja is the recipient of an NYFA Fellowship, an Iowa Review Award, and an Arts and Letters Essay Prize.

ALEXANDRIA MARZANO-LESNEVICH is the author of *Any One of Us*, a work of combined family memoir and literary journalism, forthcoming in 2017. She received a National Endowment for the Arts fellowship and a Rona Jaffe Award. Her essays appear in the *New York Times, Oxford American, Iowa Review, Hotel Amerika, TriQuarterly Online, Rumpus,* and many other publications and have won the Annie Dillard Award from *Bellingham Review* and been cited in *Best American Essays*.

BRENDA MILLER is the author of *An Earlier Life, Listening against the Stone: Selected Essays, Blessing of the Animals,* and *Season of the Body*. She coauthored with poet Holly J. Hughes *The Pen and the Bell: Mindful Writing in a Busy World* and coauthored *Tell It Slant: Creating, Refining, and Publishing Creative Nonfiction,* second edition. Her work has received six Pushcart Prizes. She is a professor in the MFA program in creative writing at Western Washington University.

MICHELE MORANO is the author of *Grammar Lessons: Translating a Life in Spain*. Her work has been honored with fellowships and awards from the Rona Jaffe Foundation, the American Association of University Women, and others. Her essays have appeared in many journals and anthologies, including *Best American Essays* and *I'll Tell You Mine: Thirty Years of Essays from the Iowa Nonfiction Writing Program*. She directs the MA in Writing and Publishing Program at DePaul University in Chicago.

KYOKO MORI is the author of three nonfiction books, *The Dream of Water, Polite Lies,* and *Yarn,* and four novels, *Shizuko's Daughter; One Bird; Stone Field, True Arrow;* and *Barn Cat*. Her stories and essays have appeared in *Harvard Review, Fourth Genre, Ploughshares, American Scholar, Conjunctions, The Best American Essays,* and other journals and anthologies. She teaches in George Mason University's MFA Program in Creative Writing and Lesley University's Low-Residency MFA Program.

BICH MINH NGUYEN, who goes by Beth, is the author of three books: the memoir *Stealing Buddha's Dinner,* which received the PEN/Jerard Award from the PEN American Center; the novel *Short Girls,* which won an American Book Award; and most recently the novel *Pioneer Girl*. She directs the MFA in writing at the University of San Francisco.

ADRIANA PARAMO is a cultural anthropologist, writer, and women's rights advocate. Her book *Looking for Esperanza*, winner of the 2011 Social Justice and Equity Award in Creative Nonfiction, was one of the top ten best books by Latino authors in 2012, the best Women's Issues Book at the 2013 International Latino Book Awards, and an award winner at the 2012 BOYA, Book of the Year Awards. She is also the author of *My Mother's Funeral*.

JERICHO PARMS is the author of the forthcoming *Lost Wax*. Her essays have appeared in *Hotel Amerika, Fourth Genre, Brevity, Normal School, American Literary Review*, and elsewhere. Her work has been nominated for a Pushcart Prize, noted in *Best American Essays 2014*, and anthologized in *Brief Encounters: A Collection of Contemporary Nonfiction*.

TORREY PETERS is an editor at Topside Press, which publishes the work of transgender writers. Her work has been published in *Epoch, Shenandoah, Prairie Schooner, Fourth Genre, Gawker, Pinch, Brevity*, and elsewhere. She is also the editor of a forthcoming collection of new nonfiction by transgender writers.

KRISTEN RADTKE is a writer and illustrator based in Brooklyn. Her first book of graphic nonfiction, *Imagine Wanting Only This*, will be published by Pantheon Books in 2017. She is the managing editor of Sarabande Books and the film and video editor of *Triquarterly* magazine. She has a master of fine arts from the University of Iowa's Nonfiction Writing Program.

WENDY RAWLINGS is the author of two books, *The Agnostics* (winner of the Michigan Literary Award) and *Come Back Irish* (winner of the Sandstone Prize from the Ohio State University Press). Her fiction and nonfiction have appeared most recently in *AGNI, Creative Nonfiction*, the *Cincinnati Review*, the *Florida Review*, and the 2016 Pushcart Prize anthology.

CHERYL STRAYED is the author of the number one *New York Times* best-selling memoir *Wild*, the *New York Times* best sellers *Tiny Beautiful Things* and *Brave Enough*, and the novel *Torch*. Strayed's essays have been published in *The Best American Essays*, the *New York Times*, the *Washington Post Magazine, Vogue, Salon*, the *Sun, Tin House*, and elsewhere.

DANA TOMMASINO's essays have appeared in *Narrative, Brevity, Seneca Review*, and *Rumpus*. She is the chef and owner of Gardenias restaurant in San Francisco and the former chef-owner—for twenty-two years—of Woodward's Garden in the Mission District. She curates literary events at her restaurants.

SARAH VALENTINE is the translator of *Into the Snow: Selected Poems of Gennady Aygi*. Her poems and translations have appeared in journals such as *Callaloo*, *Zoland Poetry*, and *diode* and in the anthology *Two Lines: Some Kind of Beautiful Signal*. Her essay "The Divine Auditor" won *Prairie Schooner*'s 2013 Bernice Slote Award; it is an excerpt from her memoir project, *Miss America*.

NEELA VASWANI is the author of the short story collection *Where the Long Grass Bends*, the mixed-genre memoir *You Have Given Me a Country*, and the middle-grade novel *Same Sun Here*. Her literary honors include the American Book Award, a PEN/O. Henry Prize, the Foreword Book of the Year Gold Medal, and the Italo Calvino Prize for Emerging Writers.

NICOLE WALKER's forthcoming books include *Processed Meats* and *Egg*. A chapbook, *Micrograms*, is forthcoming in early 2016. She is the author of a collection of essays, *Quench Your Thirst with Salt*, which won the Zone 3 Press Award for Creative Nonfiction, and of *This Noisy Egg*, a collection of poems. She coedited with Margot Singer *Bending Genre: Essays on Creative Nonfiction* and curated with Rebecca Campbell *7 Artists, 7 Rings: An Artist's Game of Telephone* for the *Huffington Post*.

AMY WRIGHT is the author of two poetry collections, *Everything in the Universe* and *Cracker Sonnets*, and a third collection written in collaboration with William Wright, *Creeks of the Upper South*. She is also the nonfiction editor of Zone 3 Press and coordinator of creative writing and associate professor at Austin Peay State University. Her first prose chapbook, *Wherever the Land Is*, was released in 2016.